The Environmental Case for Nuclear Power

Economic, Medical, and Political Considerations

by

Robert C. Morris, Ph.D.

PARAGON HOUSE
St. Paul, Minnesota

Published in the United States of America by

Paragon House
2700 University Avenue West
St. Paul, Minnesota 55114

Copyright   © by Robert C. Morris

Cover photo:
Digital imagery® copyright 1999 PhotoDisc, Inc.

Library of Congress Catalog-in-Publication Data

Morris, Robert C., 1929-
    The environmental case for nuclear power / by Robert C. Morris.
    P. cm.
    Includes bibliographical references and index.
    ISBN 1-557-78780-8 (alk. paper)
      1. Nuclear power plants–Risk assessment. 2. Nuclear engineering–Safety measures. 3. Electric power production–Environmental aspects. 1. Title.

TK9152.16.M67 2000
333.792'4 21–dc21

                                                        99-042981

10 9 8 7 6 5 4 3 2

For current information about all releases from Paragon House,
visit the web site at http://www.paragonhouse.com

Dedication

Usually, scientists report their discoveries to the media, and the media puts what the scientist has to say in the language of the layman and reports it to the public. However, in the case of nuclear power, the media has completely ignored what most scientists have had to say and has, instead, reported the frightening, unsubstantiated claims of the anti-nuclear power activists.

In an attempt to rectify this breakdown of reliable information, a few scientists took time from their main interest and left their laboratories and classrooms long enough to defend the use of nuclear power plants. One of these scientists particularly stands out: Dr. Bernard Cohen, D. Sc., who along with his other efforts has written two outstanding pro-nuclear power books.

Dr. Cohen is past Chairman of the American Physical Society Division of Nuclear Physics, and Chairman of the American Nuclear Society Division of Environmental Sciences. He was awarded the American Physical Society Bonner Prize in 1981, and is a prolific researcher. I think that Dr. Cohen would rather not have had to assume this new role, but he undoubtedly saw it as a worthwhile task which cried out to be done. Dr. Cohen also made a substantial contribution to my education in this matter, and I appreciate and applaud his efforts.

Table of Contents

Preface

Superstition can be defined as an unreasoning belief born out of fear which persists due to ignorance. This book was written in the hope that as a science educator, I might be able to play a part in correcting a superstition which has indirectly led to the deaths of one million Americans in the last twenty years. Unless the media and the American public sees this superstition for what it is, it could kill five million Americans during the twenty-first century, wreak terrible damage on the environment, and destroy our prosperity. The superstition which I speak of is the belief that nuclear power plants are too unsafe and should not be built. Read on, and I'll tell you more about this highly detrimental superstition.

It is a fact that without the consumption of energy, modern civilization cannot possibly exist. Without energy, homes grow cold, and factories close. The farmer's tractors, seeders, harvesters, and combines must sit idle, and he is forced to do his work in the same back-breaking, inefficient way that farmers used two hundred years ago. But, now his efforts won't feed forty or fifty people. If he's lucky, he's able to feed his own family very inadequately. Without the use of energy, almost all civilized endeavors cease as 90 percent of the population is forced into bare subsistence farming.

Today, only two large-scale methods of generating energy are available to us: burn the fossil fuels—coal, oil, and natural gas—or use nuclear power. Solar energy is not capable of satisfying our energy needs at present, and, it may never be up to the job. The same can be said for hydroelectric power, nuclear fusion, and windmills.

For almost eight hundred years, coal served civilization well. In the 1800s, coal powered the new machines of the Industrial Revolution, and mankind took a giant leap toward the prosperity which we now enjoy. Then, as more and more people crowded into our cities during the last century, coal's most deadly flaw became more evident. Burning coal releases sulfur dioxide, and a wide assortment of other dangerous air pollutants which are capable of damaging the human respiratory system. By the 1960s, scientific evidence began to accumulate which linked air pollution with the death of 50,000 Americans a year. Despite efforts to control air pollution, it killed 46,000 Americans in 1996.

At about the same time, environmental scientists began to be concerned about acid rainfall, which was damaging our forests, lakes, and streams. One of the sources of acid rain was the substances released during the combustion of coal and oil. Soon, a number of countries, including Canada, had declared acid rain to be their number one environmental problem.

In the 1990s, a new danger associated with burning the fossil fuels surfaced: global warming. Climatologists noted that atmospheric levels of carbon dioxide were increasing, an event which closely paralleled the consumption of greater amounts of coal and oil, and the increased release of carbon dioxide by these fuels. This carbon dioxide was apparently trapping the sun's heat and causing the earth's average temperature to rise.

In 1997, the industrialized nations agreed to reduce the levels of their carbon dioxide emissions by the year 2012. If this treaty is ratified by the U.S. Senate, we would have to cut our emissions—and the energy which we use—by 33 percent as compared with the levels otherwise expected by 2012. It is worth noting that energy usage only decreased by 8 percent during the Great Depression of 1929, so one might reasonably worry what a 33 percent reduction would do to our economy. Would millions of Americans become jobless in an attempt to solve this problem, or was there a better, more sensible solution available?

When the first nuclear power plants went into operation in the late 1950s, almost everyone viewed them favorably. Engineers and city planners saw them as a solution to the rapidly worsening problem of air pollution. The utility companies, tired of trying to cope with soaring oil prices and O.P.E.C.'s oil embargoes, saw nuclear power as a more dependable, more reasonable source of energy.

Then, in the early 1970s, public opinion abruptly shifted against nuclear power. There had been no nuclear power plant accidents worthy of mention, and no loss of life, which is very unusual for a large industry in its infancy, so this change of attitude surprised many people.

The reason for this sudden change in the public's perception of nuclear power plants can be traced to the rise of anti-nuclear power activist groups. These groups issued a continual barrage of press releases which claimed that nuclear power plants were unsafe and too dangerous to be used.

Next, the media broadcast these frightening claims, thus providing publicity to the group making the claim. This publicity enabled these groups to gain new members, notoriety, and political power. Later, two of the leaders in the anti-nuclear power movement attempted to capitalize on the notoriety they had gained by making runs at the presidency, but both were unsuccessful.

By the time Three Mile Island occurred in 1979, the anti-nuclear power groups had become so powerful that they were able to bring a halt to the normal development of nuclear power.

They were even successful in halting the construction of a number of nuclear power plants which were well along in their construction. Utility companies suffered huge financial losses whenever this occurred, of course.

In 1986, when a nuclear power plant blew up at Chernobyl, in Russia, killing two people in the blast, the public was never told that it was a chemical or steam explosion. Nor were they ever told that Chernobyl was not Western-built and was so unsafe that it never could have been licensed to operate in any Western nation. And, people have yet to learn that statistics show that five hundred nuclear accidents as severe as Chernobyl will have to happen before nuclear power's yearly death toll will equal that of the fossil fuels.

For some reason, the media has chosen to report only what the anti-nuclear activists had to say. The scientists who sought to defend nuclear power were never allowed to speak on TV, and their side of the story has never reached the American public. Organizations having a total membership of almost one million scientists, including the American Medical Association, have endorsed the use of nuclear power plants, but the public is unaware of this. Dozens of scientific studies show that it is much more dangerous to burn coal than it is to use nuclear power, but none of these studies were ever even mentioned on prime-time television. Instead, the biased, unsubstantiated opinions of a handful of anti-nuclear power activists were given extensive coverage.

Time has passed, and forty years of experience with nuclear power plants should have vindicated their use. The facts now show that during this time, Western-built commercial nuclear power plants have never blown up; they do not release radiation which kills our children, and no one—not a single nuclear power plant worker nor a single member of the public sector has ever died or even been exposed to a dangerous level of radiation. Meanwhile, we've been forced to burn increasing quantities of coal, and the fossil fuels continue to kill tens of thousands of Americans each year.

Surely, it is time to set aside the superstition that nuclear power plants are too unsafe to use. Unless we begin replacing fossil fuel burning power plants with safer, environmentally benign, more economic nuclear power plants, air pollution will kill twenty million people worldwide—five million of them will be Americans—during the twenty-first century, as it did during the twentieth century. Acid rain will continue to cause terrible damage to our lakes, rivers, streams, and forests, and our foolish attempts to prevent global warming could destroy our prosperity.

Finally, I'd like to mention that I have no ties to the nuclear power industry and that this book was not subsidized in any way by the nuclear power industry. I simply saw a bad mistake and believed that over forty years of research and study on the topic uniquely qualified me in my attempt to help correct it.

I would also like to acknowledge several people who provided me with valuable help in this project. First, and foremost, is my wife, Jacquie, the English major, who gave me much valuable criticism and prevented me from abusing the English language. Three longtime friends, Clyde Dilley, Ph. D., former Professor of Mathematics at the University of Toledo, Donald Humphreys, Ph. D., Professor of Environmental Engineering and Coordinator of the Program at Temple University, and Walter Raczynski, M.S., Chairman of the Science Department at Addison Trail High School, Addison, Illinois, all read my manuscript closely and provided me with many valuable suggestions. Dr. Michael J. Higatsberger, of the University of Vienna, Institute of Experimental Physics, in Austria, acted as technical editor and made a number of valuable suggestions and changes. Lastly, Dr. Gordon L. Anderson, the Executive Director of Paragon House, had the wisdom and courage needed to publish this book even though it refutes what the media believes.

Robert Morris, Ph.D., 1999

CHAPTER 1

The Fossil Fuels: Civilization's Troubled Servant

Having access to a source of energy other than one's own muscles has always been the key to civilization's progress and prosperity. When people first learned to use the energy of fire to ward off the cold of a bitter winter night, the chance of freezing to death diminished. Centuries later, when man discovered how to utilize the energy of the wind to push his great sailing ships across vast oceans, the inhuman work of the galley slave became unnecessary, and people were able to enjoy the new things which distant lands had to offer.

In the early 1800s, the invention of the steam engine made it possible to use the heat produced by burning coal to produce motion. For the first time, the energy of coal could be used to turn the wheels of all kinds of machines, and civilization took one of its biggest steps forward. Soon, coal-powered machinery was sawing wood, spinning thread, weaving cloth, making nails, pumping water, grinding grain, and moving huge loads great distances on rails.

The heat produced by burning coal did all of these things faster and more efficiently than either man or animal had been able to do in the past.

In only about 20 years, the use of these new coal-powered machines enabled England to change from a small agricultural country to the world's richest industrial nation. The Industrial Revolution was underway, and it was destined to bring about enormous changes which would ultimately greatly improve the lives of all of those who were fortunate enough to be able to embrace it. Today, Americans owe much of their prosperity to the fact that we took part in the Industrial Revolution and began to industrialize. Countries such as Ethiopia which, for various reasons, did not industrialize are still deeply mired in the poverty of preindustrial times.

Several generations later, when the energy of oil and its derivatives, such as gasoline, became available, civilization took another big step forward. In the 1820s, using a scythe and a lot of hard physical effort, a farmer was able to cut about two acres of oats in a day. Today, with the help of a diesel—or gasoline—powered combine, one man can easily harvest 65 acres in a day, and not sweat a lot as he does it.

Life Was Simpler Then, but—

Before man learned how to use the energy of coal and gasoline to power machines, nine out of ten people were needed as farmers. Yet, despite the large number of farmers, famine was commonplace, even in the advanced countries. Only the richest people got enough to eat, and even their diet was so poorly balanced that they suffered from an assortment of nutritional diseases including beriberi, scurvy, and rickets.

As late as well into the eighteenth century, almost everyone worked a long, hard 12-hour day, often at some backbreaking task. For this effort, a worker received the sum of two cents an hour, or $1.44 for a 72-hour week. Almost every penny that a worker earned was needed to feed and house his family, most of whom also worked long hours. When a family moved, all of the goods they had been able to accumulate in 20 years could be placed in one small handcart.

Entire families lived in a single ten-foot by twelve-foot room. Often there was little or no heat. Water to drink and wash with had to be carried from the town pump, which might be a mile away. There were no electric lights, no television, no radios, no refrigerators, no air conditioning, and no automatic anything. Garbage and toilet wastes were dumped out of a bucket and into the nearest open sewer. Travelers approaching a town frequently smelled it before they saw it.

Entertainment was virtually nonexistent. Aside from the larger cities, most people were lucky to get to see a juggler, a puppet show, or a trained monkey perform. A hanging was an eagerly awaited event, except for the man of the hour, of course.

Medical treatment was based on ignorance and superstition. More children died than lived. Antibiotics were yet to be discovered, and a scratch could turn into a fatal infection. Great epidemics of bubonic plague, typhus fever, typhoid fever, and cholera ravaged civilization periodically. Tuberculosis, malaria, smallpox, and other endemic diseases were waiting to claim the young, the old, the weak, and the unlucky. No wonder the average life span was less than 40 years.

Between 1870 and 1979 as more coal and oil came into use, hourly productivity began to increase until it reached a spectacular 1,100 percent on the average. Gradually, most things began to change for the better.

First hundreds, then thousands, and finally millions of people were no longer needed as farmers. These people became factory workers, clerks, doctors, teachers, and engineers. In the decades to follow, they produced an ever increasing flow of the material goods we now enjoy. They solved the problem of the great epidemics, purified water, built sewer systems, and educated millions, some of whom invented the automobile, radio, television, air conditioning, the telephone, the computer, and all of the other useful devices we now take for granted.

As the farmer's productivity increased, fewer farmers were needed. The unneeded farmers were then free to enter other occupations, and their efforts led to the better life we enjoy today.

Figure 1.1: People Fed by One Farmer 1830–1965

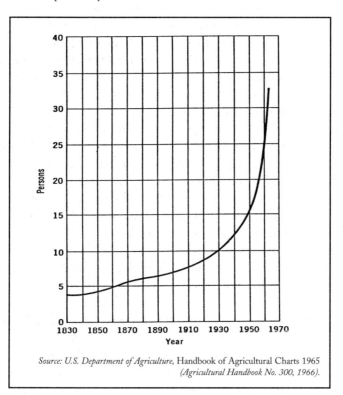

Source: U.S. Department of Agriculture, Handbook of Agricultural Charts 1965 (Agricultural Handbook No. 300, 1966).

Doubts about Coal and Oil Arise: The Killer Fogs

Clearly the energy of coal and oil has played an indisputably huge role in civilization's ascent to the pleasant life which we now enjoy. But by the

1970s, information had begun to accumulate which indicated that both fuels had serious drawbacks and were no longer the perfect solution to civilization's ever increasing need for energy.

The first inkling that it might not be wise to continue burning large quantities of the fossil fuels—coal, oil, and oil derivatives such as gasoline and diesel fuel—came from a series of air pollution episodes in which sudden large increases in the concentration of air pollutants were accompanied by soaring fatality rates caused by bronchitis, other respiratory diseases, and heart disease.

Although air pollution episodes had been observed as early as 1873, the most spectacular of these occurred on December 4, 1952, when a stagnant air mass settled over London. The coal-burning furnaces of homes, factories, and businesses poured fine airborne soot and the dangerous respiratory irritant sulfur dioxide into the air mass. The exhaust from thousands of autos, trucks, and buses added poisonous carbon monoxide and the oxides of nitrogen to the smoky mix. Trapped by a temperature inversion (an unusual atmospheric condition), the air mass blanketed London for four days.

Soon the media dubbed the air mass a "killer fog." And, the name was an accurate assessment of the situation. Prior to the arrival of the killer fog, an average of 292 Londoners per day had died. With the arrival of the stagnant air mass, death rates immediately increased. By the third day hospitals were so overcrowded that they turned away all but emergency cases. On the fourth day 910 people died, a figure more than three times the normal rate. In all there were 4,000 more deaths than usual during the two-week period following the onset of the killer fog. And, another 4,000 excess deaths occurred during the next three months. A flu epidemic struck London in the months following the killer fog; so, some of the latter 4,000 deaths may have been due to the flu. Unfortunately, it's very difficult to be sure how many people were flu victims and how many were air pollution victims. A good number probably died from a combination of the two.

Lower Levels of Air Pollutants Are also Deadly

In 1966, Dr. Leonard Greenburg, head of the Department of Environmental Medicine at Albert Einstein College of Medicine in New York, released a study which indicated that the extremely high concentrations of pollutants usually in the air during the killer fogs need not be present in order for air pollution to kill people: Apparently, lesser concentrations could be deadly, too. Greenburg produced data which showed that the concentration of air pollutants which existed in many cities from time to time was also capable of killing people. Up until Greenburg's study, few scientists were aware that air pollution was killing city dwellers much of the time.

Other air pollution-mortality rate studies by dozens of reputable scientists followed. Soon sufficient data existed to convince most scientists that the air pollutants released largely by burning coal and oil were responsible for the deaths of approximately 50,000 Americans each year.[1]

The combustion of coal and oil derivatives produces sulfur dioxide, carbon monoxide, airborne ash in the form of fine particulates, nitrogen's oxides, and many poisonous, radioactive, and cancer-causing substances. When these dangerous air pollutants are breathed over a long time period, they add to the death toll claimed by bronchitis, emphysema, lung cancer, and heart disease.

According to the Environmental Protection Agency's records, large quantities of these unhealthy substances have been released into our air since 1910.[2] And despite strong regulatory efforts by the government, 155 million tons of these dangerous pollutants were still being released into the nation's air as late as 1996.

Years from now, people may consider us foolish for having continued to use such a dangerous source of energy as the fossil fuels, especially since a much safer alternative exists.

Some Other Problems with the Use of Oil

Few substances are more crucial to modern civilization than oil and its derivatives. With sufficient oil, we prosper and grow. Without oil, our homes grow cold. The lights go out. Factory assembly lines stop. Shops and businesses close. No cars move. Lack of diesel fuel stops trains, tractors, and trucks. Less food and other goods are produced. We lose most of the 80,000 valuable products, including many of our medicines, made from oil. Without oil, modern civilization ceases to exist.

In 1973, an oil embargo by the Middle Eastern oil exporting countries—the Organization of Petroleum Exporting Countries (OPEC)—demonstrated just how easily the flow of this critical substance could be disrupted. Angered by U.S. support of Israel, OPEC announced its intention to drastically cut back and then stop all exports of oil to the industrial countries.

The source of all numbered statements appears at the end of this book.

As U.S. supplies of gasoline dwindled, motorists drove from gas station to gas station in hopes of finding enough gasoline to drive home on. Like gasoline, heating oil is also extracted from crude oil, so people were forced to set their thermostats in homes, businesses, and shops at uncomfortably cold levels. Workers were laid off as industry was forced to curtail production.

When OPEC raised oil prices over 500 percent, business was forced to pass this cost on to the consumer, and inflation set in. As the purchasing power of American households shrank, people made fewer purchases, and a severe recession set in. All over the nation, housewives went to work to offset their family's loss of purchasing power. It wasn't long before everyone in the industrial nations became painfully aware of just how much their prosperity depended on the capricious decisions made by the powerful, rich Middle East's ministers of oil.

Six years later, in 1979, a revolution toppled the pro-American government in Iran, and the world's oil market again went through another cataclysmic upheaval. This time the oil cartel increased the price of oil 1,560 percent, and the economic problems of 1973 and 1974 were repeated. Things became so bad that scary books about the economic collapse of civilization became best-sellers, and many people started to accumulate bags of silver coins which they hoped might retain their value in the face of a monetary collapse.

Unfortunately, the problems associated with our dependence on foreign oil were not over. On August 2, 1990, the Middle East was plunged into war as Iraqi dictator Saddam Hussein invaded his small, oil-rich neighbor, Kuwait. When Saddam's tanks rolled through Kuwait and then began to mass on the border of Saudi Arabia, U.S. President George Bush had no choice but to act fast, flying U.S. troops to Saudi Arabia. Had Saddam overrun Saudi Arabia, he would have controlled 45 percent of the world's known oil reserves. On a whim, he could have sent oil prices soaring, which would have caused raging inflation, massive unemployment, and severe economic depressions in all of the industrialized nations. Economies that took decades to build would have been destroyed in a matter of days.

Fortunately the Soviet Union had troubles of its own, and chose not to honor the mutual defense pact it had made earlier with Iraq. Had we been forced to fight against Russia and Iraq, we might have found out just how costly foreign oil can be.

The Trade Deficit

Unfortunately, the ease with which our supply of oil can be disrupted isn't the only economic problem associated with its use. For some years now, the U.S. has imported more goods than it exported. This is known as a "trade deficit" and the purchase of foreign oil often accounts for almost one-half of this deficit. Certain economic ills usually accompany a trade deficit. For example, it was estimated that our trade deficit cost the U.S. five million jobs in 1987. A country which imports, or purchases, more goods than it exports, or sells, is in effect spending its savings, and to do this is to become poorer.

The Worst Risk Associated with Depending on Oil

Finally, the world's supply of oil is limited, and unless the world's oil shales and tar sands prove useful, we could run out of oil in only a few decades. Various estimates place the date at which the world's oil supply will be gone at from 20 to 100 years, depending on how much more oil still awaits discovery and how fast it is consumed. Consumption rates are continually increasing—they tripled between 1960 and 1990. This trend will probably continue as more and more countries seek a better life by industrializing.

We desperately need to begin replacing oil with some other source of energy so that we won't be forced to do without energy when we run out of oil. Once our oil is gone, our coal reserves won't last long. At best, coal represents only a temporary reprieve from freezing to death. Installing a replacement for oil could easily take ten to twenty years, and so much uncertainty surrounds the world's oil reserves that they might run out without giving us this much warning. If this happens, the world will suffer massive famines, worldwide epidemics, and the painful relocation of hundreds of millions of people as civilization is forced to take a giant step backward toward bare subsistence farming as a way of life.

Several highly respected scientists, including a former chief scientific adviser to the British government and a U.S. Nobel Prize winner, have warned of the seriousness of this problem.

Shouldn't We Be Cutting Down on the Oil We Use?

So, not only is the flow of foreign oil easily disrupted, but our purchase of it is a major contributor to our trade deficit, which is very damaging to the economy. And, both of these extremely serious problems are dwarfed by the possibility that we could run out of oil without sufficient time to develop a replacement and build the the massive facilities needed to use it.

All of these very serious problems with oil suggest that we should be moving away from the use of oil, not increasing it, as we are now doing: By 1998 we were importing almost twice as much oil from the Persian Gulf as we did in 1973, when our supply was first disrupted.

(These problems are discussed more fully in chapter 6.)

The Latest Problem with the Fossil Fuels

When the fossil fuels—coal, oil, and natural gas—burn, they produce largely water vapor and carbon dioxide. Both gases are capable of acting as a sort of atmospheric blanket, which lets the heat of sunlight reach the earth but prevents a good part of this heat from escaping from the earth. This process is known as the "greenhouse effect" and, theoretically, it might cause a warmer earth, or "global warming."

Between 1800 and 1992 atmospheric levels of carbon dioxide have risen about 25 percent. This increase is thought to have come from our increased use of fossil fuels, which started when civilization began to industrialize.

Most scientists believe that the theory on which the greenhouse effect is based is sound. But, as late as 1998 there was far less agreement among atmospheric scientists as to whether the earth was actually becoming significantly warmer, and, if so, was our burning of the fossil fuels responsible for this warming?

If global warming does occur, it could result in some very severe problems: Huge ice fields in the Antarctic and Greenland could melt, resulting in a rise in ocean levels and the flooding of low coastal areas all around the earth. Many islands and most coastal cities would be under water, and tens of millions of people would have to flee their homes.

Global warming could also cause the atmospheric circulation to shift, turning some food-producing lands into dry and dusty deserts. Tropical diseases might respond to the warming by moving northward. Clearly, global warming could have serious consequences for almost everyone.

During 1988, one heat wave after another scorched the U.S. This apparently so impressed the editors of *Time* magazine that they skipped their usual year-end selection of "Man of the Year" and, instead, featured a dangerously overheated earth as its "Planet of the Year."

By mid-1989, officials at the United Nations were certain enough that the greenhouse effect was causing global warming to select the phrase, "Global Warning: Global Warming" as the slogan for their June 5, 1989, Environment Day. And, the U.N. report warned that it was already too late to prevent the impact of global warming.

Rio and Kyoto

In June of 1992, the United Nations sponsored a conference held at Rio de Janeiro, Brazil, to discuss the problem of global warming. Over 25,000 people including 7,000 journalists attended the conference.

After scores of exhausting meetings, the Global Climate Change Treaty emerged. This treaty, which was signed by President George Bush and later ratified by the U.S. Senate, called for the industrialized nations to voluntarily cut back on their use of fossil fuels in order to reduce the amount of carbon dioxide released into the air. However, probably because the cuts were voluntary, by 1997 annual worldwide emissions of carbon dioxide had actually increased.

Five years later, in December of 1997, a second U.N. conference on global warming was convened in Kyoto, Japan. The agreements that emerged from this meeting were potentially much more serious and, if they come to pass, will drastically affect the industrialized nations. At Kyoto, 38 industrialized nations agreed to reduce the emission of their "greenhouse gases"—largely carbon dioxide and the oxides of nitrogen—to 6 percent to 8 percent below 1990 levels by the years 2008 to 2012. But, the agreement exempted developing nations, including China, from anything but voluntary cuts. And, until the Senate ratifies it, the agreement is not binding on the U.S.

In the U.S., the Kyoto agreement immediately created a storm of protest. Even before the conference was held, the Senate had voted 95-0 to reject any treaty which exempted the developing nations from mandatory reductions in greenhouse gas emissions.

Of course, it was possible that President Clinton might decide to bypass the Senate, possibly by having the Environmental Protection Agency (EPA) declare carbon dioxide a pollutant so that emissions could be monitored and limits set under this agency.

Although the developing nations need to industrialize to escape from the morass of poverty which many of them are now mired in, some of these nations are already among the worst polluters on earth. Respiratory disease caused by air pollution presently accounts for 25 percent of all Chinese deaths and was that nation's number one health problem in 1998. Without restraints, in only a few decades China will replace the U.S. as the largest emitter of greenhouse gases. Also exempted were India and Mexico. In 1995, 52,000 Indians died of air pollution-related illness. And, the World Health Organization (WHO) recently gave Mexico City the dubious distinction of selecting it as the city having the world's most heavily polluted air. In one recent five-day time period, 400,000 Mexicans checked into Mexico City's hospitals and clinics with an air pollution-related health problem. Worse, it was estimated that within only a few decades, 60 percent of the world's greenhouse gas emissions will come from unregulated developing countries.

U.S. economists and business leaders were quick to point out that the Kyoto treaty could result in a mass exodus of jobs as U.S. plants moved to unregulated developing countries, which also had the additional advantage of paying lower wages to their workers.

Some scary estimates of the effect of the treaty on the U.S. emerged. Although the U.S. Department of Energy had issued a press release in September of 1997 which said that it would be possible to cut back energy usage to 1990 levels without raising energy costs, a report by the American Petroleum Institute claimed that, if ratified, the treaty could result in a 65-cents-a-gallon price increase in the cost of gasoline and a 50 percent increase in electric bills.

Under the treaty, the U.S. would have to decrease its greenhouse gas emissions by about one-third compared to the levels otherwise expected in 2012. Of course, this means it will probably be necessary to decrease the amount of energy used, perhaps by as much as 30 percent. During the Great Depression of 1929, our energy usage only decreased by 8 percent, so a 30 percent decrease is really something to worry about.

The American Petroleum Institute Report also predicted that the treaty would cause a drop in the gross domestic product of 3.3 percent, the loss of from 250,000 to 600,000 jobs, and a loss of $350 billion in income. The economic cost of the treaty was expected to run about $2,000 per family in the U.S.

How would the various countries solve the difficult problem of reducing greenhouse gas emissions without severely damaging their economy? Japan planned to build 20 nuclear power plants. China, beset with a severe air pollution problem caused by the excessive use of fossil fuels, but exempted from the cuts, planned to build 150 nuclear power plants over the next 40 years. The U.S. rushed to buy "pollution credits" from Russia. But, a June 4, 1998, hearing of the Senate Energy Committee and the General Accounting Office revealed that the president had made no other plans as to how the mandatory reductions could be accomplished should the Senate ratify the treaty.

In the face of possible opposition from anti-nuclear power groups, no U.S. politician was brave enough to suggest that more nuclear power plants be built in the U.S.

Needed: A Better Solution

History shows quite clearly that the use of energy is very important to our standard of living and well-being. To illustrate this important point, consider Norway, which is an industrialized country, and Turkey, where industrialization has begun but has not yet been fully completed. In 1990, Norway used 32 times more electricity per person than Turkey. Some of this energy was used to power machinery, and this advantage enabled the average Norwegian production worker to earn $18.92 per hour, while the average Turk earned only 41 cents per hour. These earnings reflect the productivity of the two workers, and also say a lot about the standard of living in each of the two countries.

This disparity in wages enabled the Norwegians to support one doctor for every 441 people, while the Turks had to make do with only one doctor per 1,275 people. The difference in medical care that these figures imply undoubtedly contributed to the fact that the average Norwegian enjoyed a life span almost 12 years longer than that of the Turk.

A recent study of the health of several thousand people in the U.S. showed that those having an annual income of less than $10,000 were over three times more likely to die in a given year than those with incomes over $30,000.[3] Apparently poverty leads to conditions such as poor diet, poor health care, and disease, which are very effective killers of people.

So, for the most part, both our health and prosperity depend on our high productivity in the factory and on the farm. And, in turn, our productivity depends on our being able to freely utilize other sources of energy.

Plainly, curtailing our use of energy, as might happen under the Kyoto treaty, is a giant step backwards, and we shouldn't take it unless it is absolutely necessary, because it will cost us dearly.

In view of this and all the other serious problems which presently accompany our use of fossil fuels, perhaps we should ask ourselves if there isn't a better source of energy available, for modern civilization most certainly cannot survive without energy.

CHAPTER 2

Found:
A Substance with 2.7 Million Times
More Energy Per Pound Than Coal!

The first inkling that a huge new source of energy might be available to civilization came in 1905, when Albert Einstein announced his now famous equation relating energy and mass (weight): $E=mc^2$, in which E=energy, m=mass, and c=the velocity of light. This equation predicts that if matter is transformed into energy, a small mass will yield a tremendous amount of energy. Unfortunately, there was little experimental evidence available to confirm Einstein's work. Nor had his genius been fully recognized in 1905.

A simple calculation reveals the tremendous amount of energy promised by Einstein's equation. Suppose a gram—about 1/28 of an ounce—of matter is converted into energy. This miniscule quantity of mass will produce 9×10^{20} ergs of energy, because the velocity of light, c, is a huge figure, being 3×10^{10} cm/sec. The calculation is:

$E=mc^2$

$E=1 \text{ gram} \times (3 \times 10^{10} \text{ cm/sec})^2$

$E=9 \times 10^{20} \text{ ergs (an erg is a gram cm}^2 \text{/sec}^2)$

An erg is a very small amount of energy, being capable of lifting a postage stamp to a height of only about 1/25 of an inch. But, 9×10^{20} ergs is the same as 900 billion billion ergs, which is an almost incomprehensibly huge number. About six million pounds of coal would have to be burned to release this much energy. And, when burned in the boiler of a locomotive, this much coal would move the locomotive and a large number of box cars well over 50,000 miles. Imagine being able to replace the six million pounds of coal with 1/28 of an ounce—a single gram of matter—and you can appreciate what an astounding prediction Einstein's was.

Clearly, this was a very exciting idea laden with the promise of abundant cheap energy and a better life for billions of people. But, remember that there had been no experimental confirmation of Einstein's theory, nor had he attempted to explain how this miraculous transformation of matter into energy might ever be possible.

In the late 1930s, a number of scientists were busy bombarding various elements with neutrons. When the lighter elements were bombarded, the results were not difficult to explain; but, when the heaviest naturally occurring element, uranium, was bombarded, the results baffled everyone. Then in Berlin, early in 1939, Otto Hahn and Fritz Strassman bombarded uranium atoms with neutrons and found that atoms of several lighter elements—barium, krypton, lanthanum, and cerium—had miraculously appeared. With less than complete certainty, Hahn and Strassman concluded that some of the massive uranium atoms had split, or fissioned, forming the lighter elements which they had found. Direct measurements indicated that a surprisingly large amount of energy was released each time that a uranium nuclei fissioned, suggesting that a small amount of mass had been transformed into a large quantity of energy, as Einstein had predicted 34 years earlier.

A Jewish physicist, Lise Meitner, also correctly interpreted this experiment, and when she fled Europe to escape Hitler, she took the news of this discovery with her.

At about the same time, Fredric Joliot-Curie discovered that when a uranium atom fissions, two (or sometimes three) neutrons are released. This suggests that a chain reaction of rapidly increasing magnitude might take place if each of the two neutrons released collided with another uranium atom. As these two uranium atoms fission, at least four neutrons will be produced. Thus, with each successive generation of fissioning uranium atoms, the number of neutrons released at least doubles, going from 2 to 4 to 8 to 16, and so on. As each of these neutrons strikes a uranium atom, causing a fission, rapidly increasing quantities of energy are released, of course.

When Einstein and other U.S. scientists learned of these scientific advances, they realized that these discoveries could have great potential as a weapon. Because German scientists were undoubtedly also aware of this possibility, there was concern that Nazi Germany might be the first to develop such a weapon, with disastrous consequences for the rest of the world. On August 2, 1939, Einstein wrote to President Franklin D. Roosevelt to alert him to the possibility that this new form of energy might be useful in the construction of "extremely powerful bombs of a new type."

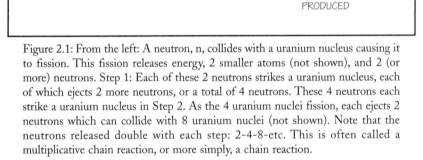

Figure 2.1: From the left: A neutron, n, collides with a uranium nucleus causing it to fission. This fission releases energy, 2 smaller atoms (not shown), and 2 (or more) neutrons. Step 1: Each of these 2 neutrons strikes a uranium nucleus, each of which ejects 2 more neutrons, or a total of 4 neutrons. These 4 neutrons each strike a uranium nucleus in Step 2. As the 4 uranium nuclei fission, each ejects 2 neutrons which can collide with 8 uranium nuclei (not shown). Note that the neutrons released double with each step: 2-4-8-etc. This is often called a multiplicative chain reaction, or more simply, a chain reaction.

The First Nuclear Reactor

By 1942, money to investigate the possibility of making a bomb which used nuclear fission had been appropriated by the U.S. government. And, a team of 31 outstanding scientists under the Nobel prizewinning Italian physicist Enrico Fermi had been assembled. Like Meitner, Fermi had also fled Europe to escape Fascism. Working on a squash court under the stands of the football field at the University of Chicago, the team of scientists had assembled what was then called simply a "pile," but which was actually the crude forerunner of the hundreds of nuclear reactors which were to follow. Only about as large as a two-car garage, this pile consisted mostly of highly purified graphite. (In lesser purity, this substance is used in today's pencils.) The pile also contained lesser quantities of uranium, uranium oxide, and a number of cadmium control rods.

Like that of most nuclear reactors, the operation of this prototype was based on the fact that an isotope, or type, of uranium atom, U235, is particularly easy to split. When the nucleus of a U235 atom is struck by a slow moving neutron, the nucleus splits, releasing two or more neutrons as described previously. But, things are not as simple as indicated earlier: The neutrons released may escape from the pile before colliding with a U235 atom. Or, the neutrons may be captured by the atoms of the lighter elements produced by the fission, by the other isotope of uranium present, U238, or by impurities in the graphite. These events are known as "non-fission capture," because no fission results from this capture.

To decrease non-fission capture, it is necessary to slow down, or moderate, the speed of the neutrons released by the fission of U235 nuclei. More slowly-moving neutrons are still able to split U235 nuclei, but they are not so likely to undergo non-fission capture. The moderator used in the first reactor was graphite, which is a planar arrangement of carbon atoms. When the fast-moving neutrons ejected by the fissioning U235 nuclei collide with carbon atoms, they impart some of their momentum to the carbon atoms, and decrease in speed. Now, the neutrons are traveling slowly enough that they are able to avoid non-fission capture, but they are still capable of splitting U235 nuclei.

Elements such as cadmium capture slow-moving neutrons which collide with them. So, to be able to control the rate of the chain reaction, cadmium control rods were provided. These rods can be slid into holes which have been made in the pile. When these control rods are slid all the way into the pile, they absorb so many neutrons that they stop the chain reaction. When the control rods are slid out of the pile, fewer neutrons are captured, and this allows the chain reaction to accelerate until the maximum possible power of the reactor is reached.

Can Nuclear Reactors Explode as the Atomic Bomb Did?

In the 1970s, a number of anti-nuclear power organizations spread the idea that the chain reaction in a nuclear power plant might increase so rapidly that the reactor could explode, as the atomic bomb did.

However, for a nuclear power reactor to undergo a nuclear explosion is, and has always been, a complete impossibility. To begin with, nuclear power reactors contain only 3 percent U235. Nuclear bombs must contain over 90 percent U235, or they don't satisfy the first of several physical conditions which must be met before a nuclear explosion can occur. (Nor is it possible for a reactor which uses plutonium to explode as did the atomic bomb.)

For those readers who might be thinking, "What about the Russian nuclear power plant at Chernobyl? Didn't it explode?" The explosion at Chernobyl was a chemical or steam explosion, not a nuclear explosion. The fact that only two people were killed by the initial explosion is ample proof that a nuclear explosion did not occur at Chernobyl; a nuclear explosion would have killed thousands. Even at a primitive nuclear power plant like Chernobyl, a nuclear explosion is an impossibility. For the time being, suffice it to say that Chernobyl was such an unsafe design that it could never have been licensed to generate electricity in the U.S., or in any of the Western European nations. (More about Chernobyl appears in a later chapter.)

When the first nuclear reactor was tested in December of 1942, Fermi allowed it to generate only about a watt—enough energy to light a flashlight bulb. But, with the help of this first primitive reactor, Fermi was able to prove that a chain reaction could be generated and controlled.

Direct measurement of the energy released and Einstein's equation showed that when one gram of uranium fissions, forming less massive atoms and several neutrons, only a small fraction of a gram of matter is converted into energy. But, this transformation enables one gram of uranium to yield 2.7 million times more energy than is released when one gram of coal burns.[1] (The reader will note that a full gram of matter was transformed into energy in an earlier calculation.)

Any time that scientists discover a new substance which can actually yield 2.7 million times more energy per gram than the old standby, coal, it is a monumental breakthrough.

The First Atomic Bomb

Following Fermi's demonstration that a chain reaction could be generated and controlled, much work still remained to be done before the atomic bomb could become a reality: A tremendous industrial effort had to be mounted. In nature, only one uranium atom out of every 140 atoms is U235; the remainder is another isotope, U238, which is unsuitable for bomb-making. So, one of the first of many problems was to mine mountains of uranium ore so that a small molehill of U235 could be separated from it. And, because both U235 and U238 behave the same chemically, separation is very difficult and costly. This effort ultimately required the labor of almost 500,000 men and women and an investment of two billion dollars.

While the separation of the isotopes of uranium was underway, a team of bomb designers at Los Alamos, New Mexico, was also busy. This team of engineers and other scientists knew that most of the neutrons produced by the fission of U235 nuclei must be captured by other U235 nuclei if a chain reaction were to occur. But, neutrons close to the surface of the uranium were likely to escape into the air, rather than being captured by other U235 nuclei. Therefore, there must be a large enough mass of at least 90 percent pure U235 present, preferably in the form of a sphere, if a chain reaction is to occur. (A sphere has the largest volume-to-surface ratio; hence, the capture of neutrons is more likely than their escape.) A sphere which is of sufficient mass to sustain a chain reaction is said to have a "critical mass."

It might seem foolish to load a sphere of U235 of critical mass onto an airplane and expect to be able to transport it several hundred miles before dropping it on a target. But, surprisingly, if this were done, no premature explosion would occur. Instead, the sphere would heat up, and then break apart into pieces, each of which would be smaller than the critical mass needed for a nuclear explosion.

One way to get around this problem would be to load two half spheres, each of which are of less than critical mass. These two half spheres are then placed at opposite ends of a cylindrical device much like the barrel of a gun, except that both ends are closed. Then, when a nuclear explosion is desired, TNT, which has been placed behind one half-sphere, can be exploded, propelling this half-sphere at the second half-sphere, and holding them firmly together for about a millionth of a second. During this brief span of time, the chain reaction rapidly multiplies, an enormous number of U235 nuclei fission, and a nuclear explosion occurs.

A second possible method of bringing about a nuclear explosion is to surround a mass of fissionable material of sufficient size with a "shaped charge" of explosives. If all of the sections of the shaped charge are exploded at exactly the right time, this explosion can briefly compress the fissionable material, suddenly allowing more neutrons to be captured and a nuclear explosion to occur. (It should be noted that much of the preceding is supposition. No nation has ever released information about the triggering mechanism actually used in nuclear bombs.)

It is also worth noting that when India tested its first atomic bomb, the arrangements made to explode it were not correct, and the explosion fizzled, as small sections of fissionable material heated up and broke apart. This failure occurred despite the fact that India has a rather well-trained scientific community. Apparently, atomic bomb making is not as simple as many people would like to believe.

Obviously, no gun barrel-like devices, no half-spheres of 90 percent pure U235, and no shaped charges of explosives are ever present in nuclear reactors; consequently, no nuclear explosion is possible. This is why, in the 58 years in which nuclear reactors have been on earth, not one of the thousands of reactors now present has ever undergone a nuclear explosion.

It is easy to understand why, in the dark days immediately after our entry into World War II, the first thought was to use this huge new source of energy as a weapon of war. After all, the Japanese Army was threatening to invade New Zealand and Australia and had driven the U.S. Army out of most of the South Pacific. The Bataan Death March was bitter history, and both the Hawaiian Islands and our own west coast were blacked out because of the fear of Japanese air raids.

In Europe, Hitler had conquered all of Western Europe except the British Isles, and was driving on Moscow in the East. The Allies reeled from defeat after defeat; everywhere, the Axis was winning.

Later, rumors that Hitler's scientists were at work on an atomic bomb were taken seriously enough to cause British commandos to stage a raid on Telemark, Norway, where work on a German atomic bomb was thought to be underway. Fortunately, Hitler had placed the task of building an atomic bomb in the wrong hands: He had selected the Nobel prizewinning theoretical physicist Werner Heisenberg for the job. But, Heisenberg lacked the practical experience needed, and he nearly died in June of 1942, when some powdered uranium accidentally got wet, reacted with the water, and released hydrogen gas which exploded. Despite this accident, Heisenberg's team was on the verge of determining what the critical mass of U235 was, when U.S. troops overran his laboratory on April 22, 1945.

On July 16, 1945, the massive U.S. effort to produce an atomic bomb resulted in a successful test explosion at Alamogordo, New Mexico. On August 6, the first atomic bomb was dropped on Hiroshima, Japan. When no surrender was forthcoming, three days later a second bomb was dropped, this time on Nagasaki. With this event, the world became painfully aware that a new source of tremendous energy was available which civilization could choose to use wisely, or otherwise.

The Cold War and Nuclear Weapons

When, in 1949, the Russians exploded an atomic bomb, fear of this new weapon increased. Then, in 1957, when the Russians launched the first earth-orbiting satellite, it became apparent that the same engines which launched a satellite could also propel an intercontinental ballistic missile. After that, the Cold War intensified, and people all over the world became fearful that nuclear bombs might be the weapons which would end civilization.

With the breakup of the Soviet Union, the world breathed a little easier, but the problem still remained. When irresponsible, power-mad people gain control of a nation, they represent a danger to the entire world, and it is very difficult to keep any of the various weapons capable of mass destruction out of their hands. Plainly, this is a problem which the leaders of the world need to work on, and there probably will be no easy solution.

Using Nuclear Reactors for Peaceful Purposes

A hint of how nuclear energy might be useful was provided when the first nuclear reactor-powered submarine, the Nautilus, was launched on January 21, 1954. On its first voyage, this vessel traveled 62,599 miles without refueling, a feat which would have been impossible without nuclear energy. This was the first of many oceangoing ships to use a nuclear reactor as its power plant.

Nuclear Research Reactors

Even while nuclear weapons reactors were producing plutonium for use in nuclear bombs, another kind of nuclear reactor, the research reactor, was at work producing the radioactive isotopes which are so useful in scientific research, industry, and medicine.

About 10 million diagnostic tests are carried out in the U.S. yearly with the help of radioactive isotopes. If you've ever had an MRI, you have benefited from a nuclear-based diagnostic procedure. Incidentally, the correct acronym is NMRI, which stands for "Nuclear Magnetic Resonance Imaging," but the "Nuclear" is usually dropped in the U.S. because many Americans are unreasonably fearful of anything nuclear.

It is estimated that even before 1960, the medical use of nuclear research reactor-produced isotopes had saved the lives of more people than were killed at Hiroshima and Nagasaki combined.[2] This was accomplished by the more accurate early diagnosis of serious medical conditions.

Nuclear research reactors also produce the radioactive isotopes—usually cesium or cobalt—that generate the radioactivity used to sterilize most of the medical and surgical supplies used in any modern hospital. The same isotopes are also used to irradiate and sterilize such common consumer goods as first aid kits, bandages, tampons, and cotton gauze.

What makes irradiation such a valuable tool is that the item to be sterilized can be sealed in a package, and then irradiated with gamma rays from radioactive isotopes. The gamma rays pass through the packaging, kill any bacteria present, and are gone without a trace. Gamma radiation emitted during the sterilization process not only kills bacteria, but also kills parasitic worms, mildew, and the fungi which causes fruit to rot.

Radiation from isotopes could be even more useful if the political activists who are against its use would let us use it to sterilize meat, poultry, and eggs. This use would go a long way toward preventing most of the 6.5 million cases of bacterial-caused food poisoning and the accompanying 9,000 deaths which occur in the U.S. yearly.

The irradiation of food is endorsed by the American Medical Association, the U.S. Department of Agriculture, the federal Food and Drug Administration, the American Dietetic Association, the Council for Agricultural Science and Technology, the Institute of Food Technologists, and the United Nations Food and Agriculture Organization.

Forty-two nations now approve of irradiation as a method of sterilizing food; but, until recently, the U.S. was not among them. China, which lags behind the U.S. by almost every socioeconomic measure, has five large irradiation plants under construction and plans to build a plant in every large city.

Many smoke detectors use the research reactor-produced isotope Americium 243. Yearly, smoke detectors save thousands of lives by warning people of fires while there's still time to get out of the building.

Other reactor-produced isotopes have been used to power thermoelectric generators in many space explorations. Cassini, the spacecraft sent to probe the rings of Saturn, got all of its electric power from 72 pounds of plutonium oxide. (Plutonium is a manmade element produced by bombarding U238 with neutrons.) The heat released by the fission of this substance was converted into electricity by solid-state thermoelectric generators.

The use of research reactor-produced isotopes during the last five decades has been responsible for much of the spectacular progress in biology, agriculture, and medicine; these isotopes have proven to be one of science's most useful research tools. A final example of the value of research reactors is provided by Frederick Reines' discovery of the neutrino, for which he won the 1995 Nobel Prize in physics. This achievement was accomplished with the help of scientist Clyde Cowan and a research reactor. Cowan died before the Nobel Prize was awarded.

Using Nuclear Reactors to Generate Electricity

Late in 1957, a larger nuclear reactor was used to generate electricity when the nation's first commercial nuclear power plant came on line at Shippingport, Pennsylvania. Figure 2.2 shows the essential details of this plant in simplified fashion.

This design became the model for the nuclear industry in Japan and in many Western European nations, as well as in the U.S. It is still in use today, although a new, even safer generation of nuclear power plants is poised to replace it.

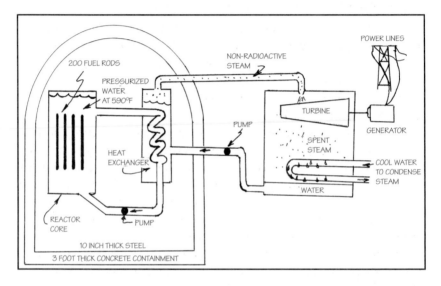

Figure 2.2: The basic design of the pressurized water reactor commonly used in the U.S., Japan, and many Western European countries. The reactor core, which is where fission occurs, is on the far left. The water in which the fuel rods are immersed is heated to 590ºF by the fission, but it doesn't boil, because it is under such high pressure. This water acts as the moderator, and also serves to transfer heat to the water in the heat exchanger. The water in the heat exchanger boils, forming steam. (From here on, nuclear and fossil fuel plants are identical.) The steam strikes the blades of the turbine, causing it to turn very rapidly. The turbine then turns a generator, which converts the energy of motion into electrical energy. An important point to note is that all radioactivity is contained in the first loop. The steam which turns the turbine is not radioactive. Thick metal jackets and a three-foot-thick concrete containment shell surround the radioactive part of the reactor. This containment is designed to prevent the escape of radioactivity in the event of an accident.

In the early 1960s, nuclear power plants were greeted with widespread public acceptance. City planners and public utility engineers alike saw them as a way to solve a rapidly worsening air pollution problem largely caused by coal-burning power plants.

By December of 1970, there were 19 nuclear power plants in the U.S. which generated 2 percent of our electricity. An additional 53 plants were under construction, and 34 more were in the planning stage. The orders increased rapidly, and only six months later, 63 plants were on order. The Federal Power Commission predicted that nuclear power's share of the nation's electricity would grow to 24 percent in 1980, and 41 percent by 1990. (Unfortunately, usage fell short of this, reaching only 20.6 percent in 1990.)

Opposition to Nuclear Power Grows

Then, without any accident or similar event to trigger their formation, anti-nuclear power groups began to form all over the nation. Although everyone was fearful of nuclear weapons, the antinuclear groups directed most of their effort not against nuclear weapons reactors but, instead, began a campaign to stop the construction of nuclear power plants which generated electricity.

Although commercial nuclear power plants had experienced no accidents with the nuclear aspect of the plants which caused injury or loss of life on the part of either plant workers or the public, the anti-nuclear power groups questioned power plant safety. While this was going on, coal-burning power plants were releasing air pollutants which scientists estimated were killing over 50,000 people a year, but this fact seemed not to matter to the anti-nuclear power groups.

During the rest of the 1970s and well into the 1980s, anti-nuclear power groups circulated one falsehood after another about nuclear power plants. The media was supplied with these falsehoods, and in numerous instances, repeated them. For example, the fictional bit about a nuclear power plant exploding was discussed on prime-time television news as illustrated by the following 1976 exchange between ABC science editor Jules Bergman and newscaster Harry Reasoner:

> Reasoner: "In a nuclear accident, you might kill a million people, right?"
> Bergman: "It's possible. You might more likely kill a hundred thousand or so, if the thing blew up."[3]

These remarks were nearly an echo of what anti-nuclear activists had been claiming for several years. But the statement had no basis in fact. Both ABC's science editor and newscaster had been badly misinformed by the political activists.

Some of the other falsehoods circulated by the antinuclear power organizations and individuals include the following:

- Nuclear power plants emit deadly radiation which kills babies and damages the gene pool.
- Nuclear power plants emit so much heat that they will cause our rivers to boil and evaporate.
- Nuclear power plants are too expensive to build.
- The disposal of nuclear wastes is an unsolvable problem.
- Nuclear wastes—and especially plutonium—are the most toxic substances known.
- In the event of a meltdown, a couple of hundred thousand people would die immediately, and hundreds of thousands would die later from cancer.
- Nuclear power plants are so unsafe that they should all be shut down, and no new ones built.

With one exception, time has proven all of these statements to be completely false. For example, have you heard of any U.S. nuclear power plants which have blown up? Or have you seen any boiling rivers, lately? Have you heard of any nuclear power accidents in which even one person, let alone "a couple of hundred thousand people" died?

The exception which is true is the statement that nuclear power plants are too expensive to build.

Until 1982, nuclear power was our cheapest source of electricity.[4] Then, the cost overruns caused by frivolous lawsuits filed by antinuclear groups that were intended to delay or stop construction began to have an effect, and the cost of nuclear power plants became as much as 10 times greater than the original construction estimates. Regulatory changes by the government during construction which were designed to appease the antinuclear power groups also added to construction costs.

In other countries where these delaying tactics were not so successful, nuclear power is still the cheapest energy. A 1982 study by the European Economic Community reported that for power plants started at that time, nuclear-generated electricity would be only 59 percent as expensive as coal in both France and Italy, and only 77 percent as expensive as in Belgium and 71 percent as in Germany.[5]

There's more than a bit of irony involved when a group which did its best to increase nuclear power plant construction costs brags, "They're too expensive to build."

Over the years, repetition of these falsehoods began to have an effect, and the public became much more fearful of nuclear power plants than they had been in the 1960s and early 1970s.

Three Mile Island

In 1979, when a loss of coolant accident occurred at a nuclear power plant at Three Mile Island, in Pennsylvania, the stage was set, and the event became front page news for almost six weeks. At Three Mile Island no one was hurt, killed, or exposed to a significant amount of radiation, but this didn't seem to matter to the anti-nuclear power activists, who treated the accident as an event which threatened the life of everyone in the area.

Subsequently, 65,000 antinuclear activists marched on Washington and demanded that all nuclear power plants be shut down. Later, a commission appointed by the president looked into the matter and concluded that "Three Mile Island had never threatened the public in any way."[6] But the weeks of hysteria had taken their toll, and the commission's report did little to alleviate the public's fear.

After Three Mile Island, antinuclear activists stepped up their efforts to stop the use of nuclear power plants. Not only were they successful in stopping the construction of any plants ordered after 1974, but they also forced many utility companies to tear down billions of dollars worth of nearly finished nuclear power plants.

The antinuclear activists were able to accomplish this by filing thousands of frivolous lawsuits, each of which halted the construction of a nuclear power plant. Although almost all of these lawsuits were ultimately either defeated or thrown out of court, they accomplished their purpose by stopping construction while each lawsuit slowly made its way through the courts. And, as soon as one lawsuit was resolved, a new suit was filed, stopping construction again. These delays cost the utility companies billions of dollars because they had to continue paying interest on the money previously borrowed for construction, even though construction was held up.

For example, suppose that a utility company had borrowed a billion dollars to build a nuclear power plant, and a lawsuit was filed which held up construction for six months. At 10 percent yearly interest, that loan would cost the utility company 50 million dollars during the delay. If a dozen such lawsuits were filed at various intervals during construction, the total additional interest could reach 600 million dollars. Frivolous lawsuits resulted in delays which often doubled the cost of building a nuclear power plant by increasing the average construction time from the usual six years to twelve years.

Today, the utility companies are so frightened by the tactics of anti-nuclear activists that not one utility company in America is brave—or foolish—enough to place an order for a nuclear power plant, despite the fact that the first generation of Western-built nuclear power plants has had an absolutely spotless safety record which shows that these plants are far safer than those of any other comparably-sized industry. And, a new, much improved second generation of nuclear power plants is waiting to be built.

Has Nuclear Power Been Correctly Evaluated?

Two decades have passed since the antinuclear activists stopped the normal development of nuclear power in the U.S. Does it matter that we let this happen? Or was it a bad mistake which should be corrected?

Several things indicate that stopping the growth of nuclear power was a big mistake. First of all, nuclear power is alive and doing well almost everywhere else in the world. France now uses nuclear power to generate 77 percent of its electricity, almost four times our present figure of 20 percent. Another 17 countries also use nuclear power to generate a higher percentage of their electricity than we do. Thirty-two countries now operate nuclear power plants. Obviously, building nuclear power plants is the strongest endorsement possible. Surely if nuclear power were more unsafe or more expensive than the cheapest fuel, coal, many of these countries wouldn't be building nuclear power plants.

Second, the following professional organizations endorsed nuclear power years ago. These are the people who know the most about it and would be the first to warn us if a problem existed. All of the following organizations are made up of medical doctors, scientists, and engineers, and all of them have passed resolutions approving the use of nuclear power plants:

- The 18,000 members of the Power Engineering Society.
- The Energy Committee of the 170,000-member Institute of Electrical and Electronics Engineers.
- The 69,000 members of the Society of Professional Engineers. (The three previous groups are closest to the problem of generating electrical energy, and they are among the most knowledgeable about nuclear energy.)
- The Board of Directors of the 3,400-member Health Physics Society. (These people best understand the effects of radiation on the human body.)
- The National Council of the 39,000-member American Institute of Chemical Engineers.[7] and, last but certainly not least,
- The 500,000 members of the American Medical Association.[8]

Furthermore, every reputable scientific organization which has looked into the matter has come to the conclusion that burning coal is more dangerous than using nuclear power. Some of these organizations include the following:[9]

- The American Medical Association's Council on Scientific Affairs.
- England's United Kingdom Health and Safety Executive.
- The National Academy of Sciences Committee on Nuclear and Alternative Energy Systems.
- The Brookhaven National Laboratory.
- The U.S. Office of Technology Assessment.
- The Legislative Office of Science Advisor, State of Michigan.
- The Environmental Protection Agency.
- The Stanford Research Institute.
- The Nuclear Energy Policy Study Group.
- The Science Advisory Office, State of Maryland.
- The Norwegian Ministry of Oil and Energy.

If you are wondering whether some of these groups which endorsed nuclear power did so because they had a vested interest in it, this question has been studied by neutral, professional researchers. In the 1970s, several prominent antinuclear activists suggested that any professionals in the field should disqualify themselves from passing judgment on nuclear power plants because they had a vested interest in the success of nuclear power. The activists wanted us to "let the people decide" without any input from the experts. (My suspicion is, however, that the next time these same antinuclear activists have moles which are changing color and rapidly enlarging, they will consult doctors instead of "letting the people decide" if it's cancer or not.)

Two researchers decided to see whether the nuclear experts had given nuclear power their approval simply because they worked in the field and earned their living there.[10] The researchers sent a questionnaire to dozens of energy experts, some of whom worked in the field of nuclear power, and some of whom did not. The researchers' conclusion: Both groups were almost equally supportive of nuclear power.

Incidentally, these researchers also found that when 72 nuclear experts were queried, 99 percent agreed that the risks of nuclear power were acceptable, and 98 percent of this group said that they would be willing to see nuclear power plants located in the city in which they lived, even though this is almost never done.[11]

Reevaluating Nuclear Power

Nuclear power plants have now been used to generate electricity for over 42 years. There are now 442 such reactors on earth. Some of them were Western-built and have a spotless safety record. A few, like Chernobyl, are dangerous and could never have been licensed to operate in the Western world. But we have little control over what other countries do, of course.

If we define a "reactor-year" as one reactor in use for one year, then by the year 2000 we will have had almost 10,000 reactor-years of experience with nuclear power reactors. Surely this is a long enough period of time so that a thorough study of the established record of the various kinds of energy will provide good, factual answers to the following questions:

1. Which has recent history proven to be more dangerous, nuclear wastes, or those produced by the fossil fuels?

2. Which source of energy, nuclear power or the fossil fuels, has proven to be more detrimental to the environment?

3. Which source of energy has caused us to run the greater economic risks?

4. From the standpoint of accidental death, which source of energy has proven itself to be safer?

5. Are there any better alternatives to the fossil fuels and nuclear power?

No longer should intelligent people bother to consider questions such as, "What will happen if a nuclear power plant explodes?" Over 42 years have passed since the first nuclear power reactor was put into service. The record of what has happened during this time period is there to be studied, and judgment should be based on this record and not on imaginative supposition of "what might happen," or misinformation. Let the factual record of the last 42 years and good, sweet common sense prevail.

CHAPTER 3

The "Unsolvable Problem" of Waste Disposal

All indications are that a good many very intelligent, well-read Americans now believe that the disposal of nuclear wastes is an unsolvable problem.

Actually, nothing could be further from the truth. No real experts in the field of nuclear waste disposal view this problem as "unsolvable." In fact, most experts agree that the safe disposal of nuclear wastes is a rather simple, easily solved engineering problem.

How did the ridiculous idea that nuclear waste disposal was an "unsolvable problem" ever get started? Because nuclear power plants produce miniscule amounts of waste, only very small quantities of waste had piled up, and temporary, on-site storage was not a problem.

However, because the antinuclear activists had made such a potentially dangerous political issue out of nuclear waste disposal, no politician wanted to approve of the burial of nuclear wastes in his state. The result was that every politician from the president on down ducked the issue. Because it was not a pressing problem, no one in either the state or federal government was forced to act.

Having succeeded in creating this bureaucratic stalemate, the antinuclear activists then went on to convince the media that no nuclear wastes were being buried anywhere because the disposal of nuclear wastes was an unsolvable problem.

The reader may wonder why the media was so quick to accept the antinuclear activists' point of view. After all, few activists have any scientific training, and almost none are experts in the field of hazardous waste disposal.

Journalists have a saying, "No problem, no news." In the early 1970s, when antinuclear activists first claimed that nuclear power plants might explode, killing hundreds of thousands of people and contaminating entire states, this seemed to be a big problem—so, it was big news, and the media gave these threats big coverage. After this threat became old news, the activists simply invented a new threat. The latest in the long line of threats is that "the disposal of nuclear wastes is an unsolvable problem."

When television newscasters first reported these activists' threats in the 1970s, they quickly found out that reporting the threats drew, and held, viewers. To the newscasters, this was similar to discovering gold, because well-paid careers in television rise—or fall—depending on the newscaster's ability to attract viewers. Soon, most of the networks were reporting almost every news release issued by the antinuclear activists.

Television newscasters repeated the misinformation put out by the antinuclear activists so often that they, and many of their viewers, seemed to forget that these reports were simply the unfounded opinion of the scientifically untrained. Both newscasters and viewers were apparently unaware that the reports were untrue.

Unfortunately, a very effective, informal, mutually advantageous alliance had fallen into place. As the antinuclear activists reported each new nuclear power threat, the media rushed to report it. The activists got the publicity they needed to gain political power, and the media got the story it needed to draw an audience. The result was that soon only the antinuclear activists' views were heard by the public. Science, and the real experts, had been denied a voice in what was really a scientific matter.

Nuclear Waste Disposal as Reported by the Media

For over a decade now, the media has been hard at work trying to sell the American public on the antinuclear activists' lie that nuclear waste disposal is an "unsolvable problem." Here are a few examples:[1]

CBS, November 8, 1976: "Another environmental concern about nuclear energy is what to do with the radioactive leftovers of power plants. Both *scientifically* and economically, it's *the big unsolved problem* of the nuclear industry."(Italics added.)

NBC, October 17, 1977: "Dumping or storing nuclear garbage is going to be a *big problem* in years to come, and not much is known about it." (Italics added.)

NBC, December 1, 1977: "Disposal of nuclear waste remains a *worrisome problem with no good answer*. (Italics added.) "What to do with nuclear garbage is now a *national problem.*" (Italics added.) "At Hanford, Washington, they still have the radioactive garbage from the first atomic bomb made there in 1945. It may all be safe by the year 250,000,000 A.D."

ABC, December 9, 1977: "Around the United States, there are sixty-five nuclear power plants generating electricity. *Each plant creates radioactive waste equivalent to 300 Hiroshima bombs each year.* And that waste remains radioactive for 200,000 years." (Italics added.)

"The Federal government has not *figured out* what else to do with *the radioactive waste equivalent to 20,000 Hiroshima bombs produced by our electricity-generating nuclear power plants* each year." (Italics added.)

CBS, April 5, 1978: "One of the *thorniest problems* of the nuclear age is how and where to dispose of the nuclear waste." (Italics added.)[1]

By August 1986, this continual barrage of misinformation had begun to take effect, and a Roper Poll showed that 67 percent of the U.S. public were "very concerned about radiation exposure from nuclear waste disposal." The more the public read or listened to the news, the more misinformed they became.

How We've Solved the "Unsolvable Problem" for the Past Fifty-five Years

To show how wildly exaggerated the claim that nuclear waste disposal is an "unsolvable problem," we need only look at what has been done in the past. Nuclear wastes from power plants, reactors used for research and medical purposes, and those used in weapons production have been accumulating since the early 1940s. And, since that time, these wastes have simply been stored in shallow tanks of water near the site where they were produced. The radioactivity coming from these wastes has been carefully monitored periodically, and the level of radiation has never been high enough to pose even a minor health threat to anyone, not even to those who work near these temporary storage tanks. So, no deaths—not even one—have resulted from this simplest, easiest method of temporary storage. In other words, the "unsolvable problem" has already been solved, even though the antinuclear activists will not accept either this simple solution or the more thorough long-term solution now ready to be put into use. But, the political activists were never interested in the safe disposal of wastes: They want to stop the use of nuclear power by preventing the disposal of wastes.

How Dangerous Are Nuclear Wastes?

All fuels produce wastes. When coal and oil burn, the substances in the coal and oil combine with oxygen and form gaseous and solid waste products. And, when uranium atoms undergo fission in a nuclear reactor, they produce a radioactive waste which must eventually be disposed of.

Although most people think that nuclear wastes are the most deadly wastes ever produced, this simply isn't true. The wastes from a coal-burning power plant are potentially ten times more deadly than the *untreated* wastes from a nuclear power plant. According to waste disposal experts and the U.S. Department of Energy, if all of the air pollutants produced during a single day by a coal-burning power plant reached the lungs of people, these poisons would kill ten times as many people as would die were they to inhale or ingest all of the wastes produced during one day by a nuclear power plant.[2,3]

Contrary to what you may have heard, nuclear wastes are far from being the "most toxic substances known to man." If you have the least doubt about this statement, consider the fact that over the last 20 years, one million Americans have died from breathing the air pollutants produced by burning fossil fuels. During this same time period, the *untreated* nuclear wastes held at temporary storage sites haven't killed a single person. These are the facts, and they are hard for a reasonable person to ignore.

Once nuclear wastes are treated, they are only about as toxic as selenium compounds, some of which occur in nature.[4] And, after the treated wastes from a nuclear power plant have been in storage for 100 years, their toxicity diminishes, and is then equal to that of arsenic trioxide, which we often spread around the food crops in our gardens to kill various pests. It is worth noting that while the toxicity of nuclear wastes diminishes with time, the toxicity of arsenic trioxide will never diminish. Whatever arsenic trioxide was added to our gardens this year simply lies on the soil along with all the arsenic trioxide which has been added over the past years. And, each year, we produce enough arsenic trioxide to kill 10 billion people. It would be more sensible if we'd worry more about arsenic trioxide and less about nuclear wastes.

Disposing of Nuclear Wastes

Of course, the wastes from a nuclear power plant aren't dangerous unless they are breathed or somehow get into our water or food chain. To prevent this from happening, present disposal plans call for the wastes produced by nuclear power plants to be mixed into molten glass, cooled, and thus made part of a solid, corrosion-proof unbreakable glass. This process, known as "vitrification," has been used by the French for over 20 years without any serious problems arising.

Because we are used to thin layers of glass we think of it as being very fragile, but in thick layers, glass is as hard and unbreakable as a rock. In fact, many rocks are actually glasses, and they are as unbreakable as many other rocks. More important, glass is virtually insoluble, even in running water. Glass artifacts several thousand years old have been discovered in riverbeds, where running water has failed to dissolve them. And, a Canadian experiment indicates that glass buried in water-soaked earth will last for roughly 100 million years.

According to plans, while still molten the vitrified nuclear wastes will be poured into stainless steel containers, allowed to cool, surrounded by backfill materials which provide additional support and also resist the entry of water, and then be buried 1,200 feet below the surface of the earth.

The site selected for burial, Yucca Mountain in Nevada, has been thoroughly studied at a cost of $30 million, which was raised by placing a tax on nuclear-generated electricity. Three hundred test holes have been drilled to determine such things as how deep the water table lies. Because of its suitability, in the past an adjoining area was used for over 600 below-ground tests of nuclear weapons. Each below-ground test site is already a small storage site for nuclear wastes generated by the tests. Apparently none of these wastes have surfaced despite the fact that they were not vitrified and placed in stainless steel containers.

The area receives on average only six inches of rainfall a year, and all but about one-third of an inch of this evaporates. As you might expect in such a dry area, the water table is 2,500 feet below the surface. Plans are to bury the nuclear wastes at a depth of 1,200 feet. Geologists estimate that it will take from 2,000 to 8,000 years for surface moisture to reach the buried wastes.

Of course, it is highly unlikely that this small amount of moisture will ever be able to penetrate the special backfill materials used and dissolve the stainless steel container and the glass surrounding the nuclear wastes.

If this extremely unlikely event were ever to somehow occur, the water bearing any dissolved wastes must move 1,300 feet downward, and then flow through layers of underground rock for 30 miles before it could surface in the Amargosa desert. Water might make this trip in only 150,000 years, but the dissolved nuclear wastes would move hundreds or even thousands of times slower. And, after this trip of over 15 million years, the water carrying the nuclear wastes would surface in a natural basin from which there is no escape. Once there, the water would rapidly evaporate, leaving stranded whatever small quantity of nuclear wastes had made the trip. And, by this time, the radioactivity of those wastes would be so diminished that they would pose less danger than naturally occurring uranium-bearing rocks in many areas.

This is probably the safest waste disposal procedure ever planned. What makes it possible is the fact that nuclear power plants produce only miniscule quantities of waste—equal to about one aspirin tablet in volume yearly for each person for whom they generate electricity.

So, what the antinuclear activists call an "unsolvable problem" is solved simply by incorporating the nuclear wastes into an insoluble glass encased in rustproof stainless steel, and then burying them over a thousand feet below the surface in one of the driest areas in the world from which escape is nearly impossible. Under these conditions, chances are very good that none of the nuclear wastes will ever escape from their burial ground.

Surely this method of disposal is safer than simply placing the waste in tanks of water, which is what we do now. And even this simple method of temporary storage has proven to be completely safe.

Over a Long Period of Time, Using Nuclear Power Could Save Even More Lives

There's one more very important fact about waste disposal which few people stop to consider. Nuclear fuel originally came from nature and, therefore, when used and then returned to the ground as waste adds nothing to nature which wasn't originally there. Nature distributed the uranium at random. Some of this uranium is undoubtedly near enough to groundwater to be washed into water supplies. Some of it is close enough to the surface so that the radon gas it emits poses a threat to our health, possibly killing as many as 14,000 people per year. Nature selected these places without concern for man, of course. When this naturally occurring uranium is mined, used, and finally made a part of glass, and buried, man removes a dangerous substance from the environment and places it in a much safer place. Man improves on nature.

Professor Bernard Cohen is past chairman of the American Physical Society Division of Nuclear Physics, and past Chairman of the American Nuclear Society Division of Environmental Sciences. And, he's extremely knowledgeable about the problem of nuclear waste disposal. According to Dr. Cohen, over extremely long periods of time, in the future, today's mining of uranium for use in nuclear power plants could ultimately save the lives of many hundreds of millions of people.[5] Dr. Cohen's calculations are based on the following facts: Uranium spontaneously undergoes radioactive decay by ejecting sub-atomic particles and forming radon gas, which is radioactive. When the radon gas is released within a yard or so of the surface, it enters the air we breathe, and this is now thought to cause about 14,000 lung cancer deaths per year in the U.S. (You may have seen the small radon test kits now sold in drugstores in many states. These are designed to detect the presence of radon gas in your home.)

Each ton of uranium in the earth has the potential for causing 3.3 deaths, and there are roughly 66 million tons of uranium in the upper yard of U.S. soil. So, just the uranium in this dangerous top yard of soil has the capacity to ultimately kill 220 million people.

If the uranium is buried more deeply, it poses no *immediate* threat, because at greater depths any radon which is released has time to fission and form a solid which is not likely to enter the air. But, falling rain washes the topsoil away at the rate of about one inch every 550 years; so, in time, most uranium atoms, no matter how deeply buried, will ultimately reach the surface, where they will pose a dangerous health hazard to future generations.

To operate one large nuclear power plant requires that 180 tons of uranium be mined each year. So, because each ton has the potential of causing 3.3 lung cancer deaths, each year that a nuclear power plant is in operation, enough uranium is removed from the soil to save about 600 lives. This figure must be adjusted for some other factors, so the final figure is 420 future lung cancers prevented for each year that a single nuclear power plant is in operation. If 500 nuclear power plants were in operation, over 200,000 lives would eventually be saved for each year of their operation.

It is true that this is a long-term effect, but it has to be considered as another very strong argument for nuclear power.

Fossil Fuel Waste Disposal

Earlier we pointed out that modern civilization can't exist without the use of energy. At present there are only two ways to generate the massive quantities of energy we need—by nuclear power plants, or by fossil fuel-burning power plants. The disposal system planned for nuclear wastes will effectively prevent almost 100 percent of them from ever entering the air we breathe, or the water we drink. Is the fossil fuel waste disposal system now in use anywhere near as effective?

When fossil fuels are burned, most of the wastes are simply released into the air as gaseous smoke. Coal burning also produces a solid waste known as ashes. Let's begin by looking at the gaseous waste products released by burning coal.

Gaseous Wastes Produced by Coal

In the U.S., we burn about one billion tons of coal a year, and it produces about 22 percent of the energy we use, including most of our electricity. But, of the three fossil fuels—coal, oil, and natural gas—coal is by far the worst air polluter.

The world's coal began its formation 200 million years ago when the giant ferns, reeds, and mosses of the time fell into swamps. Over the next 50 million years, heavy rains washed all kinds of minerals into the swamps; and as the coal-to-be was compressed and hardened, these minerals became part of the coal. Even though much of the coal used today is crushed into a powder before its use, it would be far too difficult and prohibitively expensive to remove these minerals prior to burning the coal. The result is that as coal burns, most of these minerals enter the air we breathe, and the remainder becomes part of the solid waste—ashes—which must be disposed of eventually.

[In the sections that follow, except for the figures pertaining to energy, most of the figures come from the Environmental Protection Agency's (EPA) December 1997 report, *National Air Pollution Emission Trends, 1900-1996*, and are for 1996.[6]

In 1996, coal was responsible for 88 percent of the 19 million tons of sulfur dioxide released. Additionally, coal produced 27 percent of the 23 million tons of the oxides of nitrogen released.

Although the EPA doesn't include many of these substances in its reports, the use of coal also results in the yearly emission of at least 1,000 tons each of mercury, beryllium, manganese, selenium, and nickel, and lesser amounts of lead arsenic, cadmium, asbestos, benzo(a)pyrene, and other related hydrocarbons. Surprisingly, *coal-burning power plants* release several hundred times more radioactivity per day than do nuclear power plants.[7,8] This radioactivity comes from the uranium, radium, thorium, and polonium which were trapped in the coal during its formation. Each year, about 20,000 tons of uranium is mixed in with the one billion tons of coal now mined.[9]

What's So Dangerous about the Pollutants Released by Coal?

Sulfur dioxide was present in high concentrations during all of the infamous killer fogs. And, for a long time sulfur dioxide has been considered one of the most dangerous of all air pollutants. Current research indicates that sulfur dioxide can form sulfate aerosols, a major component of fine particulate matter in the eastern part of the U.S.[10] Both sulfur dioxide and the sulfate aerosols have been linked to bronchitis and other serious respiratory diseases, and to most of the deaths associated with air pollution. These substances also aggravate existing cardiovascular disease, which is the number one cause of death in the U.S.

Mercury is a cumulative poison that collects in the small blood vessels of the brain and can lead to insanity or serious neuromuscular problems. In 1980, half of the mercury entering our biosphere came from the combustion of coal.

The reduction of lead emissions is one of the EPA's biggest success stories. Not only did it get the lead out of gasoline, but while doing so it also cut lead emissions from all fossil fuel combustion from a peak of 192,314 tons in 1970 to only 1,057 tons in 1996. This was an important reduction because lead tends to accumulate in the body, where it can cause retardation and other serious health problems.[11]

Beryllium is especially toxic if inhaled. Selenium and cadmium are both poisonous and possible carcinogens; that is, they are suspected of causing cancer. Arsenic compounds were used by the "great poisoners" of medieval times, who invited their enemies over to dinner and then served them arsenic trioxide in their pasta. Arsenic, asbestos, benzo(a)pyrene, and other cyclic organic compounds emitted by coal burning are known to cause lung cancer. Benzo(a)pyrene is also found in cigarette smoke. And, some research suggests that it could be the leading cause of lung cancer in smokers. Radium, thorium, uranium, and polonium are all radioactive carcinogens.

Obviously, not even small quantities of these poisonous, dangerous substances should be breathed. This is especially true because many of these substances have an accumulative effect. That is, over long periods of time, the damage builds up, and often does not make itself known until it's too late to do much about it. And, the damage is usually irreversible.

The emission of large quantities of sulfur dioxide and nitrogen oxides, along with so many other dangerous air pollutants makes coal by far our most dangerous fuel. *Every scientific study ever carried out indicates that coal is much more dangerous to use than nuclear power.*[12] Even nuclear power's most determined foes, such as the Union of Concerned Scientists, are forced to admit that coal is more dangerous to use than nuclear power. Coal is thought to be responsible for most of the 50,000 air pollution-related deaths which occur yearly, on the average, in the U.S.

Natural Gas

From the most dangerous fossil fuel, coal, we turn to our safest fossil fuel, natural gas. In 1996, natural gas was used to generate about a quarter of the energy produced by the three fossil fuels. But, it contributed only about 548,000 tons of sulfur dioxide and about 1.8 million tons of the nitrogen oxides to the 155 million tons of pollutants released yearly. Natural gas is definitely our cleanest, least polluting fossil fuel. It is unfortunate that there is not enough of it to replace all of the coal and oil now burned.

Oil and Its Derivatives

In terms of the pollutants it releases, oil falls in between coal and natural gas. During 1996, oil and its various derivatives such as diesel fuel and gasoline produced almost 50 percent of the energy generated by fossil fuels. Roughly 60 percent of this energy was used in automobiles, tractors, airplanes, and trucks. These sources were responsible for approximately 50 percent of the nitrogen oxides released, over 40 percent of the volatile organic compounds, and almost 80 percent of the carbon monoxide emitted. Fortunately, most of the sulfur in crude oil is removed during the refinery's production of gasoline, so automobiles and trucks released only about 1.6 percent of the sulfur dioxide emitted. This fact is significant, because most air pollution mortality studies link sulfur dioxide with the death rate. From the standpoint of sulfur dioxide emissions, automobiles only kill 1/46 as many people as do stationary coal-burning sources such as electricity-generating power plants.

Automobiles and other vehicles released nearly 70 million tons of carbon monoxide into the air during 1996. Carbon monoxide combines with the hemoglobin of the blood and prevents it from carrying oxygen. At very high concentrations, such as those produced when an automobile engine is run in a closed garage, unconsciousness and death can occur in a matter of minutes. Just how many automobile accidents are caused by carbon monoxide-impaired judgment is unknown. But a good percentage of the millions of tons of carbon monoxide released along our streets and highways must find its way into the lungs and bloodstream of a large number of drivers.

Automobiles also release the oxides of nitrogen. This pollutant is a major component of the photochemical smogs which have posed a severe problem for the larger cities of southern California for over six decades. When high temperatures are attained during combustion, nitrogen, which is ordinarily unreactive, reacts with the oxygen in the air to form nitrogen dioxide. Nitrogen dioxide irritates the respiratory system and lowers the lungs' resistance to respiratory diseases such as influenza. And, from time to time, research surfaces which indicates that nitrogen dioxide might cause lung cancer. In the presence of sunlight and other pollutants such as unburned hydrocarbons, nitrogen dioxide reacts to form ozone and other dangerous air pollutants such as peroxyacetyl nitrate. Ozone can damage both the lining of the bronchial tubes and the lungs. And it, too, reduces the ability of the lungs to resist infection.

Stationary sources such as oil-burning electrical power plants and industrial furnaces released less than 10 percent of the sulfur dioxide emitted during 1996. From the standpoint of the quantity of sulfur dioxide released, oil-burning stationary sources such as furnaces are over five times more dangerous than automobiles and trucks, but only one-eighth as dangerous as coal-burning sources.

Changing to Electric Cars Could Increase Air Pollution's Death Toll

We should mention a problem which is rapidly reaching the critical stage in many cities. Because of air pollution levels, plans are underway to eliminate, or at least greatly restrict, the use of automobiles in major cities. Los Angeles plans to completely bar the use of gasoline-powered automobiles within only a few years. And, as of November 20, 1989, Mexico City took steps to reduce the number of automobiles entering the city. In May of 1994, Athens, Greece, barred cars from the heart of the city.

As they become more common, these measures will undoubtedly result in greater efforts to produce electrical cars. When electric cars are in use, their batteries will have to be recharged by connecting them overnight to a source of electricity, say an electrical outlet in a garage. Of course, this electricity will have to be generated in power plants. If it's generated by coal-burning power plants, the death toll from air pollution could easily increase rather than decrease as many people expect.

This is based on the fact that most air pollution studies indicate a relationship between sulfur dioxide and increased death rates. But, automobiles presently release only about 1.6 percent of the sulfur dioxide emitted each year. Coal burning, on the other hand, releases 88 percent of the sulfur dioxide generated. And, when coal is used to produce electricity, two-thirds of the energy of the coal is unavoidably lost in the conversion. So, not only would we be exchanging a small source of sulfur dioxide—gasoline—for coal, which is the major source of sulfur dioxide, but we will also encounter big energy losses in doing so. This will necessitate the burning of much more coal, leading to a higher death toll.

If this doesn't happen because the cities delay in barring gasoline-driven cars, it will most certainly happen when we run out of oil. Then, battery powered cars will come into widespread use, and the increased coal burning necessary to recharge these cars will almost certainly increase the air pollution-related deaths.

The Problem of Mutations

Respiratory disease isn't the only problem which accompanies the use of fossil fuels. Here's one which you seldom hear about, possibly because so little is known about it.

As you know, our characteristics are determined by the genes we receive from our parents. Genes can change, or mutate, from time to time. Most of these changes normally occur spontaneously in nature, but a number of things are known to cause mutations. For over 95 years, it has been known that radioactivity, X-rays, and certain chemicals can produce mutations in plants and lower animals. These mutation-causing substances are known as "mutagens."

Some of the over 3,000 substances known to cause mutations in the lower animals are the bisulfites, which form when sulfur dioxide dissolves in water, and the oxides of nitrogen. On the average, fossil fuels release over 40 million tons of these two mutagens into the air each year.

About 3 percent of all human live births exhibit a mutation of some kind, so the possibility that some major air pollutants might be human mutagens is disturbing, to say the least.

In the past, some of the more artistic antinuclear activists have routinely cranked out sketches of grotesque mutants in the shadow of nuclear power plants, and then claimed that the miniscule, carefully monitored amounts of radiation which escapes from these plants could cause such mutant monsters. But the fact is, people who live right at the fence line of a nuclear power plant only receive about one-fifteenth as much radiation as they get from nature. And, the radiation from nature is not thought to cause any mutations. (Those not living at the fence line, which includes most of us, receive far less radiation from nuclear power plants than we do from our television sets.)

Long-term scientific studies of the victims of even very high levels of radiation show no excess mutations in their offspring. For example, at Hiroshima and Nagasaki, where the atomic bombs were dropped, radiation levels were thousands of times higher than the levels near nuclear power plants. But, studies of the offspring of the survivors of these bombings reveal only normal mutation rates.

Figure 3.1: Anti-nuclear art. The monster supposedly was a mutant produced by the slight amount of radiation released by nuclear power plants. (Based upon an illustration appearing on the cover of the *Southern Sierran* of January 1976.)

If these high levels of radiation failed to produce a visible change in the mutation rate, it is extremely unlikely that the much smaller amount of radiation released by a nuclear power plant would do so.

And, if you think about it, you can see how ironic the entire situation was. At the same time that the antinuclear activists were claiming that nuclear power plants cause birth defects, the fuels which they were forcing us to use were releasing 40 million tons of known chemical mutagens into the air each year.

Who Is Responsible for Air Pollution?

In case you're wondering who is responsible for the release of these poisons into the air, the real cause of air pollution is simply people going about their business in an industrialized society. All of us drive cars. But, cars are the biggest single emitter of carbon monoxide and the oxides of nitrogen. And, cars are the second largest emitter of volatile organic compounds. We live in homes, attend schools, go to shopping malls, and consume goods. All of these activities require electricity. In 1996, the generation of electricity produced 66 percent of the sulfur dioxide emitted.[13] And, electrical utilities were the second largest producer of the oxides of nitrogen.

This is not to say that there are no industrial plants which contribute more than their fair share to the problem of air pollution. Such plants do exist. But, generally speaking, industrial plants and processes are not the major source of most pollutants—we are.

A Brief History of Air Pollution in the U.S.

Table 3.1 shows some figures for the various pollutants at five-year intervals from 1900 to1996. The figures shown are from the EPA's 1997 report *National Air Pollutant Emission Trends, 1900–1996*.

Table 3.1: Air Pollution Emissions in the U.S. from 1900–1996
(In millions of tons)

Year	Carbon Monoxides	Nitrogen Oxides	Volatile Organic Compounds	Sulfur Dioxide	Particulate Matter (PM-10) w/o fugitive dust	Total, Only Pollutants Shown
1900	* NA	2.611	8.503	9.988	NA	21.102
1905	NA	3.314	8.850	13.959	NA	26.123
1910	NA	4.102	9.117	17.275	NA	30.494
1915	NA	4.672	9.769	20.290	NA	34.731
1920	NA	5.159	10.004	21.144	NA	36.307
1925	NA	7.302	14.257	23.264	NA	44.823
1930	NA	8.018	19.451	21.106	NA	48.575
1935	NA	6.639	17.208	16.978	NA	40.825
1940	93.615	7.374	17.161	19.954	15.956	154.060
1945	98.112	9.332	18.140	26.373	16.545	168.502
1950	102.609	10.093	20.936	22.384	17.133	173.155
1955	106.177	11.667	23.249	21.453	16.346	178.892
1960	109.745	14.140	24.459	22.245	15.558	186.147
1965	118.912	17.424	30.247	26.380	14.198	207.161
1970	128.761	21.639	30.817	31.161	13.190	225.568
1975	115.968	23.151	25.895	28.011	7.803	200.828
1980	116.702	24.875	26.167	25.905	7.287	200.936
1985	115.644	23.488	24.227	23.230	4.695	191.284
1990	96.535	23.792	20.985	23.136	4.639	169.087
1995	89.721	23.935	20.586	18.552	4.068	156.862
1996	88.822	23.393	19.086	19.113	4.068	154.482

*"NA" indicates that this data is not available. Note that the totals for 1900–35 do not include any figures for carbon monoxide or particulate matter, and therefore should not be compared with the totals for 1940–96.

At the turn of the century, there were only 76 million Americans. Most homes were without electricity, and there were no air conditioners, no television sets, no automatic washers and dryers, and no refrigerators. No wonder that the electric utilities only accounted for about 4 percent of the sulfur dioxide emitted. But, coal was being used as a fuel to heat many homes, which probably accounts for the fact that one-third as many people produced 50 percent as much sulfur dioxide as was produced in 1996, even though much less electricity was being used than today.

By 1925, as electricity was brought into more homes, the demand for electricity had increased so much that electric utilities were responsible for 20 percent of the sulfur dioxide emitted. Coal was still being burned in many homes for heat, so it's not surprising that a population of only 115 million people was responsible for the release of more sulfur dioxide than were 250 million people in 1996.

During the depression years, millions of people were out of work and many factories shut their doors. The gross domestic product, which fell from $103 billion in 1929 to $56 billion in 1933, reflects the slowdown in industrial activity, as does the drop in sulfur dioxide levels. After the depression ended, sulfur dioxide emissions by the electric utilities roughly doubled every ten years from 1940–1970. These increases were due to increases in coal burning.

The 1970s saw two economic recessions as the Middle East oil supply was disrupted and oil prices were raised. As a result, the nation became more energy conscious, and greater care was taken not to waste energy. Efforts by the newly established EPA also began to have an effect, and sulfur dioxide levels dropped after peaking in 1970. This was accomplished despite a population increase of 45 million people between 1970 and 1990, a 1.7 times increase in coal burning, and a gross domestic product of $5.2 trillion, which was 173 times greater than it had been at the turn of the century.

This decrease in sulfur dioxide emissions came about because of governmental pressure, and was accomplished by the use of more low-sulfur content coal and by the installation of "scrubbers," which remove sulfur dioxide while it's in the flue. The fact that 20 percent of our electricity was being generated by nuclear power plants by 1990 didn't hurt, either.

The Clean Air Act Amendments of 1990 called for sulfur dioxide emissions to be reduced to 10 million tons below 1980 emissions, which was 25 million tons. But, the EPA predicted that 16 million tons will be released as late as 2010.

As you can see, thirty years of effort have resulted in significant reductions in the level of sulfur dioxide, our most dangerous pollutant. But, reducing the oxides of nitrogen has been much more difficult to accomplish, and 1996 levels of this pollutant were 1.7 million tons greater than 36 years earlier. A 40 million ton reduction in carbon monoxide emissions was brought about between 1970 and 1996, despite increases in the number of vehicles and miles driven.

Despite these gains, the total tonnage of pollutants released in 1996— 154 million tons—was almost exactly the same as it had been 56 years earlier, in 1940.

Perhaps it is time to try another solution to the problem of air pollution.

Disposal of Solid Wastes from Coal Burning and Coal Mining

As you know, we simply release the gaseous wastes from coal burning into the air, and some of these deadly respiratory irritants, chemical carcinogens, radioactive substances, and poisons are taken into the lungs of people as they breathe. There, they cause millions of cases of respiratory illness and an average of 50,000 deaths per year in the U.S.

In addition to these gaseous wastes, there's the problem of the ashes and sludges which result from the burning of coal. These wastes weigh hundreds of millions of tons. And they, too, are dangerous.

Because such enormous quantities of solid waste are generated by coal usage, these wastes are seldom even buried. They are simply used as landfill. Where these landfills are located has not been carefully regulated in the past. This means that these wastes have been placed where land is cheap, often without regard to whether they will drain into lakes, rivers, or underground water supplies which may be used as drinking water.

Proof of the careless way in which these poison-containing wastes have been disposed of is provided by two accidents: In 1966, at Aberfan, South Wales, 144 people, mostly children, were killed when a massive pile of coal mining wastes slid down a hill, burying a school.[14] And, on February 26, 1972, a dam built of coal mining wastes failed, killing 125 people in Logan County, West Virginia.[15] Of course, the presence of a dam means water. Water dissolves the poisonous wastes and carries them into lakes and streams, adding them to our drinking water. So, in addition to the people killed by these two accidents, the location of these coal mining wastes may have been instrumental in causing the sickness and even death of others. And, this is probably true of many places where huge quantities of coal mining wastes and ashes have been carelessly dumped.

How dangerous are the solid wastes produced by burning coal? These wastes contain many of the same substances present in coal smoke, and inhaling coal smoke kills tens of thousands of people yearly. These solid wastes contain selenium, vanadium, mercury, and other metals, many of which are known to be poisonous. For example, mercury is a cumulative poison which collects in the small arteries of the brain, causing insanity, serious neuromuscular problems, and death. Suspicion of its detrimental effects dates back to the nineteenth century, when people noticed that hatters, who used mercury compounds to block and shape hats, frequently went insane; hence, the phrase "mad as a hatter," and the "Mad Hatter" in *Alice in Wonderland.*

One-half of all the mercury which entered our biosphere in 1980 did so when coal was burned.

Disposal of the Nuclear Wastes Produced by Coal Burning

The ash produced by burning coal is also radioactive because it contains uranium, radium, and thorium. Coal ashes are roughly 180 times more radioactive than the level of radioactivity permissible for nuclear power plants.[16] In 1988, when British Nuclear Fuels dumped 300 kilograms of uranium into the Irish Sea, the event drew lots of media attention even though nuclear regulators had approved of the dumping. Walter Marshall, chairman of Britain's Central Electricity Generating Board (C.E.G.B.), which generates electricity by burning coal, said this of the event:

> I have to inform you that yesterday the C.E.G.B. released about 300 kilo-grams (660 pounds) of radioactive uranium, together with all of its radio-active decay products, into the environment. Furthermore, we released some 300 kilograms of uranium the day before that. We shall be releasing the same amount of uranium today, and we plan to do the same tomorrow. In fact, we do it every day of every year so long as we burn coal in our power stations. And, we do not call that 'radioactive waste.' We call it coal ash.[17]

Although these comments come from an English administrator, much the same thing happens all the time in the U.S. Roughly 20,000 tons of uranium is brought to the surface along with the one billion tons of coal mined in the U.S. each year. When this coal is burned, most of the uranium enters the air. But, an estimated 500 tons of uranium remains behind in the coal ashes. Because there are virtually no regulations regarding the disposal of coal ashes, they are dumped almost anywhere without much regard for our health.

Surely, the method of nuclear waste disposal used by coal-burning power plants is far less safe than the waste disposal method planned for the wastes from nuclear power plants.

This thought is supported by the fact that if the U.S. Nuclear Regulatory Commission had anything to say about coal-burning power plants, and applied the same safety measures to them that it holds nuclear power plants to, it would have to close down every single coal-burning power plant in the U.S. until they solved their own unsolvable problem of waste disposal.

Even More Waste Is on the Way

There's yet another source of solid wastes from coal-burning power plants on the way, too. As scrubbers, which spray an alkaline solution over rising flue gases to help remove sulfur dioxide, come into more widespread use, the solid wastes from coal burning will accumulate even more rapidly.

In 1975, the head of the Environmental Protection Agency (EPA) estimated that if all new stationary coal-burning sources were to use scrubbers to meet EPA air pollution standards, 120 million tons of sludge would be generated each year.[18] This would amount to almost 1,000 pounds of sludge per year for each person in the U.S. This sludge would constitute an increasingly larger reservoir of poisons with each passing year. In only 10 years, there could be over *1.2 billion tons* of sludge scattered in landfills around the country. Of course, these wastes can't be incorporated into solid, insoluble glass as will be done with nuclear wastes—there is far too much of it.

Earlier, we mentioned that removing uranium from the earth, using it, and then making what is left of it into corrosion-proof, unbreakable glass is much safer than simply leaving it where it is. What about coal? Is this true of coal as well?

Right now, air pollution is the most detrimental health effect of burning coal. But, as the chemical carcinogens and nuclear wastes from burning coal begin to pile up, they may begin to claim as many or even more victims than air pollution does.

Prior to being mined, coal deposits are not particularly dangerous. Many of these deposits are deep underground. The carcinogens and poisons are there, but they pose little threat deep in the earth. The sulfur and carbon present in the underground deposits of coal also pose no threat to people.

However, when coal is burned, some of the carbon is converted into poisonous carbon monoxide. The sulfur is converted into sulfur dioxide or sulfates, which are related to 50,000 air pollution-related deaths per year in the U.S. Along with sulfur dioxide and carbon monoxide, the carcinogenic hydrocarbons and poisonous metals present in coal are released into the air of our cities, which is the most dangerous place possible. Only a small fraction of these air pollutants are breathed, but this causes 50,000 deaths a year. Most of these pollutants are periodically washed out of the air by rainfall or settle to the ground, and many will eventually be washed into our water supply.

Millions of tons of ashes produced by coal-burning power plants also contain some of the same dangerous carcinogens and poisons. And, these wastes will also remain with us forever.

The long-term effect of these dangerous chemical wastes is that eventually they will kill 70 people per year for each large coal-burning power plant which is in use.[19] With 500 such plants, the death toll could reach 35,000 people per year.

Coal also contains uranium which undergoes radioactive decay, forming radon gas. Underground, this uranium in the coal poses no threat, but when mined and the coal is burned, the uranium is set free at the surface, where any radon it releases will be dangerous. Professor Cohen estimates that the net long-range effect from this aspect of coal burning is that there will eventually be 30 additional lung cancer deaths for each year of operation by a single coal-burning power plant. With 500 coal-burning power plants in operation, there would ultimately be 15,000 additional future lung cancer deaths for each year that these plants are in operation.

So, the long-range outlook if our energy is generated by 500 coal-burning power plants, in addition to the death toll by air pollution, coal's addition of uranium and chemical carcinogens to our environment will ultimately cause 50,000 additional deaths per year.

These comparisons of the waste disposal method for fossil fuels and nuclear power should be enough to convince any reasonable person that waste disposal is, indeed, an "unsolvable problem"; but, the problem of *safely* disposing of the enormous quantities of dangerous wastes produced by burning *fossil fuels* is the real "unsolvable problem."

CHAPTER 4

Air Pollution:
Twentieth-Century Scourge

The first brush with air pollution probably took place when a prehistoric man or woman built a fire too far back in the cave and was forced to exit, coughing and eyes watering. But on a large scale, the problem of air pollution probably first appeared during the thirteenth century, when the smoke from a poor grade of coal which Londoners burned became so thick that its use was forbidden on penalty of death. As you might guess, this decree stimulated a brief switch to wood. But within a hundred years or so the forests near London had all been cut down, and Londoners were again forced to burn coal, regardless of how bad the air became.

When the Industrial Revolution began to get underway in the 1800s, the use of coal increased tremendously. And, the air of most large, new, industrial cities quickly worsened. More and more, people complained about the smoky, soot-filled air. But, over 100 more years passed before anyone had any idea of how really dangerous breathing this air could be.

It took a series of major environmental disasters, which later came to be known as the "killer fogs," to alert people to the real dangers of polluted air. One of these disasters occurred in the heavily industrialized Meuse Valley in Belgium on December 2, 1930.

Ordinarily, air at the earth's surface warms and rises and is dispersed by the wind. However, if the air aloft is warmer than the surface air, the surface air is prevented from rising as it normally would. This condition is known to meteorologists as a "temperature inversion," or more simply as an "inversion."

When an inversion occurs, the earth's surface air is not dispersed but remains in place, often for days, until weather conditions change and the inversion moves off.

On December 2, 1930, an inversion settled over the Meuse Valley in Belgium. Hills line both sides of part of the Meuse River Valley, and factories, steel mills, and power plants fill it. Coal was burned in all of these plants and most of the homes. Normally, the gaseous waste products produced by these furnaces would have risen and been dispersed, but now everything which went up the smoke stacks and chimneys in the entire Meuse Valley was trapped by the inversion, as shown by Figure 4.1.

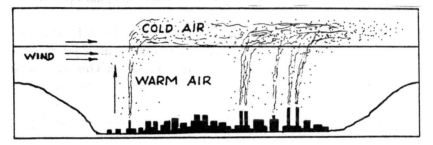

Figure 4.1: Conditions usually present. Ordinarily, the air aloft is colder. Since warm air rises, the warmer surface air rises, carrying the air pollutants with it.

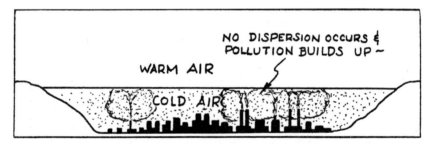

A temperature inversion. When a temperature inversion is present, the air aloft is warmer than the surface air. Under these conditions, the warmer air aloft keeps the colder surface air from rising. Under these conditions, pollutants will build up rather than being dispersed.

By the end of the first day, almost everyone in the valley was complaining of breathing difficulties, sore throats, and watering eyes. As the pollutants continued to build up over the next three days, the hospitals filled to capacity. By the time heavy rainfall washed the pollutants out of the air five days later, 63 people had died and over 6,000 had been sickened. Death rates for the elderly and for people with a past history of respiratory disease soared to ten times the normal rates.

When the disaster was carefully studied, 30 different air pollutants were identified. The inversion had trapped the air, allowing these pollutants to build up to levels which badly stressed almost everyone's respiratory system. Apparently this stress was too much for many people who already had some type of respiratory or heart disease.

Again, on October 30, 1948, Nature demonstrated the dangers of breathing heavily polluted air when an inversion settled over the industrial city of Donora, Pennsylvania. Twenty people died and 5,900 out of a total population of 14,000 became ill before the inversion moved off three days later and the gaseous waste products which had built up were dispersed.

Other serious air pollution episodes followed. In 1952, London suffered the first, and worst, of its killer fogs. Only four more years passed before London endured another air pollution episode. This one caused 1,000 deaths. And, only six years after this, 850 more Londoners died during an air pollution episode.

Unfortunately, even worse news was on the way. Deaths from air pollution were not restricted to the relatively few times when the air was exceptionally bad. Air pollution-caused deaths were occurring most of the time in most industrialized cities.

Table 4.1: Some Air Pollution Disasters

All of these disasters occurred prior to the setting of national standards for air quality.

Date	Place	Sulfur Dioxide Level (ppm)	Excess Deaths
Dec. 1873	London	N.A.	300-700
Feb. 1880	London	N.A.	1,000
Dec. 1892	London	N.A.	1,000
Dec. 1930	Meuse Valley, Belgium	9	63
Oct. 1948	Donora, Pennsylvania	1	20
Dec. 1952	London	1.50	8,000
Nov. 1953	New York City	0.20	360
Jan. 1956	London	0.30	240
Dec. 1956	London	0.50	1,000
Jan. 1959	London	0.20	200
Dec. 1962	London	1.00	850
Dec. 1962	Osaka, Japan	0.10	60
Feb. 1963	New York City	0.46	405
Nov. 1966	New York City	0.50	168

(Source: Atmospheric Pollution, *Derek M. Elsom, p. 26.)*

The Greenburg Study

In 1963, Dr. Leonard Greenburg, who was head of the Department of Environmental Medicine at the Albert Einstein College of Medicine in New York, began research which would help alert scientists to the fact that killer fogs need not be present in order for air pollution to kill people.

Dr. Greenburg noticed that air pollution levels in New York were abnormally high from January 30 to February 12, 1963. Sulfur dioxide, normally present at a concentration of 0.20 part per million, had reached 0.46 parts per million. A temperature inversion was not present and no thick cloud of haze hung over the city, but the sulfur dioxide level was over twice normal levels. This was probably due to a cold wave which resulted in furnaces burning more coal, but otherwise conditions were not unusual. Other than Greenburg, no one suspected that an air pollution episode was taking place.

Greenburg quickly organized a team of researchers and collected mortality and pollution data for the winters of 1963, 1964, and 1965. During 1964 and 1965, air pollution levels were normal, so the abnormally high levels of January 30 to February 12, 1963, stood out. When mortality rates for the three winters were carefully compared, Greenburg discovered that there had been 405 deaths from January 30, to February 12, 1963, which could only be attributed to the abnormally high levels of air pollution.

What was so significant about Greenburg's study was that it showed that *air pollution could be killing large numbers of people much of the time without anyone even being aware of it.*

The same weather conditions and the same pollution levels which had existed in New York City in 1963 had also existed from time to time in many other large cities. Apparently, air pollution had been killing people in cities such as Chicago, Pittsburgh, and Los Angeles all along, with little attention paid to it. Both the high pollution levels and the excess deaths caused by this pollution had simply gone unnoticed.

This is one of the most disturbing things about air pollution's death toll: Outside of the scientific community, very few people are aware of it. As a result there has been no public outcry, and, hence, for a long time little was done to reduce it.

The Fossil Fuels' Role in Air Pollution

By the late 1950s, scientists were convinced that the air in most big cities had become dangerously polluted. Spurred on by deteriorating conditions in their own cities and by reports of the Donora and London killer fogs, an increasing number of serious attempts were undertaken to study the problem and identify the sources of air pollution.

In the 1960s, scientists and governmental agencies began to regularly monitor air pollution levels, and some facts about fossil fuels and their role in air pollution began to emerge. After the Environmental Protection Agency (EPA) was established in 1970, the careful measurement of pollutant levels at numerous sites increased. Today our knowledge of air pollution is much closer to being complete compared to only a few decades ago.

Why Breathing Polluted Air Is So Dangerous

To understand why breathing polluted air is so dangerous, it is necessary to look at the human respiratory system and to consider the effect which air pollution might have on it.

If you remember your high school biology, you know that air enters the trachea, or windpipe, which then subdivides into two bronchial tubes. Each bronchial tube enters a lung and then subdivides again many times like the branches of a tree. The smallest branches terminate in clusters of tiny, balloon-like air sacs. The tissue in the wall of these air sacs is rich in tiny blood vessels, or capillaries. The wall of each air sac is only about 1/10,000 of an inch thick, but if the walls of all of the air sacs were spread out, they would cover an area of 2,000 square feet, about the size of a tennis court. When you take in a breath, these air sacs fill with air and expand. Oxygen from the air diffuses into the blood vessels in the wall of the air sacs. At the same time, gaseous carbon dioxide leaves the blood vessels and diffuses into the air sacs so that it can be exhaled. This interchange of gases, which occurs through the tissue of the air sacs, keeps us alive. Figure 4.2 shows these parts of the respiratory system.

Some of the substances present in polluted air irritate and damage the bronchial tubes and delicate tissue lining the air sacs. For example, most coal contains from 0.5 percent to 5 percent sulfur. When coal burns, this sulfur combines with oxygen to form sulfur dioxide.

At one time, scientists suspected that the particulates, sulfur dioxide, or the sulfates formed from sulfur dioxide were the the cause of most air pollution-related deaths. More recently, the possibility that sulfur dioxide could be acting in conjunction with a second pollutant has drawn a lot of scientific interest. Or, it may be that the villain is not sulfur dioxide or particulates, but a third substance produced along with these two substances. But the fact remains that most studies relate sulfur dioxide or the particulates with increases in the death rate.

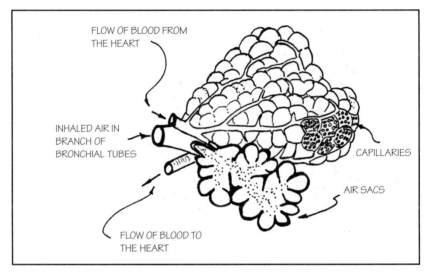

Figure 4.2. The part of the human respiratory system in which oxygen is exchanged for carbon dioxide during breathing. The air sacs at the end of the bronchial tubes expand, pulling inhaled air into them. Oxygen, which is present in the inhaled air, then diffuses into the capillaries of the bloodstream which surround the air sacs.

As one might guess, smoking is very similar to breathing heavily polluted air, except that in smoking the concentration of pollutants is much greater. However, the time of exposure in smoking is much less. Some of the same pollutants such as carbon monoxide and benzo(a)pyrene are present in both cigarette smoke and polluted air.

Emphysema: Death by Slow Suffocation

The lungs of both smokers and nonsmokers who have spent much of their lives in cities that have heavily polluted air show similar changes. In the respiratory disease known as emphysema, the damage is done to the air sacs where the interchange of oxygen and carbon dioxide takes place. Exposure to air pollution apparently causes the walls of adjacent air sacs to break down, and these tiny air sacs then become part of a single, larger air sac as shown in Figure 4.3.

This single, larger air sac does not have as much surface area as did the many smaller air sacs, so an emphysema victim gradually loses his capacity to transfer oxygen from the air to his bloodstream. As more and more small air sacs disappear, the victim becomes progressively shorter of breath. Climbing a flight of stairs becomes an impossible task. By the time that their lungs have lost 95 percent of their original capacity, most emphy-

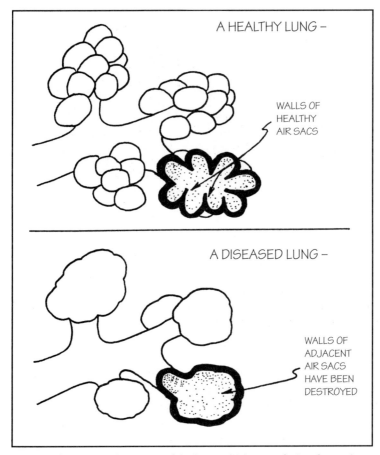

Figure 4.3. Changes in the air sacs of the lungs which occur during the respiratory disease, emphysema.

Top: The structure of normal, undamaged air sacs. Note that a wall separates each air sac from adjoining air sacs.

Bottom: The structure of a diseased lung. Note that the walls between many air sacs have been destroyed, greatly diminishing the surface area in which oxygen can enter the bloodstream.

sema victims are confined to bed.

There, they have only the promise of a slow, gradual death by suffocation to look forward to. There is no cure. Life can be extended briefly by breathing oxygen, first through plastic tubes inserted into the nostrils, and then, later, when the muscles are unable to pull the oxygen from the nose down into the lungs, the emphysema victim's windpipe can be slit, and a plastic tube to supply oxygen inserted into it. This kind of slow suffocation is not a pleasant way to die.

Between 1950 and 1957, the death rate of emphysema in California rose from 1.5 deaths per 100,000 to 5.8 deaths per 100,000 for an increase of 286 percent. During roughly the same period of time, automobile registration increased from 2 million to 3.5 million vehicles in the Los Angeles area, or a 75 percent increase. Of course, as the number of automobiles increased, so did the air pollutants they emitted. And, the air pollution emitted by industrial sources also increased during this time period.

In 1935, there were only 135 emphysema deaths in the U.S.; but, by the late 1960s and early 1970s, emphysema was the fastest growing cause of death in the United States. During 1962, 12,500 people were forced into early retirement because they were unable to work due to emphysema. In the 1960s, only heart disease disabled more men than emphysema. By 1986, emphysema was killing at least 15,000 people a year, and some physicians suspected that the actual death toll could be several times higher than this.

It should be pointed out that smoking is the major cause of emphysema. But, studies show that the death rate due to emphysema is about twice as great in metropolitan areas, where air pollution levels are greater, than in rural areas, even after adjustments are made for smoking differences.

Bronchitis

Another serious respiratory disease, bronchitis, often accompanies emphysema. Breathing polluted air causes the tiny branches of the bronchial tubes to narrow, thus diminishing the quantity of air entering the lungs. The narrowing of these tiny air passages is due to an increase in the number of layers of cells in the lining. The formation of more layers of cells is the body's attempt to deal with irritation. You've probably had calluses form on your feet as the body attempted to deal with the irritation caused by a poorly fitting pair of stiff new shoes. Of course, with air pollution the irritation is chemical.

Bronchitis is exceedingly common in England, where, until recently, a poor quality of coal with a high sulfur content was burned. As the birthplace of the Industrial Revolution, which was powered by coal, England has had a serious air pollution problem for a much longer time than the United States. In the 1960s, bronchitis was responsible for 10 percent of all deaths in England, and it was the leading cause of death in men over 45 years old in that country. It was the fourth leading cause of death overall.

In 1996, obstructive respiratory diseases such as bronchitis and emphysema were also the fourth leading cause of death in the United States, claiming 106,000 victims. This was surpassed only by diseases of the circulatory system, cancer, and accidental death.

And, air pollution may contribute to the death toll claimed by the three leading causes of death. It is related to heart disease and lung cancer, and high levels of carbon monoxide on congested city streets may impair a driver's alertness and judgment, which could contribute to automobile accidents.

Lung Cancer

The lining of the bronchial tubes contain specialized cells which secrete a sticky fluid. Other specialized cells called columnar cells, which have short, hair-like cilia, sweep this sticky fluid up and out of the bronchial tubes. Any airborne particles such as particulates or sulfate aerosols which enter the bronchial tubes settle on this fluid and are swept out of the lungs by the action of the cilia. This is the body's way of cleansing the bronchial tubes of the small particles which enter along with the air we breathe.

Certain air pollutants can destroy the cilia-bearing cells and thus prevent this cleansing action. Once this happens, particulates which enter the lungs are no longer swept out of them, but are free to accumulate, often with serious consequences.

Smoking, a more concentrated form of air pollution, apparently destroys the lungs' cilia-bearing cells. Lung cancer rates are over 10 times higher for smokers than nonsmokers. And, asbestos workers, who breathe asbestos dust in the course of their work, are 7 or 8 times more likely to die of lung cancer than members of the general public. But, asbestos workers who smoke cigarettes are 92 times more likely to die of lung cancer than nonsmokers of the same age who are part of the general population. These data suggest that once significant numbers of cilia-bearing cells have been destroyed by the effects of cigarette smoke, asbestos dust is less likely to be swept out of the lungs, and lung cancer is much more probable. These data also suggest that pollutants in the air and airborne particulates could act together as do asbestos and cigarette smoke.

Pulmonary Heart Disease

Detrimental changes in the respiratory system such as those previously described place a heavy burden on the heart. When a respiratory disease such as emphysema is present, the heart must work harder to force the same volume of blood through the greatly reduced number of capillaries in the damaged air sacs.

In bronchitis, the flow of oxygen into the air sacs and then into the blood stream is diminished because the numerous branches of the bronchial tubes have narrowed. The result of these changes is that the heart must work harder, but it gets less oxygen. Like any other muscle which works hard, the heart must have an adequate supply of oxygen or it cannot do its job. Under these conditions, the heart enlarges as it tries to do an impossible job, and the chance of heart failure greatly increases. This particular type of heart disease has been recognized for well over a hundred years and is commonly known as "pulmonary heart disease."

The relationship between air pollution, respiratory disease, and heart disease is especially important because heart disease kills more Americans than any other cause.

Research done in Japan lends support to the suspicion that heart disease rates and air pollution levels might be related. Japanese who lived in a city (Ube) which had high levels of air pollution were found to have 120 percent more heart disease than did Japanese who lived in a comparable city (Bofu) with lower levels of air pollution. (Studies such as this, in which two similar cities are involved, rule out the possibility that "the stress of city living" might be an important factor.) This study and others like it are particularly disturbing because heart disease is the number one cause of death: It killed 733,000 Americans in 1996.

It is worth noting that the death rate due to heart disease is highest in the industrialized Northeastern and upper Midwestern states, where air pollution is most serious, and lowest in the Western states, where air pollution is less serious. In New York, where air pollution is a serious problem, 303 people per 100,000 died of heart disease during 1986. The next highest death rates were in: Michigan, 299; Rhode Island, 184; New Jersey, 278; and Illinois, 274.

By contrast, in Hawaii, the Western states, and Alaska, where air pollution levels were much lower, the death rates due to heart disease were lowest. In Hawaii, little air pollution is generated, and most of what is produced is blown out to sea. And, since no land mass is nearby, adjacent areas do not pollute Hawaii's air. These factors help to insure that Hawaiians will breathe only relatively clean air, and this must contribute to the fact that in Hawaii, the death rate due to heart disease is only 166 people per 100,000. This is only 55 percent of the death rate for heart disease in New York.

The next lowest death rates were found in the sparsely populated, less-industrialized Western states and Alaska, which have comparatively little air pollution. There, the death rates are: New Mexico, 284 deaths per 100,000 people per year; Utah, 189; Idaho, 190; and Alaska, 190.

Thus far, the belief among some researchers is that people in the more heavily populated urban areas lead a more inactive lifestyle, and that this inactivity is a major cause of much heart disease. However, there is little or no doubt that air pollution makes a major contribution to pulmonary heart disease, which is included in the total for death by heart disease.

The Death Toll Claimed by Air Pollution

Over the years, numerous studies have shown that higher air pollution levels are accompanied by higher death rates caused by respiratory diseases and heart disease. Some of the best, and earliest, evidence that increasing air pollution levels cause the death rates for respiratory diseases to increase comes from the killer fog episodes at the Meuse Valley, Donora, and London. In each of these instances, unusual atmospheric conditions caused air pollution levels to suddenly increase. These increased air pollution levels were almost immediately followed by spectacular increases in death rates due to respiratory diseases.

Later, researchers designed studies which compared air pollution levels and death rates in various U.S. cities. Other studies dealt with counties, standard metropolitan statistical areas, and so on. Where conditions other than air pollution levels differed, careful statistical analysis was used to eliminate the effect these variables might have on the death rate. Of course, when air pollution levels and death rates are studied on a day-to-day basis for the same city, much of this problem is eliminated. All of these studies indicate that air pollution levels and death rates are statistically related: As air pollution levels increase, so do death rates.

Most of the studies compare sulfur dioxide or particulate levels with the death rate. However, a word of caution is in order: Sulfur dioxide may not be the killer, because other pollutants are produced along with sulfur dioxide. The killer could turn out to be one of these other pollutants, or it could turn out to be two acting together.

In almost all studies, a strong relationship was found between sulfur dioxide or particulate levels and the death rates of lung cancer, emphysema, chronic bronchitis, influenza, pneumonia, and pulmonary heart disease.

For our purposes, the most important question about air pollution is, "How many deaths in the United States each year are related to air pollution?"

In a series of papers[1, 2, 3] published during 1970–71, statisticians L. Lave and E. Seskin used 1961 data and calculated the total number of sulfate-related deaths in the U.S. to be 60,000 per year, and airborne particulate-related deaths to be 80,000 per year. (The sulfates are produced by sulfur dioxide.)

Writing in *Health Effects of Fossil Fuel Burning Assessment and Mitiga-*

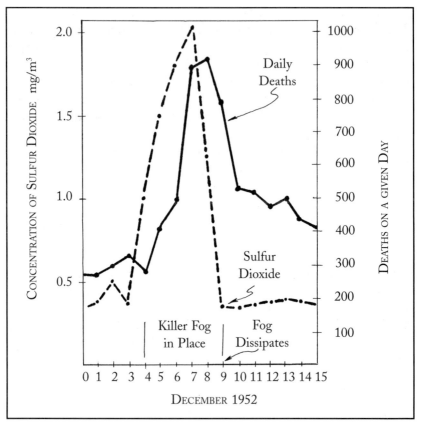

(Source: Atmospheric Pollution, Derek M. Elsom, p. 26.)

Figure 4.4. Graphic evidence of the effect of increased levels of sulfur dioxide. Note how increases and decreases in the death rate take place right after the concentration of sulfur dioxide increases or decreases, which implies that one change causes the other. These data pertain to the Killer Fog which hit London in December of 1952. (Source: Derek M. Elsom, *Atmospheric Pollution*, p. 26.)

tion, Harvard's Richard Wilson, working in conjunction with S. Colome, J. Spengler, and D. Wilson, considered almost 700 research reports in an attempt to assess the extent of the problem.[4] Wilson's team focused on research done to determine the total number of air pollution-related deaths per year in the U.S. by Lave and Seskin (1977), Mendelsohn and Orcutt (1978), Schwing and McDonald (1976), Lipfert (1978), Smith (1977), Gregor (1976), Winkelstein and others (1967), Bozzo (1978), Koshal and Koshal (1973), Thibodeau, Reed, and Bishop (1979), and Hamilton (1979). After careful analysis of these studies, Wilson settled on an estimate of 53,000 people dying in the U.S. each year due to air pollution.

This estimate of 53,000 deaths was based on evidence which indicated that for each 1 million tons of sulfur dioxide released into the air, 2,400 more people died. Thus, when 22 million tons of sulfur dioxide were released into the air, 52,800 air pollution-related deaths could be expected. By 1977, roughly 29.7 million tons of sulfur dioxide were being released into the air, which according to Wilson's earlier figures would lead to over 71,280 air pollution-related deaths in the U.S. By 1996, sulfur dioxide emissions had been reduced enough so that 45,871 deaths were predicted by Wilson's figures.

Citing over three dozen studies and references on the topic, in 1983, Bernard Cohen reached a similar figure of 50,000 air pollution-related deaths in the U.S. each year. [5] In 1982, Lave and Chappie tried to update Lave and Seskin's earlier studies and found the same "strong, consistent, statistically significant correlation between sulfates and mortality" that Lave and Seskin had found earlier.[6]

In 1979, the U.S. Office of Technology Assessment, which reviews scientific matters for Congress, predicted that air pollution from burning coal and oil will *continue* to be linked to the deaths of 50,000 Americans per year between 1979 and the turn of the century.[7] This estimate was based on work done by the prestigious Brookhaven National Laboratory. Gains resulting from improvements in air pollution control technology were expected to be offset by the increased demand for energy and the subsequent increased burning of coal.

In their 1985 publication *Acid Rain and Transported Pollutants*, the U.S. Office of Technology Assessment reiterated its position, giving a figure of 51,000 deaths for the U.S. and Canada in 1980, assuming 1978 emission levels.[8] And, then they went a step further and predicted that 57,000 deaths would occur in the year 2000, assuming that the population grew to 291 million but pollution levels remained unchanged. Table 4.2 on the following page shows these figures.

Perhaps these predictions helped convince politicians of the dangers of air pollution, because between 1986 and 1996, sulfur dioxide emissions were reduced from 22.5 million tons to 19.1 million tons. And, the Clean Air Act Amendment of 1990 promised a further reduction to about 16 million tons.

There can be little doubt that the figure of roughly 50,000 air pollution-related deaths is the best estimate available at the present. Many top-notch scientists and statisticians spent years studying the matter prior to arriving at a figure in this range. These are highly competent, careful people, and they do not carelessly attach their names to a figure such as this without giving the matter a lot of study. Given the data and knowledge available in 1992, the figure of approximately 50,000 air pollution-

related deaths was the most reliable figure science could produce at the
the time.

Table 4.2. Data from the Office of Technology Assessment's 1985 Report: *Acid
Rain and Transported Air Pollutants*

The first scenario predicts the number of air pollution-related deaths occurring in
the United States and Canada for 1980 population levels. The second scenario
makes the same prediction for the expected population in the year 2000. In these
scenarios, pollution is held to the 1978 level. In the third scenario, the sulfur dioxide,
sulfate-particulate mix is cut by 30 percent, a measure which would result in saving
an estimated 17,000 lives.

Scenario	Population (millions)	Excess deaths total
1. 1980 population, 1978 emissions, United States and Canada	249	51,000
2. 2000 population, emissions unchanged, United States and Canada	291	57,000
3. 2000 population, sulfate-particulate mix 30% below 1978 levels, United States and Canada	291	40,000

*(Source: Brookhaven National Laboratory, Biomedical and Environmental Assessment Division, "Long-
Range Transport Air Pollution Health Effects," OTA contractor report, May 1982.)*

However, in 1993, studies by the Environmental Protection Agency
and the Harvard School of Public Health indicated that even this appall-
ing figure could be too conservative, and suggested that air pollution could
be killing 60,000 Americans yearly.

And, a later study by the Harvard School of Public Health released in
March of 1995 found that air pollution was even more deadly than had
been previously thought.[9] This nationwide study followed the health history of 552,138 adults in various metropolitan areas from 1982 through
1989. Deaths in each area were compared with the level of fine particulates and sulfates in the air. The findings revealed that high levels of particulates and sulfates caused a 17 percent and 15 percent increase respectively in the overall death rate.

There was a 30 percent difference in the death rates from heart disease, respiratory disease, and lung cancer between the cities having the
least and the most polluted air. These differences in air quality led to a
year or more drop in life expectancy for the average person, depending on
how polluted the air was.

Plainly, air pollution generated by fossil fuels kills a lot of people and
shortens almost everyone's life.

A Century of Air Pollution

You may recall Table 3.1, which showed the EPA's figures for the emission of sulfur dioxide and other pollutants at 5-year intervals from 1900 to 1995. We can use these figures to estimate the total number of deaths in the U.S. due to air pollution during the twentieth century.

To do this, we simply calculate the average tonnage of sulfur dioxide released per year: This turns out to be 21.64 million tons. Next, we use Harvard professor Dr. Richard Wilson's figure of 2,400 deaths per million tons of sulfur dioxide to estimate the average number of yearly air pollution deaths in the twentieth century. This figure is 51,936 deaths/year. Finally, we multiply this number by 100 years/century to arrive at the total number of air pollution deaths in America during the twentieth century.

During the twentieth century, there have been 5.2 million deaths in the U.S. due to air pollution.

In all of the wars we have fought in the 224 years since 1776, a total of 650,604 men have died on the battlefield. This total is dwarfed by the death toll from a century of air pollution. During the twentieth century, air pollution has killed eight times as many people as died in all of the ten wars we have fought.

For several decades at least, the U.S. has used a quarter or slightly more of the energy generated worldwide. This means that we've burned just over one-quarter of the fossil fuels consumed. Ordinarily, this would imply that we have endured a fourth or slightly more of the world's air pollution. But, we've been more successful in controlling air pollution than many countries. For example, a 1984 report by the World Health Organization showed the sulfur dioxide levels of 17 countries. Chicago, which is not our most polluted city by any means, was tied for third least polluted.[10] One Chinese city, Shenyang, had sulfur dioxide levels almost ten times higher than Chicago. Calcutta, India, was over twice as high, as were Frankfurt, Germany, Glasgow, U.K., Santiago, Chile, and Sao Paulo, Brazil. Zagreb, Yugoslavia was 3.5 times more polluted than Chicago, and Zagreb is probably representative of most cities in the former Eastern Bloc countries.

So, we should be safe in making the assumption that since the U.S. burns just over one-fourth of the fossil fuels used on earth, we have suffered roughly a quarter of the air pollution casualties the world endured during the twentieth century. *This places the worldwide death toll due to air pollution at not less than 20 million people during the twentieth century.*

Granted, this is only a rough estimate. But, the complete data needed for a better estimate is probably not available. If this estimate is anywhere near correct, it makes air pollution one of the worst scourges of the twentieth century, placing it right up there with the great worldwide influenza epidemic of 1918–21, and the combined military and civilian deaths in World War II. Surprisingly, the death toll due to a century of air pollution exceeds the figure of 12.6 million military and civilian deaths during World War I, which is often referred to as the "Great War."

I think the figure of 20 million air pollution deaths will come as a big surprise to almost everyone, with the possible exception of a few researchers working in the field.

Perhaps it is appropriate to wonder when we are going to wake up and take steps to stop this. The next section suggests a safe and sane way to prevent a large percentage of these unnecessary deaths.

A Simple Plan to Prevent 40,000 Unnecessary Deaths a Year

Because most air pollution studies link the production of sulfur dioxide or particulates to the air pollution deaths which occur each year, sulfur dioxide (and the substances that accompany its production) must be decreased if these deaths are to be prevented. Coal is by far the most dangerous fuel because it emits much more than its share of sulfur dioxide. Oil also emits sulfur dioxide, but nowhere near as much as coal. Natural gas is considered our safest fossil fuel because it releases comparatively little sulfur dioxide when it burns.

Of course, nuclear power releases no sulfur dioxide, so it is safer than any of the fossil fuels.

Table 4.3 shows the sources of sulfur dioxide for 1996.

Inspection of Table 4.3 suggests that a lot of lives could be saved by simply replacing the sulfur dioxide-producing, fossil fuel-burning stationary sources with the new, improved second generation of nuclear power plants now available.

Most coal now burned is used to produce electricity. This is both unnecessary and unwise, because nuclear power is better suited for this job. Nuclear power is safe, clean, and cheap—everything which coal and oil are not. Even if we ignore the health aspects of the two fuels, the fact that we wouldn't have to mine and transport almost a billion tons of coal would be sufficient to make nuclear power a better choice than coal. Proof of nuclear power's superiority for this use is the fact that the utility companies would prefer to build and use nuclear power plants, but for over two decades this has been blocked by antinuclear activists. The utilities' preference for nuclear power has nothing to do with profits, because state

Table 4.3: 1996 Emissions of Sulfur Dioxide

Source	(In millions of tons)	
Electrical Power Plants which burn coal and oil	12.604	
Industrial Plants which burn coal, oil, or gas	3.399	Stationary sources: 87.8 percent of the sulfur dioxide emitted.
Commercial, Institutional, and Residential use of coal and oil	0.782	
Industrial Processes which release sulfur dioxide, and Misc. sources	1.653	
Vehicles	0.675	
Total sulfur dioxide released	19.113	million tons

(Adapted from the EPA's 1997 report, National Air Pollutant Emission Trends, 1900-1996.*)*[11]

regulatory boards usually set the rates which in turn determine profits.

Further proof of nuclear power's superiority is provided by the former Iron Curtain countries, all of whom are building nuclear power plants despite the fact that they have some of the largest coal reserves in the world. China, where air pollution-caused respiratory disease is the number one killer, has plans to build 140 nuclear power plants over the next 50 years.

China has the third largest coal reserves in the world, so the decision to build nuclear power plants was not influenced by a shortage of fossil fuels in that country. Nuclear power is simply the best, cleanest way to generate electricity. Russia has the largest coal reserves, and is also building nuclear power plants.

Replacing the fossil fuel-burning stationary sources of sulfur dioxide with nuclear power plants would have eliminated 87.8 percent of the sulfur dioxide released during 1996. This reduction would have decreased air pollution-related deaths from an estimated 45,871 deaths to only 5,596 deaths, thus preventing 40,275 deaths.

There are several other worthwhile advantages to this simple plan. By eliminating the use of oil for stationary heating, it delays the time when we'll run out of oil. Since we use oil as a raw material for 80,000 valuable products, including many of our medicines, we should be deeply concerned about making our oil supplies last as long as possible. Also, by eliminating our need to import oil, this plan decreases our trade deficit by 40 to 50 percent, which should give our economy a big boost. Further, decreased use of oil should result in lower prices for gasoline as the oil-producing nations are forced to once again compete for sales. In 1985, U.S. drivers spent $92 billion on gas and oil. A 20 percent price reduction would save us $18 billion per year.

Finally, less burning of coal and oil would save the cost of medical treatment and lost wages now due to the millions of cases of air pollution-related respiratory disease. In 1990, the American Lung Association estimated that passage of the Clean Air Act Amendment of 1990, which sought to decrease sulfur dioxide emissions by only ten million tons per year, would save $50 billion in reduced health care expenses. The plan described here would certainly increase that figure to well over $100 billion a year. Of course, the replacement of fossil fuel power plants and furnaces with nuclear power plants would take place over time as the fossil fuel plants wore out, so these advantages would not occur overnight. And, although this replacement might appear costly, the savings would far outweigh the costs over the long run.

Political activists may point to the fact that the measure proposed will throw thousands of coal miners out of work. Of course, the change will occur over several decades, and some coal will still be mined as a raw material used in the manufacture of other goods. However, the decrease in the cost of energy which accompanies the use of nuclear power should create some jobs. And, since our trade deficit cost us an estimated 5 million jobs in 1987, it isn't too hard to see how the loss of even 100,000 to 200,000 jobs could be offset. Besides, 15 years or more in a coal mine almost always leads to black lung disease, which is definitely something miners should be spared.

When the automobile appeared, thousands of blacksmiths were thrown out of work. But, hundreds of thousands of jobs in automobile plants, steel mills, glass factories, garages, and service stations were created. Progress almost always creates more jobs than it makes obsolete. And, progress is what this book is advocating. Nuclear power is going to be the energy source of the twenty-first century, and unless something unforeseen occurs, the energy source for many centuries to come.

CHAPTER 5

The Environmental Effects of Using Fossil Fuels and Nuclear Power

Whenever coal, oil, or natural gas burn, the major gaseous waste products are water vapor and carbon dioxide. The water vapor causes no harm, of course. And, the carbon dioxide isn't dangerous to breathe unless it is present in such quantities that it prevents us from getting enough oxygen. However, since 1861, scientists have suspected that carbon dioxide might play a role in what is known as the "greenhouse effect." Let's take a look at this interesting theory.

The sun's energy travels to the earth in the form of short wavelength radiation in the visible and near-ultraviolet end of the spectrum. Energy of this wavelength passes freely through the atmosphere without being absorbed and strikes the earth's surface, where it is absorbed. The earth's surface warms up and radiates energy in the form of long wavelength, infrared radiation. This radiation travels upward, away from the earth. However, methane, water vapor, carbon dioxide, and several other kinds of molecules in the atmosphere absorb energy in the infrared end of the spectrum, warm up, and about half of the energy which would have escaped from the earth is now radiated back toward the earth's surface. Figure 5.1 shows this process.

Ordinarily, the absorption of energy by the atmosphere and its subsequent radiation back to the earth is a beneficial process, because it helps keep the earth warm. But as the concentration of carbon dioxide and other "greenhouse gases" in the atmosphere increases, less and less heat energy escapes. And, as more heat is trapped, the average temperature of the earth will gradually increase. The process of trapping heat is known as the "greenhouse effect," and when the heat builds up so that the earth becomes warmer than it usually is, this is now called "global warming."

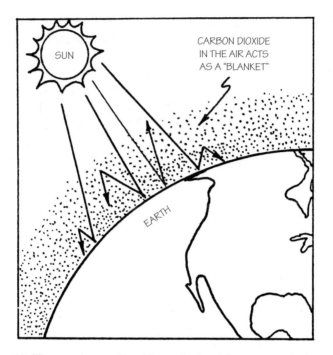

Figure 5.1: The greenhouse effect. The sun's ultraviolet rays pass freely through the atmosphere and strike the earth's surface. There, they are converted to infrared radiation and radiated outward into space. However, carbon dioxide in our atmosphere absorbs some of this energy, causing the temperature of the earth to increase. For the purposes of illustration, the height of the atmosphere has been greatly exaggerated.

Carbon Dioxide and Global Warming

Of the greenhouse gases mentioned earlier, water vapor is responsible for 98 percent of the greenhouse effect and the warming it produces. But, when the air becomes saturated with water vapor, it condenses into droplets of rain which coalesce and fall, so a natural method of regulating the amount of water vapor in the air exists.

Plants absorb carbon dioxide in the process of photosynthesis, and some of it gets washed out of the air when it rains. The analysis of glacial ice shows that with only a few exceptions, carbon dioxide levels have remained at roughly 260 to 280 ppm for 10,000 years. However, today, carbon dioxide levels are about 365 ppm, or about 35 percent higher than in the past. What caused this big increase?

Carbon dioxide enters the atmosphere by natural processes such as the respiration of plants and animals, and the eruptions of geysers and volcanoes. These natural processes add an estimated 200 billion tons of carbon dioxide to the atmosphere each year.[1] For centuries, man's contribution to the amount of carbon dioxide entering the atmosphere was insignificant.

However, beginning with the Industrial Revolution, the burning of the fossil fuels began to increase. After the Second World War ended, their use took a big jump, and today the burning of fossil fuels adds an estimated seven billion tons of carbon dioxide to the atmosphere each year.[2] A single coal-burning power plant produces 500 pounds of carbon dioxide a second, or 15 tons per minute. And, there are hundreds of such plants in the U.S. alone, and a multitude of other sources of carbon dioxide as well. During the 1980s, carbon dioxide levels were increasing each year, and the cause of this increase was thought to be the world's fossil fuel-burning furnaces and automobiles.

The Recent History of Global Temperatures

In 1958, interest in the possibility that increasing levels of carbon dioxide might be causing the earth to warm up led Roger Revelle of Harvard to begin monitoring carbon dioxide levels. But, although carbon dioxide levels were rising, yearly average temperatures were dropping slightly.

Then, in 1970, inexplicably, the downward trend in average temperature ended, and temperatures headed upward. Because the average yearly temperature normally may fluctuate from year to year, or even from decade to decade, it is difficult to tell what constitutes a normal variation and what exceeds it. But, by mid-1988, as one scorching heat wave after another burned its way into the world's record books, more scientists became convinced that the 1980s had been an extraordinarily hot decade.

Several atmospheric physicists pointed out that the world was warmer during the summer of 1988 than it had been for a very long time. This came on top of the fact that 1987 had been the warmest year, worldwide, since record keeping began in the 1880s. And, the next two hottest years on record were 1981 and 1983.

Greenhouse Hysteria

On a 99°F day in late June of 1988, James Hansen of the NASA Goddard Institute of Space Studies told the U.S. Senate that he was 99 percent certain that the greenhouse effect was responsible for the hot decade.[3] This report drew a lot of attention from the media, and overnight, millions of people who had never heard of the greenhouse effect suddenly began to worry about it.

Time magazine increased the public's anxiety when, on January 2, 1989, it skipped its usual "Man of the Year" selection and instead pictured an overheated, dying earth as its "Planet of the Year."

Stanford scientist Paul Ehrlich called global warming "the beginning of the end."[4] Station WGBH in Boston produced a ten-hour film entitled "Race to Save the Planet." And, in 1990, British science writer John Gribbin wrote: "In all probability, the greenhouse effect has already killed hundreds of thousands of people."[5] Gribbin attributed this loss of life to drought-caused famine, which he claimed had been brought on by global warming due to the greenhouse effect.

One atmospheric physicist, Michael Oppenheimer, believed that within 20 years the earth would become so warm that people would simply have to slash fossil fuel usage. Oppenheimer went on to say:

> To me the problem is as important as nuclear disarmament. What's at stake is the future of the world. It's on the same plane.[6]

By mid-1989, United Nations officials were certain enough that the greenhouse effect had arrived to adopt the phrase, "Global Warning: Global Warming" as the slogan for their June 5, 1989, Environment Day. The U.N. report warned that it was already too late to prevent the impact of global warming, and warned that the world should brace itself for rising sea levels and large-scale crop damage.[7]

What Might Be the Consequences of Global Warming?

Scientists who thought that the greenhouse effect had begun to cause abnormal global warming cranked up their computers, fed them data, and emerged with a variety of "what if" predictions. For example, James Hansen's NASA team predicted that before the year 2030, atmospheric carbon dioxide levels would have doubled and the earth would be about 2.3°F warmer on the average.[8]

Delegates to a 1988 conference on "The Changing Atmosphere" were told to expect a 7.2°F change within the next 40 years. [9] Other computer-generated models predicted that a global warming of between 6.3°F and 8.1°F would occur by the time carbon dioxide levels had doubled.[10] Everyone had their own computer model, and a variety of mostly frightening predictions emerged.

One of the more frightening predictions was that global warming might melt some ice. Normally, huge ice fields such as those which cover

Greenland and the Antarctic would melt very slowly even if the world's temperature increased by an average of, say, 9°F. But, the West Antarctic ice sheet which rests on bedrock below sea level will melt more rapidly because it extends into the ocean, where it is in contact with the warmer water.

J. H. Mercer of the Institute of Polar Studies at Ohio State University claimed that a 9°F change in the earth's average temperature might result in huge chunks of this ice shelf breaking off and drifting north, into warmer waters, where they would melt much more quickly.

Evidence seems to indicate that 120,000 years ago, during the warm interglacial period prior to the one we are now in, the level of the ocean was 20 feet higher than it now is. Some scientists think that his can only be accounted for by assuming that the West Antarctic ice sheet had broken up, drifted northward into warmer waters, and melted, causing the ocean level to rise.

What would happen if this ice sheet melted? Stephen Schneider of the U.S. National Center for Atmospheric Research in Boulder, Colorado, describes the effect which this would have:

• In the U.S., a 16 to 26-foot rise in ocean levels would flood one-quarter of Florida and inundate all but four of its cities over 25,000 people. Forty percent of all Floridians would have to flee rising waters. New York City, Atlantic City, and Boston would be under water, as would New Orleans, much of Louisiana, and the coast of Texas. Over 11 million Americans would be homeless and $110 billion worth of property would be destroyed.[11]

• Worst of all, large coastal cities all over the world would become inundated as water levels rose. Some of these cities would include Washington, D.C., London, New York City, St. Petersburg, Stockholm, Amsterdam, Hamburg, Venice, Calcutta, Bangkok, Singapore, and Jakarta. Well over 75 million people live in these cities, which are important centers of trade and commerce.

Another serious consequence of global warming is that it might reduce crop yields in many places, including the United States. As a result of the greenhouse effect having warmed the earth, some scientists believe that the atmospheric circulation would shift, making the U.S., Europe, Russia, and Japan warmer and drier.

In a 1977 symposium in Austria, W. Bach of West Germany's Center for Applied Climatology outlined some of the effects various climatic changes would have on food production in the U.S. For example:

If average temperatures rose 3.6°F and rainfall decreased 30 percent, wheat yields could decrease 27 percent in North Dakota, 21 percent in South Dakota, and 17 percent in Kansas. Even a 10 percent decrease in rainfall would result in decreased yields of 13 percent, 11 percent, and 9 percent, respectively. The Midwest corn belt could be displaced north-ward into Canada.[12] As everyone knows, American farmers are capable of producing more food than Americans can consume, so a decrease in Kansas wheat production of from 9 percent to 17 percent may not sound so bad. But, as John Gribbin, then of London's International Institute for Environment and Development, points out, a 10 percent reduction in the North American grain crop would cut off all the surplus which now goes to feed hungry people throughout the world.[13] According to Noel Brown, director of the New York office of the U.N. Environmental Pro-gram, only a 10-year window of opportunity remained in which to solve the problem of the greenhouse effect.[14] After that, the problem would be beyond human control, warned Brown.

Cutting Back on Energy Usage As a Solution to the Problem of Global Warming

In June of 1992, the United Nations joined the battle to "Save the Planet." Over 25,000 participants, representatives from 178 nations, and an esti-mated 7,000 members of the media traveled to Rio de Janeiro for what was described as an "Earth Summit." Officially, it was a conference on "Environment and Development."

Although the conference was held to consider the threat of global warm-ing, which is a scientific topic, no scientists were called on to discuss the matter, and the decisions made were done so without any input from the scientific community.[15]

A major, recurring theme of the conference was that the world was facing impending doom in the form of global warming and that this warm-ing was being caused by carbon dioxide emissions from the coal- and oil-burning furnaces of the industrialized nations. The U.N.'s proposed rem-edy: Cut back on the use of these fuels.

The Rio conference ended with the signing of the Global Climate Change Treaty, which called for the industrialized nations to formulate plans to reduce their carbon dioxide emissions. The first draft of the treaty called for every nation signing the treaty to freeze carbon dioxide emis-sions at the 1990 level and then gradually cut them by 20 percent. Fortu-nately, this disastrous motion did not carry. During the Great Depression of 1929 energy usage fell only 8 percent, so you can imagine what a 20 percent decrease would do to the economies of the industrialized nations.

Various estimates of what it would cost to reduce our level of carbon dioxide emissions have been made, and they all point to economic disaster. Here are a few of them:

• To freeze carbon dioxide emissions at the 1990 level would take a $500-per-ton carbon tax, cost $95 billion a year, and reduce U.S. economic growth rates by 1.4 percent. And, these measures would more than double the price of gasoline and home heating oil, according to the U.S. Department of Energy.[16]

• According to Yale economist William Nordhaus, to cut emissions 50 percent would cost the U.S. $200 billion a year.[17]

• Maurice Strong, secretary general of the Rio conference, estimated that the bill for reducing carbon dioxide emissions could reach $600-billion-a-year with another $125 billion going to nonindustrialized countries to help them reduce emissions.[18]

However, none of these dire consequences came to pass—probably because the cuts were voluntary rather than mandatory. Most industrial countries continued to release even more carbon dioxide as their economies grew, and they prospered.

Then, in 1997, a second meeting was held at Kyoto, Japan, with the results described in chapter 1. This time, the cuts agreed to would be mandatory in the U.S. if they were approved by the U.S. Senate.

To reduce the use of fossil fuels in order to cut back carbon dioxide emissions would mean a greatly diminished standard of living for all of us. We would all work longer hours for less money and spend a much larger percentage of our income for heat and light. We would have to endure cold homes in the winter and hot homes in the summer, because heating and air conditioning would become so expensive. And, we would all have to drive smaller automobiles, which are much more dangerous than full-sized ones. But, this danger would be reduced because few people could afford to drive very much, anyway.

Of course, when you cut back on energy usage, you cut down on industrial production, so fewer workers are needed. This not only throws the factory worker out of a job, but also hurts all of the people who depend on him for their livelihood. The factory worker and his family see fewer movies, don't eat out as much, can't buy as many new clothes, new carpet, or new cars, and can't afford to see a doctor or dentist when they should. Of course, all of these industries are forced to cut back their output, too. Plainly, when measures are taken that cut into industrial growth, everyone suffers. It is a great step backward to a harder life, and it denies everyone the benefits progress could bring.

A Better Solution to the Problem of Global Warming

At present, we are making plans to handle the problem of global warming in the worst possible way: That is, current plans appear to include a cut in our use of fossil fuels. But, we have no plans to replace this loss of energy with nuclear power, or for that matter, anything else. This cut in energy usage would be a giant step backward and would drastically affect all of our lives.

Cutting our energy usage is a very serious step, and we should be absolutely certain that it is necessary before we do it.

On the other hand, it's probably not wise to completely ignore the possibility that a problem could be developing. Global warming is the kind of problem which is best stopped in the early stages. But, more research is called for, not drastic changes in our way of life. After all, only 20 years ago some of the same people who are now most vocal about global warming were busy writing papers and books about the threat of global cooling. It is interesting to note that the same furnaces of industry now being blamed for global warming were then being blamed for the threat of global cooling.

There are those who claim that we can't afford to wait for the research to be done. This includes Vice President Al Gore, who claims that in the face of "…a rapidly deteriorating global environment, we must all become partners in a bold effort to change the very foundation of our civilization."[19]

To those who claim that it's too dangerous to wait, we suggest that they consider a change to non-polluting nuclear power. Several nations plan to do this in order to comply with the Kyoto treaty. Not only would this diminish the threat of the greenhouse effect by reducing carbon dioxide emissions, but it would also prevent the drastic, detrimental changes in our way of life which some people are now trying to force on us.

Acid Rain

In addition to the fact that fossil fuels cause 50,000 air pollution-related deaths each year and contribute to the greenhouse effect, they also contribute to another "little" ecological problem—acid rain.

Hundreds of miles north of the U.S. border lie great ice fields and glaciers. For untold centuries, falling snow has increased these deposits, adding one year's precipitation on top of another in an orderly and predictable fashion. To a team of trained scientists, this record is as readable as a library book might be to you.

What these records tell us is this: Prior to the beginning of the Industrial Revolution in the late 1700s, the rain that fell had absorbed no manmade pollutants from the air, and the acidity of the frozen layer was very low.

Following the start of the Industrial Revolution, the frozen layers of ice show gradually increasing levels of acidity. Layers closest to the surface, formed most recently, show by far the greatest acidity.

Two air pollutants released by burning coal and oil are thought to be largely responsible for this increase in acidity: Sulfur dioxide and the nitrogen oxides. Most of the sulfur dioxide presently released into the U.S.'s atmosphere each year comes from burning coal, but burning oil also releases some. Automobiles and stationary sources such as industrial furnaces and power plants contribute almost equally to the nitrogen oxides presently released.

During the 1970s, over 28 million metric tons of sulfur dioxide and over 22 million tons of the oxides of nitrogen were released into our air each year. These are enormous quantities.

Late in 1990, Congress passed a new, tough amendment to the Clean Air Act. Among other things, this law sought to reduce yearly sulfur dioxide emissions by 10 million tons by the year 2000. But, the Environmental Protection Agency was forced to give 100 of our most heavily polluted cities up to 20 years to meet these new air quality standards. However, by 1996, yearly releases of sulfur dioxide had been reduced to about 19 million metric tons.

When sulfur dioxide is released into the air, it reacts with water vapor and other substances in the air to form various sulfur-based acids. Some of these, such as sulfuric acid, can dissolve metal and limestone, and can easily damage plant tissues.

The oxides of nitrogen undergo a similar chemical transformation into an acidic form. When these acids are washed out of the air by rain and fall on a vulnerable surface, the damage starts. In 1996 we released 23 million tons of this pollutant into the air.

Acid Rainfall Damage

What kind of damage results from acid rainfall? In West Germany, the death of trees first alerted people to the problem of acid rainfall. In Norway it was the death of fish, and in Italy it was the destruction of priceless marble statuary.

During the autumn of 1980, German scientists noted that a mysterious "wasting disease" was progressively damaging and killing trees. By 1982, 60 percent of the silver firs had been damaged, as had 9 percent of the spruces, which made up 40 percent of the forests. A year later, in 1983, 75 percent of the silver firs and 41 percent of the spruces had been damaged. By 1985, 87 percent of the silver firs, 52 percent of the spruces, 58 percent of the pines, and 55 percent of the oaks and beeches had been affected. [20]

Unofficial estimates of the cost of this damage in West Germany were approximately $10 billion per year, and the damage was spreading over the woodlands of France, Sweden, Norway, East Germany, Czechoslovakia, Poland, Hungary, and, to a lesser extent, the U.S.S.R.

During the 1980s, Germany began to substitute nuclear power for her aging fossil fuel-burning power plants. This led to a significant decrease in sulfur dioxide emissions, but the health of Germany's forests did not improve. Scientists then began to suspect that the oxides of nitrogen or perhaps ozone were the villains in the decline of Germany's forests.

Nor was forest damage confined to Europe. In the U.S., a study by University of Vermont scientists showed that between 1965 and 1981, in the Camel's Hump area of Vermont's Green Mountains, approximately half of the spruce trees had died. [21] Later, scientists pointed out that the primary cause of the damage described could be due to ozone or some other substance, and that acid rain might simply be a contributing factor.

To the north, the very mention of acid rain made Canadians extremely nervous. With a $20-billion-per-year forest industry beginning to show signs of damage, the worry was well justified.

By the mid-1980s, Canada, Norway, and Sweden had declared acid rain to be their most serious environmental problem.

This same acid rainfall which fell on or about trees also fell on the ground, where it was washed into rivers and streams. There, increasing levels of acidity first killed the small aquatic organisms at the base of the food chain. As the acidity increased, larger and larger fish died. Soon, many lakes had no fish in them at all.

The U.S. Office of Technology Assessment estimates that approximately 17,000 lakes and 112,000 miles of streams in the U.S. are vulnerable to acidification, and that about 20 percent of these are now affected. Canadian estimates also indicate that about 20 percent of the 50,000 lakes in eastern Canada are also similarly affected. [22]

In the Adirondack Lake region of upstate New York, 500 lakes had become so acidic that fish were unable to reproduce in them. An estimated 150 lakes in eastern Canada had also met the same fate. Many of the best salmon rivers in Nova Scotia no longer had any salmon.

As you might expect, European lakes were unable to escape from the falling acid rain. In Sweden, 18,000 lakes were very acidic, and about 4,000 had suffered severe biological damage leading to the death of almost all of the fish and aquatic plants. To the west, in Norway, the situation was even worse. Many lakes in the entire southern part of Norway had become so acidic that almost no fish were to be found.

Later, some of these damage estimates were revised downward, but it is clear that acid rain is a major problem.

Acid Rain Is an International Problem

One of the complications of acid rainfall is that it is an international problem. Earlier, in an attempt to solve the problem of increasingly higher levels of dangerous sulfur dioxide in the cities, utility companies and other coal-burning industries had built tall smokestacks so the pollutants would be carried aloft, over the city, to be shared by the countryside. "Dilution is the solution to air pollution," decided many engineers who were confronted by the difficult-to-solve problem of providing more energy while being restricted to using fuels which pollute the air.

By 1981, there were 179 smokestacks over 490 feet in height in the U.S. And, there were 20 giant 980-foot smokestacks. England, West Germany, and other European countries also resorted to smokestacks. And, for a while, this measure, and others, worked. Sulfur dioxide levels dropped. In industrialized Manchester, England, engineers reduced winter smoke levels 90 percent and dropped sulfur dioxide levels by two-thirds. This resulted in a doubling of winter sunshine hours and cut the bronchitis death rate by half between 1956 and 1987.[23]

However, the engineers had scarcely finished celebrating when reports of increased pollution downwind began to pour in.

Sulfur dioxide generated by the industrial cities of England and West Germany began to fall on Norway and Sweden, 500 miles away. It was estimated that over 70 percent of the sulfur dioxide which fell on Norway and Sweden was generated by furnaces in England, West Germany, and, to a lesser extent, other European nations. But, a University of Stockholm study later indicated that Swedes themselves might be the source of much of the pollution. And, although England has reduced sulfur dioxide emissions by 30 percent since 1990, the acidity of Swedish lakes has not decreased. [24]

In North America, sulfur dioxide produced by coal-burning power plants in Ohio, Indiana, Illinois, Pennsylvania, and West Virginia fell on Canada. Some of these same states also contributed to acid rainfall in the hard-hit northeastern part of the U.S. But, a study by scientists working for the Environmental Protection Agency found that increased levels of sulfur dioxide in New York City could be traced to fuel oil burned in the city's apartment buildings.

Other Damage

Acid rainfall does other damage, too. When it falls on marble statuary, it reacts chemically with the marble to form a more water soluble compound, with the result that the statue is gradually dissolved and washed away by subsequent rains.

Since many building materials contain calcium carbonate, as does marble, they, too, experience deterioration when acid rain falls on them. In the United States alone, an estimated $2 billion per year is spent repairing the damage acid rain does to building materials. If you own a brick house, it probably needs tuck pointing more frequently as a result of damage by acid rain. Adding to the cost cited above is the fact that acid rain is also thought to cause much of the rust on automobiles. Your new automobile may rust out years sooner than otherwise if you live in an area which has high levels of sulfur dioxide.

Ozone, an atmospheric gas produced largely by gasoline-burning automobiles, causes an estimated loss of 6 to 7 percent of U.S. agricultural production. It is estimated that approximately $2 billion a year in crop losses could be avoided if the amount of ozone could be reduced to half of present levels.[25] Some volatile organic compounds and oxides of nitrogen act as precursors for ozone. That is to say that ozone is a secondary pollutant formed from the action of sunlight on these substances.

Attempts to Control Acid Rain

In an attempt to control acid rainfall, it was suggested that "scrubbers," which prevent some of the sulfur dioxide from reaching the atmosphere, be installed on coal-burning power plants. However these devices are so expensive to install and maintain that utility company executives estimated that the use of scrubbers could cause the cost of coal-generated electricity to increase by 25 percent. And, as expected, utility companies fought to prevent the mandatory use of scrubbers. Even without the scrubbers, the electricity generated by coal-burning power plants is almost twice as expensive as the electricity generated by pre-1982 nuclear power plants, according to a Commonwealth Edison report. Another possible route to less sulfur dioxide was to use more expensive low-sulfur coal.

Fortunately, decreasing the sulfur dioxide emissions from coal-burning furnaces proved to be cheaper than expected. According to 1994 EPA figures, it cost $150 to prevent the release of a ton of sulfur dioxide. But, even so, this brought the cost of a ten-million-ton reduction to $1.5 billion per year.

With so much at stake and so much conflicting information, the federal government did the smart thing and funded a massive research effort. Scientists working in the government's National Acid Precipitation Assessment Program (NAPAP) spent ten years and $500 million to study the problem.

Their conclusion: "There is no evidence of widespread forest damage from current ambient levels of acidic rain in the U.S."[26] The scientists of NAPAP further concluded that acid rainfall was simply one more insult to nature, rather than the primary cause of environmental deterioration. As Environmental Protection Agency administrator Lee Thomas said in 1986: "Acid rain is a serious problem, but it is not an emergency."[27]

In 1990, Congress enacted the Clean Air Act Amendment. Although there was much to be said for this law, it will cost all of us many billions of dollars in the long run. A much smarter, less costly move would have been to pass legislation making it easier to build nuclear power plants. At present, because of frequent changes in regulations and legal delays which occur *after construction has been approved,* it has become almost impossible to build a nuclear power plant.

Nuclear power plants emit none of the pollutants involved in acid rain, so every nuclear power plant built lessens the threat of acid rain. And, because nuclear power is cheaper than fossil fuel-generated electricity, this measure would save, not spend, billions, even while it decreased the danger of acid rain.

Oil Spills

There's another "little" environmental problem associated with the use of the fossil fuels. Each year, huge quantities of crude oil are pumped into the holds of tankers thousands of miles from their destination at U.S. ports. Enroute, these tankers often collide or run aground, spilling all or part of their cargo.

Some of these accidents result in large quantities of oil being spilled into the ocean. According to the 1988 World Almanac, the largest of these spills came when the tankers *Atlantic Empress* and *Aegean Captain* collided off Trinidad and Tobago on July 19, 1979, and 110 million gallons of oil were spilled. Not far behind is the *Castillio de Bellver,* which caught fire off Cape Town, South Africa, on August 6, 1983. This accident resulted in 92 million gallons of oil being spilled. And, when the *Amoco Cadiz* went aground near Portsall, France, on March 16, 1978, 82 million gallons of oil ended up floating on top of the ocean.

When the *Exxon Valdez* ran aground in the spring of 1989, it disgorged 11 million gallons of crude oil into Alaska's Prince William Sound.

Over 300 miles of shoreline were oil-covered, and in only a month the oil slick had spread out over an 1,800-square-mile area. An estimated 33,000 birds and uncounted numbers of aquatic life died as a result of the spill.

The *Exxon Valdez* spill was still big news when three other lesser spills occurred in U.S. waters.

Of these three spills, the first occurred on Friday afternoon, June 23, 1989, when the 530-foot tanker *World Prodigy* struck the well-known Brenton Reef in Rhode Island Sound. An estimated 420,000 gallons of fuel oil escaped. As the incoming surf turned orange, the governor of Rhode Island called out the National Guard and prison inmates in an effort to contain the spill and clean it up.

Hours later that same evening, a barge carrying heavy crude oil collided with a cargo vessel in the Houston Ship Channel. About 250,000 gallons of oil escaped.

Then, on the following day, a Uruguayan tanker carrying 18 million gallons of industrial heating oil ran aground in the Delaware River near Wilmington, Delaware, and lost an estimated 306,000 gallons of its cargo. Fortunately, Wilmington, Delaware's largest city, does not draw its drinking water out of the Delaware River, or the city would have been without any drinking water.

These three accidents, occurring within only a two-day period, should bring home the fact that oil spills are not infrequent disasters.

According to the Georges Bank Petroleum Study of 1973, between 1957 and 1971 there were 23 collisions, each resulting in over 42,000 gallons of oil being spilled. Also, during the same time period, there were 16 groundings, three hull failures, and 2 sinkings. The worst of these spills involved the *Torrey Canyon,* which spilled 29 million gallons when it went aground in 1967. Of the 46 major spills recorded, all but 11 involved over 100,000 gallons of oil being spilled.

Of course, large spills draw more attention from the media, but in 1970 alone there were 3,700 spills of all sizes recorded. These spills resulted in over 367 million gallons of oil getting into the oceans. According to oceanographer and author Thor Heyerdahl, the major routes of the transatlantic oil tankers are now covered with a continuous oil slick.

In February of 1993, the British secretary of transportation called the prevalence of substandard oil tankers "an international disgrace," and a report by Shell Petroleum admitted that 20 percent of the world's tankers were overdue for the scrap yard.

Spilled oil is detrimental to almost all creatures which use the ocean. The oil floats, so sea birds land in it. Their feathers become coated, and they die. Fish are killed too, but probably the smaller marine organisms are at greatest risk.

So, our continued use of fossil fuels is contributing to the destruction of valuable forests, the biological death of thousands of lakes and streams, and the befouling of once pristine beaches. Additionally, this unwise choice of fuels is leading to the destruction of priceless works of art, the more rapid deterioration of building materials, and the hastened rusting of your automobiles. This damage coupled with the agricultural losses caused by air pollution certainly cost us large sums of money each year.

What are the environmental effects of nuclear power plants? Do they also release millions of tons of environmentally-destructive, unhealthy substances?

The Environmental Effects of Nuclear Power Plants

When Tom Hayden shouted "People are willing to profit from the potential poisoning of their children," he was talking about the radiation released by nuclear power plants.[28]

And, when Ralph Nader warned students at Colorado University that "nuclear pollution" was the "modern form of suicide," he, too, was talking about the radiation released by nuclear power plants.[29]

As you'll see shortly, both these samples of inflammatory, irresponsible rhetoric are completely false. But, let's start at the beginning.

When nuclear power plants first came into use in the late 1950s and early 1960s, no one worried about the possibility that they might release radiation. It was generally taken for granted that this couldn't happen, and the public felt safe. Then, the antinuclear activists' campaign to frighten the public gathered momentum, and by August 1986 a Roper Poll showed that 55 percent of the U.S. public felt "very concerned" about the possibility of being exposed to radiation from nuclear power plants.

However, the public's fear of radiation from nuclear power plants is groundless. The effects of radiation have been thoroughly studied, and we are in a good position to be able to evaluate the activist's claims.

What We Know about Radiation

Fissionable, or radioactive, substances such as uranium are one of the sources of radiation. Whenever an atom such as uranium splits or fissions, it spontaneously ejects various fission fragments. Some of these fragments may be atoms, or parts of atoms such as electrons, protons, or neutrons. Or, an atom may release a short burst of energy known as a gamma ray. These emissions are known as radiation. X-rays are also considered a form of radiation, as are the cosmic rays which enter our atmosphere from space.

Most of these forms of radiation travel at very high speeds and can penetrate the cells of the human body. There, they are capable of disrupting the biological processes which take place within the cells.

Extremely large doses of radiation can kill people, as happened during the atomic bombing of Hiroshima and Nagasaki. (However, far more people died from the effects of the blast, which was the same as that of conventional explosives.)

Moderately high levels of radiation may lead to the development of cancer. Radiation can also cause mutations in some of the lower animals such as insects, but this has never been observed in humans. Unfortunately, we cannot escape from radiation; we are exposed to it every second of the day and night. Each second, about 15,000 particles of radiation strike each and every one of us. This adds up to 500 billion collisions per person per year and almost 38 trillion collisions per person over an average lifetime.

The source of almost all of this radiation is not nuclear power plants, but nature. This radiation comes from the soil and rocks, both of which contain a very small percentage of radioactive atoms such as uranium. Because our food is grown in the soil, food is also radioactive. Finally, cosmic rays which come from space are in the air which we breathe. Plainly, we cannot escape from radiation. This is the bad news about radiation.

Fortunately, there is some good news: At low levels, such as we are normally exposed to, there is good evidence that radiation apparently causes no damage, or so little damage to humans that the effect can't be detected. Now, in order to differentiate between the various levels of radiation, it is necessary to talk in terms of numerical values. For this discussion, we shall use the term *milliroentgen equivalent man*. This term is usually shortened to "millirem" and abbreviated as "mrem." The millirem can be thought of as a measure of the damage done to humans by radiation. Although we shall use the term *millirem*, if you read other sources, you may encounter the *rem*, which is 1,000 times larger than the millirem.

In the United States, the average person is exposed to about 250 millirems of radiation per year. This exposure seems to have little effect on our health. The International Commission on Radiological Protection sets 500 millirems as the maximum permissible annual dose an individual should receive, and people who live in certain areas of India and Brazil, where the soil is rich in radioactive thorium, often receive over 1,500 millirems per year without showing any increase in leukemia or bone cancer rates.*

About 130 millirems of the 250 millirems we absorb yearly come from cosmic rays, the earth, and stone building materials. For example, if you live in a brick or stone building, you receive upwards of 30 millirems per year from the small quantity of radioactive substances in the minerals in the stone. And, although a person living at an altitude of 5,000 feet in Denver, Colorado, receives 120 millirems per year from cosmic rays, one living at a lower altitude in Florida may receive only 35 millirems per year from the same source.

Most of our food is grown or raised on the earth, so it absorbs some radioactivity. On the average, the food we eat leads to our absorbing another 25 millirems. For the average person, this brings the total dose of radiation received from nature to about 155 millirems per year. An additional 95 millirems is added from man-made sources, largely medical X-rays. Color television accounts for roughly 1 millirem. Thus, the average person is exposed to about 250 millirems of radiation each year. Little can be done to reduce this total aside from cutting down on the number of medical X-rays, which is risky because these are a valuable diagnostic tool in medicine.

Low Levels of Radiation Are Not Particularly Dangerous

Apparently, this normal exposure is not worth worrying about. Although high levels of radiation often cause bone cancer and leukemia, there is no evidence that low levels of radiation cause these diseases. Doses of radiation below 10,000 millirems are generally considered to be low level doses.

Cosmic rays, which enter the earth's atmosphere from space, are a form of radiation. In Denver, where radiation received from cosmic rays and minerals in the ground ranges from 100 to 150 millirems depending on the elevation, the rate of both bone cancer and leukemia is lower than in both New Orleans and San Francisco, where radiation from these sources averages only about 75 millirems. If low levels of radiation caused very much bone cancer or leukemia, the rates for these diseases should be

---

*For technical purposes, the millirem has some shortcomings. So, in 1974, the international community adopted the following units:

for an absorbed dose: 1 Joule/kg = 100 rad = 1 Gy (gray)

for an equivalent dose: 1 Sv (sievert) = 100 rem.

We shall use the more familiar but less precise *millirem*.

highest in Denver, which has the highest background radiation due to its elevation, but, the opposite is true. Table 5.1 shows the data discussed.

Table 5.1: Evidence That Low Levels of Radiation Are Not Particularly Harmful. Note that cancer rates do not increase as these low levels of radiation increase.

Location	Average background radiation from natural sources	Bone cancer rate/ 10^5 people	Leukemia rate/ 10^5 people
New Orleans, Louisiana	75 mrem	2.80	6.90
San Francisco, California	77 mrem	2.90	10.30
Denver, Colorado	100-150 mrem	2.40	6.40

(Several sources, including Radiation *by Martin O. Ecker, MD.)*

These data indicate that low level radiation is not an important cause of either bone cancer or leukemia. How does the radiation produced by nuclear power plants compare with some of these sources of radiation? At the fence line of a nuclear power plant, by law, radiation may not exceed 10 millirems, which is only about one-tenth as much radiation as the average American gets from medical X-rays each year. Of course, hardly anyone lives this close to a nuclear power plant. The rest of us get less than 0.02 millirems of radiation per year from nuclear power plants. Unlike the standards set for air pollution, which are frequently violated, the standards set for nuclear power plants are closely monitored and almost never exceeded. Even during the highly publicized accident at Three Mile Island, people nearby were exposed to only about 1.4 millirems.

Incidentally, fossil fuel-burning power plants actually emit more radiation than do nuclear power plants. Fortunately, the quantities of radiation released by fossil fuel-burning power plants are small, and, at least for the time being, are nothing to worry about. Table 5.2 shows some sources of radiation, so that you can become more familiar with them.

It is worth noting that the average person receives 50 times more radiation from watching color television than from nuclear power plants. And the occupants of a brick house receive 1,500 times more radiation from the bricks and mortar than they do from nuclear power plants.

What Medical Studies Tell Us about Radiation

Now, let's look briefly at what medical studies reveal about radiation.

During the atomic bombing of Hiroshima and Nagasaki, well over 400,000 people were exposed to various levels of radiation. At least 300,000 people survived, and a joint U.S.-Japanese casualty commission studied these survivors and their descendants over the next thirty years.

Table 5.2: The Radiation Received Yearly from Various Sources

Source of radiation	Dose received in mrem/year
Average background in U.S.: Cosmic rays, earth, and building materials	130
Average, all medical x-rays	95
Food, internal sources	25
Living in a brick house	30
Watching color television	1
3-hour flight in a jet	2
Fallout from weapons testing	3
Cosmic rays at sea level	35
Maximum allowable level at the fence line of a nuclear power plant	10
All nuclear power plants: emissions over entire U.S.	less than 0.02
one coal-fired power plant: average within 20 miles	0.10

(Various sources, most notably Richard Wilson and William Jones,
Energy, Ecology, and the Environment *(New York: Academic Press,), p. 244.)*

Three possible health effects can result from being exposed to massive doses of radiation: Genetic mutations, radiation sickness, and cancer.

Although it has been known since the early 1900s that large doses of radiation can produce genetic mutations in insects, no excess genetic mutations have ever been observed in any of the children born to the Hiroshima and Nagasaki survivors after the war. We said "excess" genetic mutations, because approximately 3 percent of all live births everywhere show a mutation of some sort or other. The mutation rate at Hiroshima and Nagasaki has shown no increase since the atomic bombs were dropped, even though the survivors were exposed to various amounts of radiation.

So, although the writers of *Rolling Stone* magazine once claimed to have found a two-headed calf born just down the road from a nuclear power plant, this mutation was most certainly due to the normal mutation rate rather than to any emissions of radiation by the nuclear plant. The antinuclear activists' cartoons showing deformed monsters in the shadows of nuclear power plants are the products of artists' overactive imaginations and have absolutely no basis in truth to them.

Exposure to 400,000 millirems, such as occurs during an atomic bombing may kill as many as half of the people irradiated. People exposed to over 100,000 millirems develop "radiation sickness," the result of damage to the bone marrow which affects the production of white blood cells. Radiation sickness kills some people, but others survive, and the symptoms disappear within weeks or months. Again, this happens only to people exposed to massive doses of radiation. Below 100,000 millirems, radiation sickness usually does not occur. The maximum level of radiation which is allowable at the fence line of a nuclear power plant, 10 millirems, is 10,000 times less than the level at which radiation sickness occurs. *And, the level of radiation produced by all nuclear power plants in the U.S. is over five million times too small to cause radiation sickness.* The public need not worry about any possibility of radiation sickness being caused by nuclear power plants, no matter what anyone says.

The last health effect, cancer, which includes leukemia, is the most serious concern, primarily because of the possibility that even low levels of radiation *might* cause it. At Hiroshima, where the radiation produced involved neutrons that are especially dangerous, no excess cases of leukemia were found at exposures below 20,000 millirems, which is a lot of radiation. At Nagasaki, where electrons and gamma radiation were emitted, no excess leukemias were found at radiation levels below five times this dose, or 100,000 millirems. In all, up to 1974, there were only about 200 excess cancers among a carefully studied group of 80,000 Japanese exposed to radiation at Hiroshima and Nagasaki.[30] Expressed as a percentage, 200 cancers among 80,000 people is only one-fourth of one percent, which is a miniscule figure in view of the large amount of radiation involved. Of those Japanese exposed to radiation, 8,500 people had received from 100,000 to 600,000 millirems, which is a very large dose, indeed. Table 5.3 summarizes part of what has been learned from studying the medical history of Hiroshima and Nagasaki survivors.

The only reasonable conclusion to be drawn from the study of Hiroshima and Nagasaki survivors is that the 0.02 millirems per year the average American receives from nuclear power plants poses virtually no cancer threat.

A number of other important medical studies on the effects of radiation have been carried out on large groups of people, some of whom were exposed to radiation for years before its dangers were realized.

Some of these groups are:

1. 15,000 people who received large doses of X-rays in an attempt to treat arthritis of the spine.

Table 5.3: Radiation Levels and Health Effects, as Indicated by the Survivors of Hiroshima and Nagasaki

Radiation dose in millirems	Immediate health effects	Later health effects
over 1,000,000 millirems	Almost certain death	No genetic mutations at any level of radiation.
400,000 millirems	50-50 chance of death nausea, fatigue	Excess cancers.
100,000 millirems	Radiation sickness only below this level Temporary changes in blood cell count	No excess cancers below this level at Nagasaki.
25,000 millirems	No medically detectable immediate effects below this level	None
20,000 millirems	None	No excess cancers below this level at Hiroshima.
250 millirems (average exposure to radiation in the U.S.)	None	No excess cancers likely at this level.
0.02 millirems (average radiation received from ALL nuclear power plants in the U.S.)	None	None

(Various sources, including The Nuclear Energy Option, *Bernard Cohen, Chapter 5.)*

2. 10,000 employees of the Hanford nuclear weapons facility.

3. 36,000 hyperthyroid patients in the U.S. who underwent X-ray treatment.

4. 1,600 Brazilians who live in an area of unusually high natural radiation.

5. Thousands of uranium miners.

6. 775 employees of a watch factory who ingested radium, which is radioactive, in connection with their work.

These studies also indicate that low-level radiation poses no threat to our health. In fact, some of these studies indicate that there is a threshold below which radiation causes no damage, or may even be beneficial.

The results of all of these studies confirm that the small amount of radiation emitted by nuclear power plants poses no danger to the public or the environment.

So, when Hayden shouted "People are willing to profit from the potential poisoning of their children," and Nader called "nuclear pollution" "the modern form of suicide," both were repeating completely groundless exaggerations. Unfortunately, the public does take heed of such statements, and it is no wonder that 55 percent of the American public are "very concerned" about the possibility of being exposed to radiation from nuclear power plants. Actually, they have a greater chance of being killed by the stress brought on by such irresponsible misinformation.

CHAPTER 6

Risky Business

In the 1970s, anti-nuclear power activists claimed that nuclear power plants were too risky to be used. At first, they claimed that nuclear power plants might explode as the atomic bombs had done, killing hundreds of thousands of people. Later, the activists claimed that radiation released by nuclear power plants might kill our children. When the threat of these risks became old news, the activists began to claim that a meltdown might occur, killing 500,000 people.

Forty-two years have passed since the first nuclear power plant went on line in the U.S. To date, there have been no nuclear explosions in any U.S. reactors, nor, for that matter, in any of the 442 nuclear power reactors now on earth. Nor is there one shred of evidence that the small amount of radiation released by U.S. nuclear power plants has ever harmed anyone, even those who live right at the fence line of a nuclear power plant. Nor have any meltdowns occurred in Western-built nuclear power plants.

According to the people who should know—scientists and nuclear engineers—a nuclear explosion cannot occur in a nuclear power plant. Because of the design of U.S. power plants, the release of a significant amount of radiation is highly unlikely. Much the same can be said for a meltdown. This kind of accident is said to be nearly impossible in the new, second generation of nuclear power plants now waiting to be built. The risk of either of the latter accidents occurring must be very low, because neither one has occurred to date. And, according to committees of experts in several countries, even if one of these accidents were to occur, chances are good that there would be no fatalities. So, despite the anti-nuclear activists' earlier claims, these risks have not proven to be very serious and apparently are nothing worth worrying about.

This is not to say that there will never be a fatal accident involving the nuclear aspect of a nuclear power plant. In an endeavor as large as the nuclear power industry, sooner or later a fatal accident will probably occur. Of course, very few things are completely safe. Balloons, which children sometimes inhale while inflating them, kill a dozen or so children each year. So do drapery cords, in which small children become entangled and strangle. Bicycling and football also lead to a number of deaths each year. But no one marches on Washington to shut down these activities as they did after Three Mile Island, where no one was injured, killed, or exposed to a significant amount of radiation.

It isn't reasonable to insist that nuclear power plants operate accident-free, and then accept accidents which occur in fossil fuel-burning power plants without a murmur. But, this happens all the time. For example, on July 30, 1998, two coal dust explosions and a fire occurred at a Hammond, Indiana coal-burning power plant. Seventeen people were hurt, including four whose condition was listed as "critical." This event was far more severe than the accident at Three Mile Island, but it didn't rate space in newspapers other than those in the immediate vicinity. And, there was no mention of the accident on national television; it simply went unnoticed by most of the media.

We cannot do without energy. It's a very necessary part of modern civilization. So, what we have to decide is this: Which fuel, nuclear or fossil, poses the greatest risk to our health and prosperity?

To date, Western-built nuclear power plants have never negatively affected the public's health or prosperity. Other than several hundred uranium miners, the use of Western-built nuclear power plants has never been responsible for the injury, sickness, or death of anyone. Nor have nuclear power plants exposed us to raging inflation and recessions, or forced us into a war over vital raw materials.

What about fossil fuels? Do they have as spotless a record? Or do the fossil fuels subject us to greater risks than nuclear power?

In this chapter we'll compare the economic risks which both fuels—fossil fuel and nuclear power—force us to run. Then, in the next chapter, we'll compare accidents involving the two fuels.

It's Risky to Depend on Foreign Oil

Having access to oil is the difference between a miserable struggle to survive on the edge of starvation and fat-and-sassy prosperity. Without oil, no trucks or automobiles move over the roads. Without oil, many homes, offices, and shops grow cold, and some are forced to do without electricity. Much of our industrial grid grinds to a halt. No tractors plow the fields, and food production plummets. We lose all of the 80,000 products made from oil, including many of our medicines and insecticides. Without oil, modern civilization ceases to exist.

In 1990, few industrial nations could allow themselves to be deprived of oil from the Middle East. The U.S. relied on this dangerous, unstable area for 50 percent of its oil imports, and the Japanese and Germans for even more. If this source of energy were denied to any of these countries, and they were unable to quickly find a replacement, they would probably be forced to go to war to gain access to the oil. The alternative—to see their economies utterly and completely destroyed—would be unthinkable. With 88 percent of U.S. goods transported by truck and most of the rest by diesel-powered trains, we would be hard pressed just to keep our cities fed without access to oil. It was exactly these facts that caused a 26 nation coalition to wage war on Iraq in January of 1991.

Iraq overran oil-rich Kuwait, in 1990 and then massed troops on the border of Saudi Arabia in preparation for another easy conquest, when coalition troops hurriedly took up defensive positions on the Kuwait-Saudi border. Had Iraq been allowed to take Saudi Arabia, her power-mad dictator would have been able to ruin economies all over the world simply by raising the price of oil as it suited his whims.

A Modern History of the Turbulent Middle East

How did we ever let ourselves get into such a predicament? Let's start at the beginning. Before oil was discovered in the Middle East, most of the countries there were poor, backward, sparsely populated places. Less than 1 percent of the world's population lived in this harsh, desolate land. The Kuwaitis survived by fishing for pearls in the sea, and Libya's number one export was scrap metal left behind on the battlefields of North Africa.

In 1908, a British geologist discovered oil in what is now Iran. Fifteen years later, a huge pool of oil was discovered in Kuwait. Other discoveries followed, and soon it was apparent that most of the world's oil was located in the Middle East. The big oil companies in England and the U.S. negotiated drilling contracts and leases which the Middle Eastern rulers eagerly signed. After all, the oil companies had the expertise which would convert a thick, foul-smelling black liquid into huge sums of money. Soon the oil companies began drilling and pumping oil to meet the slowly increasing demands of a civilization gradually shifting to an oil-based economy. Except for World War II, there was generally a glut of oil, and most of the oil supplied to the Allies during the war came from the U.S.

Following World War II, the shift to an oil-based economy accelerated as Europe and Japan rebuilt their industrial complexes destroyed by the war. Cheap oil—only $1.50 a barrel—fueled this rebuilding, as it did the 25 years of rapid growth which followed.

During these years, contracts the big oil companies had signed with the various Middle Eastern countries gave the oil companies the right to set the price of oil. And, by contract, the oil companies owned the drilling rigs, the pipelines, and even the huge pools of oil they had discovered.

Originally the oil men had been welcomed to the Middle East because they brought prosperity with them. But when Kuwaitis, Arabs, Iranians, and Iraqis were treated as second-class citizens in their own countries, this viewpoint began to change. Most Middle Easterners came to view the foreign oil companies as "bloodsuckers."

OPEC

In 1960 this resentment reached the boiling point, and the oil ministers of Saudi Arabia, Kuwait, Iraq, Iran, and Venezuela joined to form an international oil cartel, the Organization of Petroleum Exporting Countries, or OPEC. Cartels are business monopolies, and the near-monopoly on oil that OPEC represented was formed for the purpose of eliminating price competition between the oil selling nations. Later, when OPEC's members each agreed to limit their production of oil, it made oil artificially scarce, which in turn enabled OPEC to demand—and get—a higher price from the industrial nations, which could not survive without oil. Now, OPEC could virtually set the price of oil at whatever it wished. It was a beautiful situation for OPEC, and an economic disaster for anyone who needed oil.

In the U.S., monopolies and the price-fixing which they result in are illegal. But there is nothing in international law to prevent their formation. The industrial nations had no choice but to pay the price OPEC demanded.

Prior to the formation of OPEC, crude oil was selling for $1.80 a barrel. Even today, Middle Eastern oil producers are able to find and pump oil at a cost of only about $1.00 a barrel. Because there was an oversupply of oil, OPEC was not particularly effective at first. However, by the early 1970s, air pollution had become such a pressing problem in heavily populated metropolitan areas such as New York City that many utility companies discontinued using coal and switched to low sulfur crude oil from the Middle East. Oil was more expensive than coal, but it also produced far less air pollution. And, the oil oversupply of the 1960s had disappeared as the world's demand for energy increased in the late 1960s and early 1970s. Whereas earlier the U.S. had been self-sufficient in oil, it now began to depend more and more on oil from the Middle East.

In March of 1971, the world's seven major oil companies met with OPEC and signed an agreement that set the price of oil at $2.18 a barrel for a period of five years.

In mid-1973, Saudi Arabia's King Faisal spoke on TV and warned the U.S. that its support of Israel made the U.S. supply of oil exceedingly uncertain. Then, on October 6, 1973, the Arabs attacked Israel. As the badly outnumbered Israeli troops fell back, the Israeli government begged the U.S. for help. When U.S. planes loaded with supplies arrived, their landing was filmed by the media and appeared later on national TV. This further angered the Saudis; the U.S. was openly helping their sworn enemy.

Monopolies, Embargoes, Inflation, and Recessions

Two days later, on October 9, 1973, Iraq announced that it was going to seize all foreign holdings. And the next day, Saudi Arabia, Kuwait, and other OPEC members followed suit. In effect these countries were canceling the long-term contracts and leases they had signed with the foreign oil companies. When the oil companies demanded payment for this seizure of their assets, they received pennies on the dollar. For example, British Petroleum asked Kuwait for $2 billion, but received only $50 million, or two cents on the dollar.

At an earlier time, either Britain or the U.S. might have fought this seizure with troops. But the U.S. was still in shock from its withdrawal from Vietnam and the recent embarrassment of Watergate. And, because Iraq and Russia had signed a mutual assistance treaty, it might have led to war with a militant Russia.

William Brown of the Hudson Institute calls this seizure "the greatest heist in history," and estimates that the oil reserves seized were worth "roughly $254 trillion, an amount comparable to the value of all the tangible property in the United States, including land, buildings, contents, and vehicles."[1]

At the same time, OPEC announced that it would gradually halt shipments of oil to the industrial nations. Then, only two months later, OPEC increased the price of oil to $11.65 a barrel, a 534 percent price increase in less than three months.

As gasoline supplies diminished in the U.S., lines of motorists waiting to buy gas became blocks long. Angry, frustrated drivers went from one gas station to another trying to buy enough gasoline to drive to work the next day. Nor was transportation the only area affected: oil is used in the manufacture of most goods, the generation of electricity, heating, as a raw material for tens of thousands of substances, and in dozens of industries.

People turned their thermostats down to uncomfortable levels to avoid running out of heating oil. Others lost their jobs when industries were forced to cut back production. Virtually everyone in the industrial countries began to realize that their warmth, convenience, and prosperity depended on the whims of OPEC.

This artificially diminished supply of oil forced the U.S. into the recession of 1974. Unemployment rose almost 50 percent, and economic growth rates fell by 50 percent. As the price of oil increased, manufacturers were forced to pass this increase on to the public. Inflation soared, and many families found it difficult to stay financially solvent. Housewives who had not worked outside the home for years returned to the workforce in an attempt to make ends meet. In the end, most of the money they earned ultimately found its way into the pockets of the already-rich men of OPEC. Federal Reserve Board Chairman Arthur Burns succinctly explained the effect OPEC's wild price increases and embargo had on the U.S. economy: "No economic event in a long generation, excluding only wartime upheavals, has so seriously disrupted our economy as the manipulation of oil prices and supplies over the past year."[2] Then, Burns pointed out that $60 billion had been transferred to OPEC in just 1974, and said, "If the price of oil remains at anything like its present level— and there are repeated stirrings in OPEC countries to move it still higher— there will be a massive redistribution of economic and political power among the countries of the world. This of itself carries dangers for our country's future." (It is worth noting that when Burns spoke, the price of oil was $11.65 a barrel. Today, it fluctuates between $15.00 and $22.00 a barrel. In March 2000, it soared to $30 per barrel.)

By 1977, the U.S. economy had partially recovered from the effect of the 1973 embargo and the enormous increases in oil prices, and it experienced moderate economic growth until 1979. Then the Iranian government was toppled by a revolution which brought the Ayatollah Khomeini to power. Possibly because the American government had a good relationship with the former Iranian government under the Shah, Khomeini was extremely anti-American. The American embassy was overrun by Iranian revolutionaries, and the American flag was burned and trampled in front of television cameras as Iranians showed their contempt for the U.S. And, in an event unprecedented in modern times, U.S. embassy personnel were held as hostages while an embarrassed U.S. counted the days of their captivity.

Worse, this event caused a total disruption of the world oil market. Between 1979 and 1981, oil prices rose to $34.00 a barrel, a 1,560 percent increase over the 1973 price of $2.18 a barrel. Were a 50 cent loaf of bread to increase 1,500 percent, its new price would be $7.50.

By June of 1979, oil buyers were so terrified that OPEC might once again shut off the supply of oil that they agreed to almost anything the oil ministers demanded. If the oil minister wanted a $4.00 premium paid on top of the agreed on price, the buyer paid it. If a $2.00 a barrel "sales commission" was to be paid to the oil minister's brother, the buyer paid it. When a retroactive price increase was demanded on oil which had already been shipped and paid for, the buyer paid it.

In short, it was a seller's market of the worst sort, because the buyer had to have the product, at almost any cost. Of course, the 1,500 percent price hike wreaked havoc all over the world. Overnight, prices were forced upward on every process using oil. Inflation rates skyrocketed in most of the industrial countries of the world. More wives went to work to offset the loss of purchasing power. As inflation raged, the price of gold shot to new levels. Scary books about the collapse of the currency system and even civilization itself surfaced. One of the more popular books suggested that every family purchase a bag of silver coins in case the dollar bill lost all value. Survivalist schools, which pretended to train people to survive in the event that civilization collapsed, flourished. Practically everyone took the possibility of a disastrous turn of events very seriously.

By late in 1979, it was estimated that the yearly flow of money from the rest of the world into the pockets of OPEC was enough to buy the entire U.S. farm crop and all of the stock in the 30 biggest U.S. industrial corporations.

In 1981 the members of OPEC had all but reached an agreement, and they were planning to fix the price of oil at $36.00 a barrel, plus a yearly 3 percent increase, when the demand for oil began to decrease. Rather than see their economies destroyed, the U.S. and other countries had taken steps to decrease their reliance on oil from OPEC.

By 1986, the lessened demand for crude oil had weakened OPEC, and prices dropped to about $15.00 a barrel. This decrease came about as a result of the increasing popularity of smaller cars which used less gasoline, conservation measures such as lowered thermostat settings and improved home insulation, and a shift to other sources of energy. For example, in the U.S., more coal and less oil was used from 1977 to 1986. Of course, from the standpoint of our health, coal is the worst fuel of all.

How to Deal with Monopolies and Embargoes

Since the 1973 oil embargo, France has been able to slash its dependency on foreign oil more than any other industrialized nation. Because it was able to deal with antinuclear activists more effectively than most countries, France shifted to nuclear energy as a method of producing electricity. In 1974, right after the first oil embargo, oil was used to generate 40 percent of France's electricity. Yet, only ten years after the oil embargo, France had succeeded in reducing the amount of electricity generated by oil to only 10 percent. By 1996, nuclear power was generating 77 percent of France's electricity. Thus, in the absence of effective political opposition, France's nuclear power industry experienced near normal growth, and it was possible to replace oil with nuclear power. In France, nuclear power has proven to be cheaper and safer than oil or coal, and there have been no problems with waste disposal, although in America, antinuclear activists have convinced many people that this is an "unsolvable problem."

Between 1973 and 1989, what little nuclear energy was used to produce electricity in the United States prevented the need to import over four billion barrels of oil, and decreased our trade deficit by the $115 billion which would have been spent for this foreign oil.

A country which imports more than it exports is, in effect, spending its savings, and no country can do this for long without becoming poorer. In the first eight months of 1989, the U.S. had a $73.6 billion trade deficit, and the purchase of foreign oil accounted for over $36 billion of this deficit. Vast sums of U.S. cash were being transferred to OPEC to buy oil.

According to one study, the trade deficit cost the U.S. five million jobs in 1987.[3] Other economists estimated that we had traded the cash equivalent of six of our 50 states for crude oil since 1973. The use of nuclear power would help cut the flow of cash out of the country for oil purchases, thus cutting the deficit, and result in the saving of several million jobs per year.

The best way to prevent OPEC from abusing the U.S. consumer is not to need their product. Once we begin to use more oil than OPEC must produce to meet their financial needs, look for really outrageous price increases and a return to the 1979 seller's market in oil, or worse.

By being unable to use nuclear power to replace oil, we are forced to deal with OPEC on the worst possible terms. Through the use of nuclear power, we could reduce our need for oil. This reduced demand could lead to more normal competition among sellers, and might even break up OPEC.

Although no one believes that the antinuclear activists are being subsidized by OPEC, they might just as well be. Even if the anti-nuclear activists were working for OPEC, they could hardly do more to force us into OPEC's hands. When oil costs $15.00 a barrel, each year's delay of just one nuclear power plant puts $150 million into OPEC's pocket. Assuming that the antinuclear activists have prevented the construction of 100 nuclear reactors over the past ten years, this delay has cost us a total of $150 *billion.* This sum exceeds the total spent by the U.S. government in 1986 for the departments of Education, Energy, the Food and Drug Administration, the National Institutes of Health, the Public Health Service, the Health Care Financing Administration, and the Human Development Services Department. You can imagine the gains which might have been made had $150 billion been spent on medical research, instead of putting it in the hands of OPEC.

Remaining Competitive in the World Marketplace

Have you or someone in your family lost their job or been forced to take a cut in pay? If so, maybe the antinuclear activists are to blame.

Almost every imaginable product requires some energy for its production. In the case of a red-hot steel ingot being rolled into sheet steel, it's easy to see the energy component.

But, it's not so easy to visualize the energy which went into the production of say, a hamburger. While the cattle were out on the range, coal generated electricity may have been used to pump the livestock's water tanks full of water. Then, diesel powered trucks transported the animals to the packing plant. Once there, electrical energy lit the plant, moved the conveyer belts, and kept the entire plant and the refrigerators cold enough so that the meat wouldn't spoil. A refrigerated truck moved the freshly ground beef to a wholesaler, and, later, on to the restaurant's walk-in coolers. Finally, a gas or electric grill was used to cook the burger. Of course, electric signs were needed to attract customers, and electric lights were used to keep the store brightly lit. And, the building had to be heated or cooled, so more natural gas or electrical energy was needed. All of this energy costs money, and a small bit of it is recaptured with each hamburger sold.

In some industries, the cost of energy may be as much as 50 percent of the total cost of the product. Obviously, the cost of energy can determine whether a product succeeds—or fails—in the marketplace.

Until recently, Americans enjoyed the advantage of having access to some of the world's cheapest energy. We had ample supplies of coal and oil within our borders, so shipping costs were low. Once the U.S. monopolies were broken up, U.S. oil and coal companies competed with each other for sales, and this competition kept the price low. In turn, these low energy costs fueled our growth and prosperity. The energy component of our goods was small, and they sold well on the world market. For a long time, we enjoyed the advantage of oil which cost less than $1.80 a barrel. Then came OPEC, and today oil is $19.00 a barrel.

However, OPEC isn't the only threat to our prosperity. The anti-nuclear activists pose an even bigger threat to our economy, and not every country is equally threatened by them. In those countries where it has been possible to control these militant groups, the use of nuclear power has grown more rapidly than it has in the U.S., which explains why 18 countries now use nuclear power to generate a higher percentage of their electricity than we do.

Nuclear Power Is Our Cheapest Source of Energy

Here's where the threat to our economy comes in: Nuclear power is considerably cheaper than any of the other common sources of energy. It's roughly one-half as expensive as coal, which is generally thought to be our cheapest fuel. And, nuclear power is even cheaper when compared with natural gas and oil.

The utility companies have carried out a lot of studies on the comparative costs of various fuels, and through the early 1980s almost all of them indicated that nuclear power was our cheapest fuel.

Table 6.1: The 1982 Cost of Electricity Generated by Nuclear Versus Coal

Fuel	Plant construction	Operating and Maintenance	Fuel	Total Cost per kilowatt hour
Nuclear	0.92	0.50	0.82	2.24 cents
Coal	1.11	0.42	2.80	4.33 cents

(Source: Commonwealth Edison, 1982.)

This table shows Commonwealth Edison's average operating costs for six large nuclear reactors and six comparable coal-fired power plants. It is worth noting that costs for plant construction and operating and maintenance were similar for both kinds of plants. But, fuel costs were over three times higher for the coal-fired plants. *Total cost per kilowatt hour, which is what counts, showed that electricity generated by coal-fired plants was almost twice as expensive as electricity produced by the nuclear power plants.*

Unfortunately, this picture has changed in the U.S. in recent years. In an attempt to placate the mobs of antinuclear activists and end the multitude of frivolous lawsuits they have filed, the Nuclear Regulatory Commission (NRC) has continually tightened regulations. Unfortunately, some of the new regulations haven't accomplished very much. For example, at one time regulations called for all welds to be x-rayed periodically so that a developing flaw could be detected long before the weld broke. This makes sense where pipes pass through metal containment, but it's an unnecessary, expensive bit of nonsense to have to x-ray the weld on a metal hand rail, which is what has to be done at nuclear power plants.

Unfortunately, none of these "improvements" was ever enough to satisfy the anti-nuclear activists. And, the NRC should have anticipated this. After all, the anti-nuclear activists were never interested in improving the safety of nuclear power plants; they have always been bent on stopping them from operating, no matter how safe they are.

Over the years, these regulatory changes have increased the cost of nuclear power plants, and they are now over twice as expensive to build in the U.S. as they are elsewhere.

When the anti-nuclear activists use the argument "nuclear power plants are too expensive to build," a bitter irony emerges. Nuclear power plants cost the same, or less, to build than coal-burning plants until the anti-nuclear activists forced construction costs up by filing hundreds of frivolous lawsuits and picketing.

More Evidence that Nuclear Power Is Our Cheapest Source of Energy

Common sense proof of the comparative costs of producing energy using coal and nuclear power plants is provided by the former Eastern Bloc countries: By 1990 these countries had built 63 nuclear power plants, despite the fact that they hold some of the world's largest coal reserves. If nuclear power was more expensive than coal, why would these countries build even one nuclear plant?

When newly-elected President Clinton outlined his plans for an energy tax in February of 1993, *energy industry figures showed that to produce a million BTUs of energy cost 50 cents if the energy was produced by nuclear power. But, coal costs were $1.10; natural gas, $2.40; and oil, $2.65 per million BTUs.*[1] So, as a result of the antinuclear activists' work, although the energy produced by nuclear power plants was only from one-half to one-fifth as expensive as that produced by fossil fuels, we weren't building any more nuclear power plants.

But, the rest of the world was building nuclear power plants. Table 6.2 shows the percentage of electricity supplied by nuclear power in a number of countries.

Table 6.2 The percentage of electrical power generated by nuclear power plants in various countries.

Note that there are a large number of countries (which many economists think are not as technologically advanced as the U.S.) that are using cheaper, healthier nuclear power to generate a larger percentage of their electricity than we do.

Country	Percentage
Lithuania	83.44%
France	77.36%
Belgium	57.18%
Sweden	52.38%
Slovakia	44.53%
Switzerland	44.45%
Ukraine	43.76%
Bulgaria	42.24%
Hungary	40.76%
Slovenia	37.87%
Armenia	36.72%
South Korea	35.77%
Japan	33.99%
Spain	31.97%
Germany	30.29%
Taiwan	29.07%
Finland	28.13%
United Kingdom	26.04%
⇨ United States	21.92%

(Not shown: The twelve nations which use an even lower percentage of nuclear energy than the U.S.)

(Figures are for 1996, and are from the 1998 World Almanac.)

The Rest of the World Is Building Nuclear Power Plants

It is sad to note that although we were once a leader in the use of nuclear power, we now lag badly behind other nations. In fact, a number of once less technically advanced nations have long since passed us by. And, there's a lot of danger in letting this happen. For example, in 1996, South Korea used cheap nuclear power to supply 36 percent of its electricity, while we generated only 22 percent of our electricity with nuclear power.

We have to compete in the world marketplace with South Korea. And, as you probably know, South Koreans will work for a whole lot less money than U.S. factory workers are happy with. So, not only will South Korea's energy costs be less, but their labor costs will also be less. This means that South Korean automobiles, computers, televisions, and other products will be significantly cheaper than those produced in the U.S. Nor are the South Koreans turning out junk—the quality of many of their products is just as good as ours. You have probably seen some of them—Gold Star television sets, Leading Edge computers, and Hyundai automobiles are examples of Korean products which have sold well in the U.S.

How to Become a Second-Class Nation

Of course, if a Gold Star television set is just as good and significantly cheaper than a comparable U.S.-made set, the U.S. public will probably buy the Gold Star. At least, that's what has happened with other products: The U.S. now imports 100 percent of its table radios and VCRs. And, we import 85 percent of the black and white TVs sold here, and 68 percent of the digital watches. Less expensive foreign products have all but crowded us out of the market for these goods. The reason that we no longer manufacture table radios and VCRs in the U.S. is that we can't make one which is price competitive in the world market place. And, whenever this happens, we lose manufacturing plants and tens of thousands of jobs. Our labor and energy costs are so high that we are no longer competitive in an increasing number of areas.

Thirty-two years ago, in 1968, our Gross Domestic Product (GDP) per person was the highest in the world. Only eleven years later, we had fallen to eighth place. After that, things stabilized a bit, but by 1990, Switzerland's GDP per person was almost 50 percent higher than the U.S.'s. If this downward trend continues, a number of nations could have a much higher standard of living than we do before too many decades pass.

The word "sabotage" originated with the European Luddites who once dropped wooden shoes—"sabots"—into machinery in an attempt to destroy it. Today, the modern Luddites are sabotaging our attempts to remain economically competitive. But, they aren't dropping wooden shoes into the machinery any more. Instead, they are stopping us from building nuclear power plants, which are our cheapest, best source of energy.

In 1991, Oil Forced Us into War, and It Could Happen Again

As serious as the threats of the transfer of huge sums of money, economy-destroying price increases, and oil embargoes are, there's a much more dangerous aspect to having to rely on the Middle East for a large part of our energy supply: *The threat of war.*

In mid-1990, Kuwait was pressing Saddam Hussein, Iraq's ruthless dictator, to begin repayment of the $10 to $20 billion Iraq had borrowed from Kuwait to finance its eight-year war with Iran. However, Saddam maintained that he had fought Iran on behalf of all Arabs, and therefore the entire $30 to $40 billion debt which he owed the rest of the Arab world should be considered paid. Naturally the lenders of this huge sum did not agree with Saddam's easy dismissal of this enormous debt.

Throughout the early months of 1990, Saddam accused both Kuwait and Saudi Arabia of exceeding the oil production quotas which OPEC had set. According to Saddam, this overproduction was preventing the price of oil from rising and, as Saddam saw it, preventing him from paying his debts. In June, Saddam warned that he would "cut some necks" before he would cut his "means of living."

Then, in July, Saddam moved 30,000 of his best troops to the Kuwait border just before an important OPEC meeting.

Although Kuwait and the United Arab Emirates had long been advocates of reasonable oil prices, the threat of Saddam's troops apparently forced them to agree to the first price hike in oil for four years, from $18 a barrel to $21.

Encouraged by the ease of his success, on August 2, 1990, Saddam sent his mechanized columns into Kuwait. And, when Iraqi armor massed on the border of Saudi Arabia for what looked like another easy conquest, U.S. President George Bush had little choice but to send American troops into Saudi Arabia to protect U.S. interests.

Why the U.S. Had to Go to War

The industrialized nations of the world can survive without oil from Iraq and Kuwait, but had Iraq's tanks plunged across the Saudi border and captured the rich oil fields there, the situation would have taken a much more disastrous turn. Had this happened, one man—Saddam Hussein— would have controlled 45 percent of the world's known oil reserves. Overnight, Saddam would have become the most powerful man on earth. At a whim, he could have sent oil prices skyrocketing, causing massive inflation, unemployment, and terrible economic depressions throughout almost all of the world. Faced with the possibility that Saddam might destroy both the Kuwait and Saudi oil fields if attacked, it might have been very difficult to remove him from his seat of power.

Once he was aware of these depressing possibilities, U.S. President George Bush had no choice but to act. Within hours after the decision had been made, U.S. warplanes and troops were on their way to Saudi Arabia. The risk of having almost half of the world's oil fall into the hands of a ruthless dictator who once used poison gas on thousands of *his own civilians* was more than could be tolerated.

The War in the Desert—and Elsewhere

Faced with the presence of U.S. troops in Saudi Arabia, Saddam halted at the Saudi border. Then, an uneasy stalemate ensued. The United Nations (UN) authorized a blockade of Iraq, and by mid-December of 1990, an international force of nearly 500,000 troops—mostly Americans—was in Saudi Arabia.

In more ways than one, Iraq appeared to be a very formidable foe. Its one-million-man army was equipped with over 5,500 tanks, 3,500 artillery pieces, and 500 aircraft. This modern equipment was in the hands of Russian-trained Iraqi soldiers, many of whom had just fought an eight-year war with Iran. And, it was in place, ready to go. The U.S. had to move its equipment over thousands of miles of oceans. All of Iraq's costly weapons had been purchased with profits from the sale of oil. It is worth reminding the reader that, by contract, this oil had once belonged to the Western oil companies which had discovered it. As you may remember, in 1973, Iraq seized these oil reserves without bothering to compensate the oil companies for their loss.

And, a few other things made Iraq even more dangerous. Thousands of Westerners, including 3,000 Americans and 4,600 British citizens, were trapped in Iraq and Kuwait at the time of the invasion. At first, Saddam vowed to use some of these people as "human shields" around potential bombing targets in Iraq. Later, as the UN authorized military action against Iraq, Saddam let large numbers leave, and the last hostages were freed during early December.

Time magazine's William Dowell and Bruce van Voorst suggested that Iraq might launch a missile attack with chemical, biological, or, later, even nuclear warheads against Tel Aviv or Jerusalem in an attempt to ignite a holy war which might unite all Arabs against any outsiders.

Then, there was the threat of a big increase in Iraqi-sponsored terrorism. In October of 1990, *Time* reported that there were signs that a network of Iraqi terrorists was being developed. Presumably these terrorists would strike targets in the U.S., Europe, and Japan. And, for the first time, terrorists might use such weapons as nerve gas or germ warfare on unsuspecting civilian targets. So, while American aircraft were leveling Baghdad, Iraqi terrorists could be releasing poison gas in the halls of Congress or the subways of New York. It was, to say the least, a chilling thought.

In the past, the antinuclear activists have sought to frighten the American public into joining their ranks by exaggerating the possibility that terrorists might steal nuclear fuel and convert it into a nuclear bomb. And, the antinuclear activists were fond of describing the "police-state," complete with martial law, which they *imagined* might develop in order to deal with this problem. (Because huge processing facilities and much technical expertise are needed to convert nuclear fuel into a nuclear bomb, nuclear fuel is not a likely target for terrorists.)

However, you can imagine the real police-state which might be necessary to prevent Iraqi terrorists from releasing a canister of colorless, odorless, but lethal nerve gas into the ventilation system at a rock concert, or a crowded high school gymnasium.

Although the Iraqi terrorist network failed to develop, our presence in the Gulf has led to various acts of terrorism. Numerous hostages have been taken and held, often for years. In 1982 a U.S. military attaché was murdered by terrorists, as were other U.S. military personnel from time to time. But, the worst death toll came when terrorists blew up the U.S. Marine headquarters in Beirut, killing 241 Americans. And, in apparent retaliation for the U.S.'s downing of a Libyan passenger plane that had been mistaken for a warplane by a U.S. Navy vessel, Libyan terrorists planted a bomb on Pan Am flight 103. The plane exploded over Lockerby, Scotland, killing everyone aboard the ill-fated flight. Then, in March of 1993, Middle Eastern terrorists struck in the U.S., bombing the World Trade Center. Only five people were killed, but over a thousand were injured.

It might be worth remembering that without the antinuclear activists, nuclear power would have been gradually replacing oil over the last 20 years. Had this happened, we would have had no need to place 500,000 men on the line in Saudi Arabia, and Iraq would have had nothing to gain by stepping up its terrorist attacks on innocent civilians.

The Economic Consequences of the War

While the stalemate in the desert continued, Western economies suffered as oil prices climbed. Oil quickly shot from about $20 a barrel to almost $40 a barrel. Gasoline prices jumped 37 cents a gallon in only 5 days. Later, oil prices dropped to $33 a barrel.

One-fourth of each barrel of oil is used to manufacture goods ranging from plastic bags to medicine. As a consequence, rising oil prices also increased the cost of 75 to 80 percent of the items in the consumer price index. In September of 1990, wholesale prices in the U.S. jumped 1.6

percent, for an annual inflation rate of nearly 20 percent. This was the biggest two-month rise in wholesale prices in almost ten years.

On September 24, 1990, the U.S. stock market hit a 14-month low, largely because of rising oil prices. The price of gold, the refuge of the fearful investor, climbed to over $400 an ounce. By September 26, the U.S. economy was at a virtual standstill, and most economists agreed that a recession had set in. Saddam's threat that he would destroy all the oil fields in the event of war did little to bolster confidence in the future.

In September 1990, the U.S. trade deficit showed its largest increase since 1982. And, higher energy costs led to a decrease in industrial production and an increase in the jobless rate. The U.S. economy had clearly been dealt a staggering blow by the increase in oil prices.

Meanwhile, the Federal Reserve Board (the "Fed") was faced with a near-impossible problem: Inflation was increasing, and the Fed usually *increases* interest rates to fight inflation. But, at the same time, the economy was in a recession, and the Fed usually responds to this problem by *decreasing* interest rates to stimulate the economy. Obviously, the Fed cannot simultaneously both increase and decrease interest rates.

The cost of keeping troops in the desert soon reached $50 billion. As more troops were sent to the Middle East, the cost was expected to rise even more. Plainly, this was not a year when a cut in military spending would be feasible.

So, by mid-December of 1990, the stalemate in the desert had already caused higher gasoline prices, a big jump in inflation, a higher jobless rate, higher interest rates, a recession, and increased military spending.

By now, it should be obvious that there are few places on earth more dangerous than the Middle East. To depend on this region for oil, which is the very lifeblood of modern civilization, is unwise by any measure.

When the January 15, 1991, deadline that the UN coalition had set neared, it became obvious that Saddam wasn't going to withdraw. Then only a day after the deadline expired, U.S. warplanes and cruise missiles struck military targets in Baghdad. The worst had come to pass—the world was at war again. It was the fourth war in the Middle East in less than 20 years. Most readers are well aware of what followed these events. After a devastating air assault which lasted 38 days, coalition ground troops quickly destroyed the Iraqi army with only exceedingly low casualties to themselves. The results surprised everyone.

As Saddam was driven from Kuwait, he set over 600 oil wells afire. But, his quest for power had been thwarted. And, partially because of Israeli restraint, his threat of a holy war had evaporated.

This time, the civilized world had escaped what could have been a catastrophic war. But, what might the loss of life have been had communism not been on its deathbed, and had the Soviet Union decided to fight alongside Iraq against us? Had this happened, we might have learned just how costly Middle Eastern oil can be.

A Note on a Frightening Scenario

When an industrial accident occurred at the nuclear power plant at Three Mile Island in Pennsylvania, in 1979, no one was hurt, killed, or even exposed to a significant amount of radiation. But, an anti-nuclear power media turned what was a minor industrial accident into scary front page news for several weeks. After 65,000 anti-nuclear protesters marched on Washington, the future of the nuclear power industry was so uncertain that the respected scientist Professor Edward Teller appeared in an unprecedented full two-page advertisement which appeared in newspapers in many major U.S. cities. Dr. Teller explained that Three Mile Island had threatened no one, and that we could not do without nuclear power if modern civilization was to survive.

Even before Three Mile Island, militant West German activists had appeared at nuclear power plants wearing gas masks, and armed with wire cutters, chains, iron bars, bayonets, and Molotov cocktails. As a result of these violent confrontations, a brief moratorium on the construction of any nuclear power plants had been declared in West Germany.

After Three Mile Island, foreign protesters followed the lead of American antinuclear activists and increased both the frequency and the violence of their demonstrations. The future of nuclear power appeared uncertain in West Germany, France, Sweden, and Great Britain.

In the U.S., a number of activists including Tom Hayden, Ralph Nader, and Barry Commoner used the incident at Three Mile Island and the media publicity accorded them to increase their name recognition and political power. Hayden made a 50-city tour, speaking about the dangers of nuclear power, and for a while, it appeared that he might be making a run for the presidency, but he settled, instead, for a seat in the California State Legislature. Commoner did run for President on an antinuclear platform, but was soundly defeated. Nader used his newly-gained popularity to form one of the largest political action groups in Washington, and did not run for president until 1996. Without the notoriety gained at nuclear power's expense, these political candidacies would have been even less successful.

But, the efforts of these people were successful in halting most nuclear power plant construction in the U.S. A strong antinuclear power movement, which had been well-publicized by the media, forced many utility companies to abandon the construction of 120 nuclear power plants in the U.S. And, no orders have been placed for the construction of a nuclear power plant in America since 1979.

So, by the late 1970s, and well into the 1980s, it appeared that nuclear power's future was dead in the U.S. and in serious trouble elsewhere. Since no other source of energy was ready to take over the role of oil, modern civilization was still very much dependent on oil.

When a militant government in Iran seized the American Embassy in Iran, the second serious threat to our oil supply in six years took place. This stimulated efforts to determine how long our oil reserves would last. One well-publicized report placed proven oil reserves in the U.S. at only nine years. Suddenly, it appeared that we might run out of oil and have no alternative source of energy available to supply our need. This, of course, meant major trouble for the entire world.

At this point, I began to look into just what would happen if we suddenly ran out of oil and had no alternative source of energy in place, ready to go. The chilling scenario which follows, in the section entitled "The World's Greatest Risk," reports what I found.

However, during the late 1980s and early 1990s, three events occurred which made the scenario much less likely.

The first event was the development of off-shore oil wells. As you may know, oil is thought to be formed from the remains of microscopic plants and animals which inhabited ancient oceans tens of millions of years ago. In the 1950s, the deepest oil well in the U.S. went down 20,500 feet in Wyoming. Offshore, oil wells were being placed a maximum of 25 miles out in the Gulf of Mexico in 50 feet of water. Then, in 1968, the exploratory ship *Glomar Challenger* dropped a line in almost three miles of water and recovered rock from the ocean floor. Other oceanic exploration followed quickly.

By 1985, a 22-nation consortium had built the oceanic exploratory ship, the *Resolution*. The Resolution could drill a 6,874-foot deep exploratory hole over 19,641 feet of water, for a total depth of pipe of 26,515 feet. This was over a mile more pipe than the deepest land well used in the 1950s. And, by late in 1998, Japan, which has to depend entirely on foreign oil, began plans to build a larger, improved vessel which could ultimately drill exploratory holes having 36,000 feet of pipe. This was over three miles deeper than the deepest land well of the 1950s.

Should this exploration reveal the existence of significant oil fields in the ocean floor, the next step would be to erect exploratory oil well drilling rigs in the most promising areas; and, if these tests confirmed the presence of oil, actual commercial drilling would quickly follow.

Much of the world's oil has been found in sedimentary rocks which were formed during the Tertiary Period which began about 65 million years ago, but a good part of the Middle East's immense pools of oil comes from the Cretaceous and Jurassic rocks which immediately preceded the Tertiary Period. Significant layers of these sedimentary rocks occur on the ocean's floor within 500 miles or less off the Pacific coasts of Canada, the U.S., Central and South America, the Southern coast of Australia, and for that matter, much of the European, South Africa, Indian, and Japanese coasts.

Should these developments lead to the discovery of a lot of oil, as they well might, we could easily have enough oil to supply our needs for over 100 years. This would give us an adequate period of time in which to agree on an alternative source of energy to be used when our oil ran out, and build the massive facilities needed to fully utilize this alternative source of energy.

The second event which made the scenario less likely to occur was the foreign public's recovery from Three Mile Island, and Chernobyl which followed in 1986, and the rapid development of nuclear power throughout most of the world, except the U.S. By 1996, a total of 325 nuclear power plants had been built outside of the U.S. Eighteen countries used nuclear power to generate a greater percentage of their electricity than we did. Most of the technology had been developed by the U.S., but other countries were taking advantage of it, even if we weren't. Of course, each nuclear power plant which is built makes the country building it increasingly less dependent on oil.

The third event which diminished the possibility of the scenario taking place was the threat of global warming. Late in the 1980s and early 1990s, when global warming became the number one concern of numerous environmental groups, a number of them began to change their unreasonable position on nuclear power. Typical of these was the misnamed Union of Concerned Scientists, in which less than 2 percent of the members were actually scientists. Several times in the 1970s, this powerful anti-nuclear organization had issued press releases calling for the shutdown of all U.S. nuclear power plants. But, by 1989, The Union of Concerned Scientists was telling their membership that it now favored the development of a second generation of nuclear power plants. This made the resumption of construction of nuclear power plants more likely in the U.S.

So, these three events made what I had called the "world's greatest risk" less likely to happen. However, in 1986, it seemed very likely.

Chernobyl had just occurred, and the media wrote that it was a nuclear explosion, which it was not. Also, the media never explained that Western-built nuclear power reactors were thousands of times safer than the unsafe reactor at Chernobyl. Everywhere, nuclear power was on the ropes, and its future was very uncertain.

In 1998, when it came time to update this book immediately prior to the final typesetting, I considered discarding the scenario. But, when I thought about it, the scenario emerged as still possible.

On November 28, 1999, Ukraine announced that it planned to restart the unsafe reactor at Chernobyl and would operate it until the U.S. paid for the completion of two new, safer nuclear reactors to replace it. Since there are about 25 Chernobyl-type reactors scattered throughout the former Eastern-bloc nations, it could cost $25 billion to replace all of them. But, these countries argue that they cannot do without the electrical energy supplied by these reactors, and they cannot afford to replace them. This means that these unsafe reactors will probably continue to operate, getting more and more dilapidated and dangerous as time goes on, unless there's a massive outpouring of cash from the U.S.

In order for the scenario which I had constructed to occur, two of these aging, unsafe reactors would have to have catastrophic accidents within a short period of time. Then, if even a moderately serious accident occurred in one of our nuclear weapons reactors—which aren't as safe as our commercial power reactors—the stage would be set. The media, which has been strongly anti-nuclear power since 1973, would probably whip the public into a near-hysteria, and the nation's environmentalists would once again march on Washington and demand that every nuclear power plant in the world be shut down, as they did after Three Mile Island. Similar protests in other countries might shut down nuclear power all over the world.

The fact that nothing had happened in a Western-built nuclear power plant would be quickly brushed aside without even being mentioned in the press. The media might even be happy, because the events that had occurred would prove that they had been right all along, or so they would think. As the ranks of the anti-nuclear power organizations grew with new members who wanted to help save the earth from nuclear power, these organizations would also celebrate.

New members of these organizations would be happy that their membership dues had been well spent, and that they had done their part in saving the planet. But, then the bills for this foolishness would come due as utility companies all over the world scrambled to build more gas turbine, oil, and coal-operated power plants. Gas and oil prices would escalate quickly, and air pollution levels would also rise. Each year, the world would have to dig another 20,000 additional graves to accommodate the latest victims of air pollution.

If the oil fields of the oceans failed to live up their initial promise, and the world's demand for oil increased due to the rapid industrialization of China and India, the chance that we would run out of oil and not have a substitute in place would be much more likely. And, if the nuclear accidents described took place, and all of the world's nuclear power plants were shut down, oil would have to fill in for nuclear power, too.

So, I decided to leave the scenario in. If nothing else, it shows how close we had come to complete, utter disaster had three important factors not changed to prevent it. And, more than anything else, it illustrates the potential danger of listening to ignorant people, who proclaim themselves as experts, win the media over and go on to set a nation's course in a near life and death matter, often for personal political gain.

Here's the scenario, slightly updated, but largely as written back in 1986, only a few months after the disaster at Chernobyl. You can breathe a little easier; as things now stand; the scenario is still possible, but less likely than it was back in 1986.

The World's Greatest Risk

As bad as the prospect of economy-destroying price increases, an oil embargo, other countries having cheaper energy, and the increased chance of a serious war in the Middle East are, there's a far greater catastrophe waiting to make its appearance. This catastrophe will have worldwide consequences probably worse than anything that could happen to civilization short of an all-out, worldwide thermonuclear war. Right now, it is probably one of the more serious long-range threats to modern civilization.

Twice in the 1970s, we displeased the lords of Middle Eastern oil, and they shut off our oil supply. This shortage launched various attempts to determine how long our oil and natural gas reserves would last. In 1975, a U.S. geological survey placed our oil reserves at 145 billion barrels. Almost 60 percent of this oil had not been discovered, but geologists were certain enough that it was present underground to include it in their estimate.

Fifteen years later, in 1990, the Administration's Annual Energy Review placed U.S. oil reserves at 26.5 billion barrels. At our current rate of usage, 5.5 billion barrels a year, these reserves would last less than five years if we were unable to import any foreign oil. However, before you rush to sell your car, you should know that enough oil was being discovered each year to maintain this reserve.

In 1990, the U.S. Energy Information Administration also released figures which indicated that the entire world had the equivalent of about one trillion barrels of oil in reserve. But, the world was consuming 22 billion barrels of oil a year. At this rate, the world's oil might last only 45 more years.

However, a steady rate of consumption is not something we should gamble on. In the 19 years between 1960 and 1979, the world's oil consumption tripled. As more countries become industrialized, this sort of explosive increase could easily occur again. If that happens, we could run out of oil in only 15 years.

And, it could happen. In the few decades since World War II, Japan has become highly industrialized. More recently, the "Four Tigers" of Asia—South Korea, Taiwan, Hong Kong, and Singapore—have emerged as newly industrialized nations. In 1960, these four countries exported only $50 million worth of products, and most of this was agricultural. Twenty-eight years later, in 1988, their exports totaled $65 billion. This over 1,000-fold increase came mostly in the manufacturing sector. Manufactured goods made up only 10 percent of the exports of these countries in 1960, but represented 96 percent of all exports by 1988. This great increase in manufacturing was accompanied by huge increases in the consumption of oil.

If this same sort of explosive industrial growth were to reach China and India, which have over two billion of the world's six billion people, the world's oil consumption could skyrocket.

One thing to realize about the estimates of our oil reserves is that they are very uncertain. Oil and its companion fuel, natural gas, do not occur in uniform deposits. Oil is trapped in irregularly shaped pools in sand and porous sedimentary rock. The area and depth of each pool varies tremendously. Even after thorough seismic studies by geologists have been carried out, drilling for oil is still a very speculative business. Most of the holes drilled produce no oil at all. And, even if a drilling company does strike oil, it may not be able to extract very much of it from the hole. Many holes have been sealed with 50 percent of the oil still present, but unextractable.

If one understands the crucial importance of oil to civilization, all of this is a bit frightening. And, because the estimates of our oil reserves and usage could change overnight, the entire problem is cloaked in a terrible uncertainty. However, it boils down to this: No one is certain how much oil remains underground. If you believe the pessimists, America's oil and natural gas—and the world's supply as well—will be gone in only about 20 years. If you believe the most optimistic estimates, our oil and natural gas could last for over 100 years.

When Being an Optimist Could Be Very Dangerous

However, this is one situation in which it could be very dangerous to be an optimist. This is one time that we'd better believe the pessimists, and act accordingly. If we run out of oil and don't have an alternative source of energy in place, ready to use, we'll be in serious trouble, the like of which most of us can't even begin to imagine.

If we are foolish enough to believe the optimists, and it turns out that they are wrong, we might get caught without enough time to develop an alternate source of energy and build the massive facilities which would be needed to process and utilize this new source of energy.

Even if we were in complete agreement as to which source of energy to use as a substitute for oil, and embarked on a crash program to build the facilities necessary for the utilization of this fuel, it could take 10 or even 20 years to carry out this massive task. The huge facilities needed to mine, refine, and process the great quantities of raw materials which will be needed for the switch from oil simply can't be built overnight.

On the other hand, if we believe the pessimists and get started on the job today, the worst that could happen is that we'll be ready for the day when we run out of oil before it happens. This wouldn't be bad, because the leftover oil certainly wouldn't go to waste. On the contrary, it would be used more intelligently; oil is needed as a raw material for the production of tens of thousands of useful chemicals which are used to make a variety of finished products ranging from plastic bags to some of our most valuable medicines. For over 100 years, some of our best minds have expressed the opinion that oil is too valuable a natural resource to burn frivolously as we now do. To paraphrase one scientist, "Burning oil for heat is comparable to burning dollar bills to keep warm."

Can Solar Energy Do the Job?

Although some people insist that solar energy or some other new source of energy could fill in for oil, they've been badly misinformed. We've been hard at work on an alternative to oil since 1973, but 16 years later, in 1989, sources such as geothermal, wind, and solar energy combined to produce only four-tenths of one percent of all of the energy consumed in the U.S. The reason that so little energy is currently being generated by these methods is that they are among the least practical ways to produce large quantities of energy.

This extremely low production of energy by geothermal, wind, and solar energy came despite the fact that the Department of Energy has spent $4 billion on research and development in these areas, and has allowed another $2 billion in tax subsidies to stimulate their growth. Yet, in spite of all of these incentives, Mobil Oil Company recently closed down its 19-year-old solar energy research program. Big oil companies do not walk away from something that shows promise. And, a 1980 poll of 279 scientists who could be considered experts in the field of energy production revealed that almost none of them felt that solar electricity would be able to make any kind of a significant contribution toward meeting our energy needs in the next 20 years.[5] Time has proven that the experts were right.

Unfortunately, it will take a major technological breakthrough to change this bleak outlook. Since the billions spent thus far have failed to produce this breakthrough, we can assume that it isn't going to be easy to achieve. The breakthrough which would make solar energy a more promising source of energy may never come, or it may happen decades in the future. But, the odds against it happening tomorrow are very high. And, yesterday is when we should have started a crash program to build the facilities needed to make the switch over from oil to some new source of energy.

If solar energy and the other newer sources of energy can't be counted on to take up the slack when we run out of oil, how about the old standby, wood? Wood was able to meet about 90 percent of our much more modest energy needs in 1850. However, then there were only 35 million Americans, and just keeping them warm was rapidly depleting our forests. Today, there are 265 million Americans, or more than seven times as many. It is almost inconceivable that wood could keep 265 million Americans warm, let alone supply even a small fraction of the electricity we now use. We'd exhaust our forests in only a few short years, and air pollution would significantly worsen.

Coal—A Temporary Reprieve from Freezing to Death

This leaves us with only nuclear power, which the antinuclear activists won't let us use, and coal. We have 28 percent of the world's coal—290 billion tons—within our borders. And, the usefulness of coal is well-proven, so on the surface, coal looks like a promising substitute for oil.

Because both our oil and natural gas are expected to run out at nearly the same time, coal will have to replace both fuels. Figure 6.3 shows the contribution of each fuel to our 1996 energy needs.

In 1996, we burned about a trillion tons of coal a year, and this met 23.73 percent of our total energy needs. But, if coal is used to replace both the oil and natural gas burned in stationary sources such as power plants, industrial furnaces, homes, offices, and businesses, we will have to burn about 2.9 times more coal.

Table 6.3 Sources of Energy Used in the U.S., 1996-1997

Source	% of Total Energy Used
Coal (incl. coke)	23.73%
Oil	38.11% ⎯ 24% transportation 14% stationary sources
Natural Gas	23.68%
Hydro (water)	4.09%
Nuclear	7.02%
Bio Fuels	2.85%
other, including. Wind, Solar, and Geothermal	0.52%

(Source: Energy Administration, U.S. Dept. of Energy.)

Coal might be a possible substitute for the oil used in our stationary sources, but what about transportation? Our gasoline and diesel fuel comes from crude oil. Without first being converted into a liquid fuel, coal can't be used to power our automobiles and trucks. However, the Germans produced limited quantities of a liquid fuel from coal when they ran low on oil during World War II. Unfortunately, the process of making a liquid fuel from coal isn't very efficient, and it uses up a lot of coal because coal is not only needed as the raw material, but also must be used to supply the energy needed to carry out the process.

If an efficient battery-powered electric car can be mass-produced, coal could be used to generate the electricity needed to recharge these batteries. However, when the heat energy of burning coal is transformed into electrical energy, only about one-third of the heat produced can be converted into electricity. And, this huge loss of energy is unavoidable.

Transportation now uses about 25 percent of all of the energy we produce; and coal met 23.73 percent of our energy needs. So, when the energy losses involved in converting coal into a liquid fuel or into electricity are considered, we find that we'll have to burn about three times as much coal as we are now doing to supply the energy needed in transportation.

When we combine the three-fold increase in coal usage for transportation with the previous 2.9-fold increase in coal burning in stationary sources, we find that when we run out of oil and natural gas, we'll have to burn roughly 5.9 times as much coal as we now do to meet our energy needs. In 1990, we burned almost a billion tons a year, so this would increase our coal burning to 5.9 billion tons a year. This is a huge quantity, of course.

Under this increased usage, our coal reserves would last only about 49 years. So, coal isn't the solution to the problem. At best, it represents only a very poor, temporary reprieve from freezing to death.

By preventing the normal development of our only proven new source of energy, nuclear power, the antinuclear activists are pushing us ever closer to the day when we'll run out of oil and not have a substitute source of energy except coal. And, if this happens, it will be the beginning of civilization's darkest hour.

The End of Civilization As We Know It

Suppose we continue to let the uneducated, misinformed, but highly vocal antinuclear activists set our national energy policy. Further, suppose that the dreaded day arrives when we run out of oil, and we still have nothing to meet this shortage except coal. In this case, the following events are nearly certain to occur.

As we increase our coal burning to compensate for the loss of oil, the first problem to arise will be air pollution. From the standpoint of air pollution, coal is by far our poorest fuel. It produces large quantities of sulfur dioxide, and this air pollutant is currently linked to 50,000 deaths yearly. So, when we increase coal burning to make up for the loss of our oil reserves, air pollution-related deaths will also increase. With a sixfold increase in coal burning, air pollution-related deaths in the U.S. could easily reach 300,000 per year.

The New Killer Fogs

As coal burning increased, it wouldn't be long before we were experiencing "killer fogs" periodically in all of our industrial cities. You may recall that one such killer fog killed approximately 8,000 people in London during December of 1952 and the first months of 1953.

As the air quality worsened, and killer fogs became more common, the government would have no choice but to order a cutback in coal burning. This would cripple our industrial production and throw the economy into a severe economic depression. Perhaps, it would take less than five years for these developments to take place.

Coming: The World's Last Great Depression

Some readers may be old enough to remember the terrible worldwide depression of 1929 to 1940. During this depression, our energy production was diminished by only about 8.5 percent. Millions of people were out of work, and there were hundreds of applicants for even the worst jobs. People lost their homes, and farmers lost their farms. Soup kitchens appeared in every major city, and homeless, out-of-work people moved about the country looking for a job of any kind.

As air pollution worsened and further production cuts were made, more and more people would become jobless. Soon, a domino effect would set in which would make even more people jobless. For example, when automobile production is cut, not only are automobile workers thrown out of work, but so are steel, glass, rubber, carpet, and plastic workers. Large quantities of these materials are used by the automobile industry.

When factory workers are unemployed, they have no money to spend, so movie theaters, taverns, fast food restaurants, and shopping malls would close, and still more workers would be laid off. Unemployed workers pay no taxes, so cities would be forced to cut back on teachers, policemen, garbage collectors, and other public employees. Streets would go unpatched, criminals would not be apprehended and would become more aggressive, and students would go untaught.

These effects would be felt very quickly, and within 10 or 15 years many cities might become virtually uninhabitable. For example, when a water main broke, it might go unrepaired, and the people served by this main would then be without water. Without drinking water, and unable to flush toilets, there would be little choice but to abandon the area. And, without jobs, there would be nothing to keep people in the city except for their homes or apartments. Of course, with few people working, the cities would become increasingly dangerous places to live.

From an ecological standpoint, *any* increase in coal burning would be a complete disaster. Acid rain produced by burning coal would damage our forests at an increasing rate, denying us the use of wood in the future when it would be needed most. And, the huge quantities of carbon dioxide produced by this increased coal burning would increase the risk of setting the greenhouse effect in action, possibly flooding many of the world's coastal cities and inundating much of our most fertile farmland.

A large percentage of the world's people farm the lands formed where rivers empty into oceans, probably because these are among the most fertile of all lands. Unfortunately, these lands would be the first to flood if the greenhouse effect melted huge ice sheets and raised the level of the world's oceans.

Food Production Plummets

As serious as these problems would be, they can't begin to compare with the effect that the loss of oil would have on our food production. The first aspect of this problem would involve our inability to produce enough synthetic liquid fuel from coal to power farm machinery. Farming generally requires more gasoline and diesel fuel than any other industry. For example, it takes the energy produced by burning a half a glass of diesel fuel just to put one glass of milk on the table. Without the use of gasoline or diesel powered farm machinery, the American farmer would lose his present high productivity and would be unable to work the big acreages he now does.

How soon this problem surfaced would depend on how successful we were in producing large quantities of liquid fuel from coal. Millions of gallons of this synthetic fuel would have to be used to transport food from the farms to the cities, so only part of the synthetic fuel produced would be available for use in farm machinery. In any event, this problem would certainly become acute as soon as people realized how fast our coal supplies were being depleted and coal rationing was instituted. This could occur within 15 or 20 years after we ran out of oil. And, if we were unsuccessful in mass-producing synthetic fuel from coal, it could happen a whole lot faster than that.

A second aspect of the loss of oil might hurt the farmer's productivity even more. The American farmer presently uses large quantities of synthetic fertilizers, insecticides, weed killers, and rodent poisons to increase and protect his crop. All of these things are presently produced from the petrochemicals which come from oil. In some instances, these things can be made from coal, but this would place an even greater strain on our coal reserves, which would then dwindle even more rapidly. They might be completely exhausted in 40 years or even less.

Today, in countries too poor to afford them, insecticides and rodent poisons are not used, and as a result these pests often claim over 50 percent of the food crop. Nor can these countries afford to purchase synthetic fertilizers. This inability further decreases their food production from 10 to 50 percent.

With the help of gasoline and diesel powered farming machinery, synthetic fertilizers, chemical insecticides, weed killers, and rodent poisons, one American farmer is presently capable of feeding 50 people. It wasn't always like this, however. In the 1800s, before the advent of diesel powered machinery and oil-based insecticides, weed killers, rodent poisons, and synthetic fertilizers, 9 out of 10 Americans were farmers and were forced to work long hours to keep everyone fed.

Then, in more recent times, diesel powered machinery and the chemical products the farmer presently relies on came into common use. The American farmer's productivity increased spectacularly with the addition of each new chemical tool. As each individual farmer's productivity increased, fewer and fewer people were needed as farmers, and tens of millions of people left the farm and headed for the city. Most of these people became factory workers, but some became scientists, teachers, sanitation technicians, doctors, and nurses.

We Become a Nation of Farmers Again

When our oil is exhausted and the farmer's productivity has dropped, it will once again be necessary for most of us to become farmers. Although each American farmer was able to feed 50 people in 1986, after the loss of our oil he'll be lucky to produce enough food to be able to feed his immediate family. This was the way it was before oil-based chemical products and fuels came into use, and we have no reason to believe that it'll be any different after we've lost them.

The only way to compensate for this loss of individual productivity would be to drastically increase the number of farmers. Otherwise, not enough food will be produced to keep people fed. This would necessitate a massive relocation from city to farm for over 240 million Americans.

As you might expect, the relocation of over 240 million people to areas having little or no housing surplus would be a tremendous problem, and it would put a severe stress on the nation's home building industry. With electrical production, sawmills, and roofing manufacturers virtually out of business, it would be impossible to build even enough sheds to house this many people. And, with no diesel powered equipment, it would be next to impossible to dig the millions of septic systems and wells needed. Nor would it be easy to supply this many new "homes" with electricity. With our factories shut down and no fuel available to operate heavy mining equipment, where would the thousands of miles of copper or aluminum wire come from? Plainly, most Americans would be forced to live in sheds having no heat, electricity, running water, or bathrooms. But, at least they would be close enough to the land to plant the food they would need to survive.

As doctors, sanitation workers, plant and animal pathologists, teachers, and research scientists were forced to become farmers, we'd lose the services of these highly specialized, valuable people. In only a short time, the age old diseases such as malaria, cholera, typhoid fever, tuberculosis, bubonic plague, and hookworm would rise from the backwaters of civilization where they have been lurking, to once again threaten mankind with great epidemics. There simply wouldn't be enough sanitation workers and medical personnel to keep these diseases in check. And, chances are that the thousands of medicines once manufactured from oil would no longer be available.

Within 35 or 40 years after we lose our oil, coal rationing will probably be necessary. By then, most people in the industrialized nations will have made the painful relocation from urban to rural areas where there is land, and where they can again become farmers. There will be severe shortages of everything, including housing, food, clothing, and medicine. People will have lived through one terrible hardship or tragedy after another, and they'll believe that nothing worse can happen. But, they will be in for a shock, because now civilization's last and greatest catastrophe will begin.

The Great Die-Off: Two Billion People Must Perish

In the late 1800s and early 1900s, the world's farmers fed 1.6 billion people without the use of diesel powered farm machinery, oil based synthetic fertilizers, weed killers, insecticides, and rodent poisons. And, except for China and India, where famine killed 23 million people between 1876 and 1899, there was little famine. But, today, the world's population isn't 1.6 billion. It had shot up to six billion by 1999 and is expected to top nine billion by 2050.

During the 1950s and 1960s, the use of DDT and improved sanitation in the underdeveloped countries cut the death rate and led to rapid growth of the world's population. Soon, many dire predictions were heard regarding the world's inability to feed itself in the face of what many termed a "population explosion." But, the world's scientists went to work on the problem and succeeded in developing such high-yielding food crops that their success became known as the "Green Revolution." Worldwide, famine decreased to all-time lows except in war torn countries such as Ethiopia, where a communist dictator prevented the distribution of food to drought-stricken areas of his country unfriendly to his regime.

The surprisingly high crop yields were due not only to the geneticists' development of exceptional new strains of old crops such as wheat and rice, but also to the use of modern high-yield farming techniques which called for lots of fertilizer and the abundant use of chemicals to protect the crop from insect pests, weeds, and disease.

Unfortunately, many of these agricultural chemicals are made from coal, natural gas, or crude oil. Of course, once we run out of oil, all of these raw materials, including coal, either will be gone or in increasingly short supply. When the world's farmers are denied these valuable tools, their ability to produce food will undoubtedly plummet. It will probably be a little better than that of the farmers of the early 1900s, but not much. One scientist estimates that we'll have to farm three times as much land as we now do to produce the same amount of food without the tools of high-yield agriculture.[6] If this is correct, we will have to increase the land under cultivation by 10 million square miles, an acreage roughly equivalent to the entire land mass of North America.

But, will this be possible? By 1967, most of the best, most fertile land had already been cleared and placed in cultivation in Asia and Europe. Table 6.4 shows the figures for the various continents. As much as 88 percent of the potentially farmable land was already being cultivated in Europe as early as 1967. Much the same was true of Asia.

Table 6.4: Acres of Cultivated Land Per Person on Various Continents

Continent	Acres of cultivated land per person	Percent of potentially farmable land in cultivation
South America	1.0 acres/person	11%
Africa	1.3 acres/person	22%
North America	2.3 acres/person	51%
U.S.S.R.	2.4 acres/person	64%
Asia	0.7 acre/person	83%
Europe	0.9 acre/person	88%

Source: *The President's Science Advisory*, The World Food Problem *(1967)*.

In the 1980s and 1990s, much of the South American rain forest was cut down so this land could be used to produce food. Of course, not all land is suitable for growing food. Some land is too far north or south and has too short a growing season. Some land is too wet, or too dry. A lot of land lacks the humus or necessary minerals needed by crops. Little grows in the desert, or on a mountaintop. Only 8 percent of the land in Russia is considered farmable. In China, where one-fifth of the world's people live, only ten percent of the land is farmable.

Further, since it won't be possible to use coal or oil to produce synthetic fibers such as Orlon and Dacron, much of the arable land remaining will have to be used to grow fibers such as cotton and flax for clothing. More land will have to be provided as pasture for draft animals—unless we plan to pull the plows ourselves. And, of course, if we plan on eating meat, making shoes out of leather, or wearing wool, pastureland must be provided for cattle, pigs, and sheep.

We'll also have to keep some land in trees if we want to be able to repair any wooden structures or build any new ones. And, presumably, we'll need some paper, which means more land in trees. Of course, wood will probably be the most widely used fuel except for coal, and as our coal runs out we'll have to rely more and more on wood.

Finally, without the insecticides and medicines now produced from fossil fuels, larger acreages will have to be used to grow crops such as the flower from which the insecticide pyrethrum can be obtained. Plainly, we're going to have to use the land to produce a lot of things besides food.

Let's make the very optimistic assumption that each one of us will require an acre of land under cultivation to survive. Only about half of this acre will be used to raise food; the other half acre will be used as previously described. Of course, insects, rodents, and plant and animal diseases will take a significant toll on whatever is raised on this acre. How many countries have enough land to meet this one acre per person minimum?

Even today most of the industrialized countries have far more people than they have farmable acres. Japan has 10 people per farmable acre, South Korea, eight people per acre, and China, four people per acre. In Europe, the Netherlands has 5.5 people per acre, followed by Belgium—4.94, West Germany—3.3, and Britain—3.1. (Fortunately, the U.S. has only 0.5 person per acre.)

The grim implication in these figures is that much of Asia and Europe are simply too densely populated and have too little farmable land to support all of their people by bare subsistence farming.

With the loss of oil and worsening shortages of coal, the production of industrial goods would be virtually halted. Yet, without these goods to sell, these nations would lack the cash needed to buy food elsewhere. And, even if they had the cash, there probably would not be any food to buy. Because of the worldwide drop in agricultural productivity, even the nations which formerly exported food would probably be hard pressed to keep their own people well fed.

The terrible consequence of this would be a massive "die-off." Any country which exceeded one person per farmable acre would have to watch large numbers of its people starve to death or die of disease until its population was reduced to one person per farmable acre.

Combined, Japan and South Korea would have to bury 147 million people, and each survivor would have to dig nine graves using only a shovel. China and India would have to dig over 1.1 billion graves, and the nations of Europe would have to bury over 150 million victims of famine and disease.

Japan would lose 90 percent of its people, and China 75 percent. In Europe, the population of West Germany would decrease by almost 70 percent. Even Britain would lose 68 percent of her people.

The total death toll from this great catastrophe could easily exceed two or three billion people worldwide, or from 40 percent to 60 percent of the earth's population. Table 6.5 shows how some of the nations of the world would be affected by this catastrophe.

Of course, not everyone who died would starve to death. As people weakened they would become more susceptible to disease, and great epidemics of the age-old killers of people would sweep over the entire world. And, these horrifying conditions would undoubtedly lead to a complete breakdown of civilization and give birth to incredibly barbaric times, as people looted, stole, and killed in hopes of gaining enough food to survive, rather than starving to death. Starvation would push even ordinary people to incredible savagery.

Table 6.5 Famine's "Hit List"

Country	People per farmable acre*	Population*	Number of people who must die in order to decrease population density to one person per farmable acre	Percentage of the population who will die
Japan	10	121,402,000	109,261,800	90.0%
South Korea	8.08	43,284,000	37,929,068	87.6%
Netherlands	5.54	14,536,000	11,912,172	81.9%
Belgium	4.94	9,868,000	7,870,429	79.8%
China	4	1,045,537,000	784,152,750	75.0%
West Germany	3.3	60,734,000	42,329,751	69.7%
Britain	3.12	56,458,000	38,362,482	67.9%
Italy	1.88	57,226,000	26,786,637	46.8%
India	1.7	783,940,000	322,798,810	41.0%
East Germany	1.33	16,692,000	4,141,624	24.8%
United States	0.51	240,856,000	0	0
U.S.S.R.	0.46	279,904,000	0	0
*Totals		2.7 billion	1.4 billion	51.80%

*These results were calculated from figures in the *1988 World Almanac* and are for 1986. However, the world's population is expected to increase by 60 percent by the year 2050. Much of this growth is expected to occur in the nonindustrial countries. We chose to ignore growth rates in our predictions because they are subject to change. But, one thing is nearly certain: If this event occurs, it will probably result in the death of more people than we've predicted.

There Have Been Other Warnings

This is not the first warning of this great catastrophe. In 1954, in *The Challenge of Man's Future*, Harrison Brown wrote:

> If our energy resources dwindle, our industrial technology will dwindle, and life expectancy and population will slowly dwindle with it. Consumption of the earth's store of fossil fuels has barely started; yet, already we can see the end. The age of fossil fuels will be over, not to be repeated for perhaps another 100 million years. Will its passing mark the end of civilization and perhaps the beginning of the downward path to man's extinction?[7]

Later in the same book, Brown says "[The] collapse of machine civilization would be accompanied by starvation, disease, and death on a scale difficult to comprehend."[8] Of Harrison Brown's effort, Albert Einstein said, "We may well be grateful to Harrison Brown," and, "This objective book has high value."[9]

In 1977, England's honored scientist Sir Fred Hoyle, writing in *Energy or Extinction?* added his voice to Brown's:

> There can be no disagreement with the statement that world reserves of coal, oil, and gas can provide an adequate energy source for only a limited future...

> Nor can it be contested that most of the world's population, presently 4,000 million, will die in a disastrous catastrophe should an adequate energy source not have been developed by the time that reserves of coal, oil, and gas become exhausted.

> Nor can there be any serious debate over the statement that the only alternative energy source *presently known to be technically viable* is energy from the nuclear fission of uranium or thorium.[10]
>
> (Emphasis in the original.)

Writing about Hoyle's book, Sir Alan Cottrell, who was once the chief scientific adviser to the British government, says:

> It (Hoyle's book) is about *energy:* about the alarming prospect that oil will soon run out and not be replaced by anything else. It shows that—contrary to an influential belief—we do not have time, and there is *no* practical alternative to nuclear energy, and that western decision makers have been frightened into immobility in their nuclear energy policies by a well-orchestrated campaign which has marched under an 'environmentalist' banner but yet has a clearly identifiable political basis.[11]
>
> (Emphasis in the original.)

And, in 1979, while the U.S. reeled under the aftereffects of Three mile Island and a Middle East oil embargo, the world-renowned scientist Edward Teller warned us: "The citizens of the United States have just begun to recognize the impact of the world's growing energy shortage. Gasoline lines, electrical brownouts, and higher prices are minor irritants. They are nothing compared to what may lie ahead. In a struggle for survival, politics, law, religion, and even humanity may be forgotten. When the objective is to stay alive, the end may seem to justify the means. In that event, the world may indeed return to the 'simpler' life of the past, but millions of us will not be alive to discover its disadvantages."[12] It is difficult to argue with the point these respected people make; yet, at this writing, their messages have largely been ignored.

We Can't Continue to Let Antinuclear Activists Dictate Our National Energy Policy

For well over two decades now, we have let antinuclear activists forcibly dictate our national energy policy. During this time, they have prevented the normal development of nuclear power, which is the only source of energy which could possibly replace coal and oil at the present. During this time we've continued to use our precious oil supplies in the most frivolous manner possible, such as using it to generate electricity, which could be done much better by nuclear power. Each year that this foolishness continues will mean that we'll arrive that much sooner at the day when there will be no liquid fuel for cars and trucks, and no more oil from which to extract petrochemicals.

Whether we have 10, 20, or 100 years of oil left makes no difference. The time to adopt an intelligent national energy policy was yesterday, and 16 million barrels of oil are used up in the U.S. each day that goes by. We'll miss this oil badly when it's gone.

Risky Business: Using Fossil Fuels, or Using Nuclear Power?

Earlier, we mentioned that none of the risks that antinuclear activists claim exist for nuclear power plants have materialized during the 42 years in which these plants have been in use.

Then, we described how precarious our supply of oil from the unstable Middle East was, and the devastating effect on our economy which disruptions of this supply have had. Next, we pointed out how our need for oil forced us to go to war with Iraq in 1990. And, then we discussed the possibility that we might run out of oil and not have an alternative source of energy in place, ready to go. If this happens, modern civilization is in big trouble, because it cannot exist as we know it without energy.

Now, we ask: Doesn't it sound as if our use of fossil fuels poses far more very real risks than nuclear power ever did?

CHAPTER 7

What the Record Shows About Accidents and Terrorism

During the first 28 years nuclear power was in use, there wasn't a single real nuclear accident worthy of the name. For this reason, nuclear scientists and antinuclear activists alike had to speculate about the results of a nuclear accident. As you might expect, the antinuclear activists took advantage of the fact that no accidents had occurred by predicting that when one did occur, the results would be almost too horrible to contemplate. Here's the way antinuclear activist Ralph Nader described the possible effects of a meltdown:

> I don't think that a society can endure the disaster of one major meltdown... I really don't think that our country can tolerate the trauma of a couple of hundred thousand people dying all at once in one place, and many more dying over a period of time from cancer, leukemia, mutations and what have you.[1]
>
> Ralph Nader, as quoted by Sheldon Novick

At an antinuclear demonstration in Washington a month after Three Mile Island, Australian pediatrician Dr. Helen Caldicott claimed that had a meltdown occurred, three thousand people would have died immediately, and from 10 to 100,000 people would have been exposed to enough radiation to cause their death within a short time.[2] Dr. Caldicott further predicted that thousands of babies would be born with small heads, or mentally retarded. She ended by predicting that hundreds of thousands of cases of cancer would appear within 15 to 50 years, and that the meltdown would have killed approximately half a million Americans, all told.

After years of listening to similar horror stories about potential nuclear accidents, finally, on April 26, 1986, a meltdown did occur at a primitive reactor at Chernobyl, Russia. Because of its design and lack of safety measures, Chernobyl had long been a disaster waiting to happen. After a

28-year wait, the world finally had a real nuclear disaster to discuss.

There are some very crucial differences between U.S.-built nuclear power reactors and Russian-built reactors. In the U.S. reactors, the uranium fuel rods are surrounded by water which acts as a moderator and also serves to transfer the heat generated by the fuel rods. If a U.S. reactor loses water, the nuclear reaction stops all by itself because the moderator, which is necessary for the reaction, is gone. But, in many Russian-built reactors, graphite is used as the moderator, and the water which is used to transfer heat actually slows down the reaction. This means that when water is lost from a Russian reactor, the chain reaction accelerates rapidly, and an engineer in the plant must act immediately to stop the rapidly increasing reaction rate and heat. Reactors of the Chernobyl type are so dangerous that they could never be licensed to generate electricity in the U.S., or in most Western countries.

Secondly, U.S. nuclear power plants are built with multiple layers of containment. Usually, several 8-inch-thick steel jackets and a steel reinforced concrete containment up to 3-and-one-half feet thick enclose the reactor and insure that nothing can escape from it. But, at Chernobyl, this kind of safety containment was completely absent. Figure 7.1 shows this containment.

Figure 7.1: The multiple containment barriers in a nuclear power plant which prevent radiation from reaching the air which we breathe.

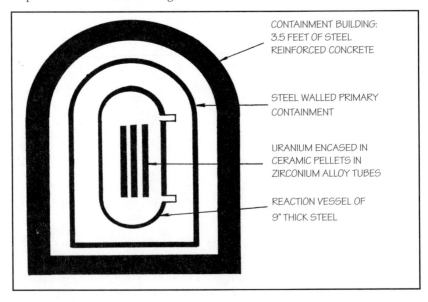

CONTAINMENT BUILDING: 3.5 FEET OF STEEL REINFORCED CONCRETE

STEEL WALLED PRIMARY CONTAINMENT

URANIUM ENCASED IN CERAMIC PELLETS IN ZIRCONIUM ALLOY TUBES

REACTION VESSEL OF 9" THICK STEEL

Unlike Western-built power reactors, Chernobyl was built to serve a dual purpose: As it generated electricity, it was producing plutonium for nuclear weapons. Because the plutonium must be removed frequently, a heavy concrete containment would be in the way and, therefore, was never built. After the accident, observers studying the situation concluded that had containment such as is used in U.S. nuclear power plants been present, there would have been no escape of radioactive materials from the plant.

At the time of the accident, electrical engineers—not nuclear engineers—were carrying out an electrical experiment which led to nuclear conditions so dangerous that plant rules strictly forbid operating under such conditions. However, the electrical engineers in charge disregarded these rules and proceeded with their experiment. Apparently, no nuclear engineers were on hand to emphasize how dangerous this was.

At 1:23 A.M., on April 26, 1986, an automatically-generated computer print-out warned plant operators that the reactor should be shut down immediately, but the operators ignored this warning. Only minutes later, two explosions occurred almost simultaneously. Although the U.S. media failed to make the point clear, the explosion was not nuclear, but was either chemical or a steam explosion such as occurs when a water heater without a safety valve becomes overheated. In addition to the fact that not enough of the fissionable isotope of uranium is present for a nuclear explosion to occur, the fact that only two people were killed in the two explosions further indicates that the explosions were not nuclear.

A nuclear power plant operator's worst nightmare quickly developed. The graphite, which, like coal, is flammable carbon, caught fire, and a five-story-high fire followed. Then, the explosions and raging fire carried two tons of radioactive graphite and uranium into the air in its most dangerous form—a fine, breathable dust. And, it took the Russians over 10 days to extinguish the fires and prevent the further discharge of the dangerous radioactive dust being carried aloft with the rising smoke.

Twenty-nine of the hundreds of workers and firefighters who fought this fire subsequently died of burns and radiation. Two hundred and thirty-seven others were hospitalized with burns, radiation sickness, smoke inhalation, and other injuries, but all recovered. No people outside the plant were injured, but they were exposed to significant radiation.

The Soviet government waited 36 hours before evacuating the nearby town of Pripyat. And, they waited three days before notifying their European neighbors. In the U.S. and other advanced countries, even chlorine or ammonia spills routinely call for prompt evacuation as a safety measure. The delayed evacuation at Pripyat insured that everyone there would get a big dose of radiation, and it greatly increased the chances for more fatalities and latent cancers, of course.

Antinuclear Activists' Exaggerations and the Reality of Chernobyl

It is interesting to compare the actual death toll at Chernobyl—31 deaths—with Nader and Caldicott's earlier predictions for an American nuclear accident. Nader claimed that "a couple of hundred thousand" would die "all at once," and Caldicott predicted that "three thousand would die immediately." The actual death toll was 31, so Nader's prediction was 6,451 times too high. Caldicott's was 97 times too high. And, both Nader's and Caldicott's predictions were made for U.S. reactors, which have multiple layers of containment, while Chernobyl had none. Nor was prompt evacuation carried out at Chernobyl, as is always done in the U.S. These two factors greatly worsened the accident by unnecessarily exposing thousands of people in the area to a lot more radiation. This made Nader's and Caldicott's predictions much more likely to come true.

It is worth noting that in terms of immediate death, Chernobyl's death toll of 31 people is not particularly high. In the U.S. alone, there have been over 50 coal mining accidents in which over twice as many people died. And, on the average, more workers in the U.S. die each day in industrial accidents than died at Chernobyl.

Remember the scary prediction that Australian pediatrician Dr. Helen Caldicott made, that thousands of babies would be born with small heads? Well, despite the fact that all expectant mothers in the Chernobyl area received a large dose of radiation because of the lack of containment and failure to promptly evacuate, thousands of babies were not born with small heads. *No* babies were born with small heads. Not one was abnormal.[3]

Although the immediate death toll was easy to ascertain, the number of cancer deaths which might occur in future years was more difficult to estimate. As you might expect, estimates varied considerably. In March of 1987, British radiologists predicted that radiation from the accident would add only about 1,000 deaths to the usual cancer fatalities which would occur during the next 50 years.[4] According to an Associated Press release of April 23, 1987, the International Atomic Energy Agency and the U.S. Department of Energy were in agreement that somewhere between 2,500 and 75,000 cancer deaths might occur in the future as a result of the accident.[5] Professor Richard Wilson of Harvard, who had visited Chernobyl, estimated that there could be as many as 20,000 excess cancer deaths during the coming years.[6] Physicist Bernard Cohen placed the death toll at 16,000.[7] The latter estimates are now more widely accepted in the scientific community.

Chernobyl's Death Toll Compared with Air Pollution's

In order to properly evaluate the seriousness of Chernobyl, it helps to compare it with the use of the fossil fuels. As we've already pointed out, in terms of immediate accidental death Chernobyl was not an exceptionally bad accident. But, how does it compare in terms of long-term cancer deaths? To make this comparison, we shall use the middle-of-the-road estimate provided by Dr. Wilson of Harvard. The 20,000 cancer deaths predicted by Professor Wilson would occur over a 50-year time period, so we divide 20,000 by 50 to arrive at the figure of an average of 400 deaths per year.

How does this possible future yearly death toll compare with that of the actual deaths caused by fossil fuel-produced air pollution? At present, worldwide, there are at least 200,000 air pollution deaths each year. This figure is 500 times larger than Chernobyl's yearly long-term death toll is expected to be. *In other words, 500 nuclear accidents as severe as Chernobyl will have to occur before the yearly death toll from the world's most unsafe reactor equals the death toll that air pollution from burning fossil fuels now claims.*

At this point, two things should be kept in mind. First, we have little control over what Russia, or any other country does. Although Chernobyl is the only accident in a nuclear power plant which ever resulted in the loss of life because of the nuclear aspect of the plant, in the future, there may be others because there are about 25 power plants of the same design as Chernobyl in Russia. Second, and more important, no loss of life has ever occurred because of an accident in a Western-built nuclear power plant. We have no reason to forsake our safe nuclear power plants because Russia builds plants of an unsafe design. And, plans exist for even safer reactors than our present ones.

It can be argued that fewer accidents have occurred in nuclear power plants than in fossil fuel power plants because nuclear power is not as widely used as fossil fuels. But, this is offset by the fact that nuclear power is a new technology, and history shows that the most dangerous period of time is right after a new technology is introduced. For example, in the 1870s and 1880s an average of 25 railroad bridges per year failed in the U.S., killing thousands of people. But, today, this almost never happens. The design of bridges has been so improved that they are now much safer.

Next, we'll compare the accident record of fossil fuels with that of nuclear power.

Coal Mining Accidents

Coal mining is an extremely dangerous occupation. In the past, coal mining has usually been the most hazardous of all U.S. industries. Between 1910 and 1940, an average of 1,900 U.S. coal miners were killed each year in mining accidents.

Surprisingly, coal dust and air mixtures are extremely explosive. Although less than 10 percent of all coal mining fatalities result from the explosion of coal dust, all of the five worst disasters were due to this reason. Ranked in order of the number of miners killed, these disasters are:

1. Honkeiko, Manchuria. April 26, 1942: at least 1,549 dead.
2. Courrieres, France. March 10, 1906: 1,060 dead.
3. Omuta, Japan. November 9, 1963: 447 dead.
4. and 5. (tie) Senghenydd, Wales. 1913: 439 dead; and, West Germany. 1946: 439 dead.[8]

The principal U.S. coal mine disasters are shown in Table 7.1. You should note that these disasters have become less frequent and less serious in recent years, as coal mining has grown into a more mature technology.[9]

Since 1907, when good record keeping in the coal industry began, over 90,000 U.S. miners have died in coal mining accidents. Most of these fatalities came prior to 1950, when the industry was comparatively young and struggling to solve its safety problems.

Improvements in safety regulations, periodic inspections of mines, and new, safer mining procedures have greatly lowered the annual death rate in recent years.

Additionally, all of the one billion tons of coal which are mined each year must be loaded at the mine, transported to the power plants, and unloaded. Transportation accidents involving coal claim an average of about 500 people each year.

Incidentally, although mining accidents are spectacular disasters which attract a great deal of public attention, they are not as serious a problem as black lung disease.

In the course of their work, coal miners breathe large quantities of coal dust. Over the years, the inhalation of this dust damages their lungs and produces a kind of chronic pneumonia which is commonly known as "black lung." At present, there are about 50,000 ex-coal miners in just the U.S. who are incapacitated by this disease. And, about 4,000 ex-miners die of this disease each year. An estimated 300,000 former coal miners have died of black lung disease during this century. In recent years, coal mine operators have done a better job of decreasing the dust present in coal mines.

Table 7.1 Principal U.S. Mine Disasters

Note: Prior to 1968, only disasters with losses of 60 or more lives are listed; since 1968, all disasters in which 5 or more people were killed are listed. Only fatalities to mining company employees are included. All accidents occurred in coal mines.

Date	Location	Deaths	Date	Location	Deaths
1867 Apr. 3	Winterpock, Va.	69	1919 June 5	Wilkes-Barre, Pa.	92
1869 Sept. 6	Plymouth, Pa.	110	1922 Nov. 6	Spangler, Pa.	77
1883 Feb. 16	Braidwood, Ill.	69	1922 Nov. 22	Dolomite, Ala.	90
1884 Mar. 13	Pocahontas, Va.	112	1923 Feb. 8	Dawson, N.M.	120
1891 Jan. 27	Mount Pleasant, Pa.	109	1923 Aug. 14	Kemmerer, Wyo.	99
1892 Jan. 7	Krebs, Okla.	100	1924 Mar. 8	Castle Gate, Utah	171
1895 Mar. 20	Red Canyon, Wyo.	60	1924 Apr. 28	Benwood, West Va.	119
1900 May 1	Scofield, Ut.	200	1926 Jan. 13	Wilburton, Okla.	91
1902 May 19	Coal Creek, Tenn.	184	1927 Apr. 30	Everettville, W. Va.	97
1902 July 10	Johnstown, Pa.	112	1928 May 19	Mather, Pa.	195
1903 June 30	Hanna, Wyo.	169	1929 Dec. 17	McAlester, Okla.	61
1904 Jan. 25	Cheswick, Pa.	179	1930 Nov . 5	Millfield, Ohio	79
1905 Feb. 20	Virginia City, Ala.	112	1940 Jan. 10	Bartley, West Va.	91
1907 Jan. 29	Stuart, West Va.	84	1940 Mar. 16	St. Clairsville, Ohio	72
1907 Dec. 6	Monongah, W. Va.	361	1940 July 15	Portage, Pa.	63
1907 Dec. 19	Jacobs Creek, Pa.	239	1943 Feb. 27	Wash, Mont.	74
1908 Nov. 28	Marianna, Pa.	154	1944 July 5	Belmont, Ohio	66
1909 Jan. 12	Switchback, W. Va.	67	1947 Mar. 25	Centralia, Ill.	111
1909 Nov. 13	Cherry, Ill.	259	1951 Dec. 21	West Frankfort, Ill.	119
1910 Jan. 31	Primero, Col.	75	1968 Nov. 20	Farmington, W. Va.	78
1910 May 5	Palos, Ala.	90	1970 Dec. 30	Hyden, Ky.	38
1910 Nov. 8	Delagua, Col.	79	1976 Mar. 9, 11	Oven Fork, Ky.	26
1911 Apr. 7	Throop, Pa.	72	1977 Mar. 1	Tower City, Pa.	9
1911 Apr. 8	Littleton, Ala.	128	1981 Apr. 15	Redstone, Colo.	15
1911 Dec. 9	Briceville, Tenn.	84	1981 Dec. 7	Topmost, Ky.	8
1912 Mar. 20	McCurtain, Okla.	73	1981 Dec. 8	nr. Chattanooga, Tenn.	13
1912 Mar. 26	Jed, West Va.	83	1982 Jan. 20	Floyd County, Ky.	7
1913 Apr. 23	Finleyville, Pa.	96	1983 June 21	McClure, Va.	7
1913 Oct. 22	Dawson, N.M.	263	1984 Dec. 19	Huntington, Utah	27
1914 Apr. 28	Eccles, West Va.	181	1986 Feb. 6	Fairview, W.Va.	6
1915 Mar. 2	Layland, West Va.	112	1989 Sep. 13	Sturgis, Ky.	10
1917 Apr. 27	Hastings, Colo.	121	1992 Dec. 7	Norton, W. Va.	8
1917 Aug. 4	Clay, Ky.	62			

(Source: Bureau of Mines, U.S. Dept. of the Interior.)

Accidents Involving Oil and Natural Gas

As you know, because of their flammable nature, oil and its derivatives such as gasoline, kerosene, and fuel oil, are dangerous to use. The top five disasters involving oil derivatives or natural gas through 1998 were:

1. Jesse, Nigeria. October 18, 1998: An explosion and fire in an oil pipeline killed between 700 and 1,000 people.

2. Cubatao, Brazil. February 25, 1984: An explosion and fire in an oil pipeline killed 508 people.[10]

3. Lagunillas, Venezuela. November 14, 1939: An oil refinery fire destroyed the town and killed over 500 people.

4. New London, Texas. March 18, 1937: A natural gas leak in a school resulted in an explosion which killed 413 students.

5. Ufa, Russia. June 5, 1989: A liquefied petroleum pipeline near a railroad line exploded just as two passenger trains passed by. The Russian news agency, Tass, initially reported 800 people missing, then revised the number of dead downward to 400.

Accidents are the fourth leading cause of death in the U.S. and the greatest killer of people under age 35. And, burns are the number four cause of accidental deaths in the U.S., killing about 4,000 people per year. Although many of these accidents undoubtedly involve natural gas or the oil derivatives such as gasoline, the exact number of deaths due to these flammable, explosive products is uncertain.

In the days before electricity came into use, some spectacular fires were the result of kerosene lanterns being tipped over. This was thought to be the origin of the Great Chicago Fire of 1871, which killed an estimated 150 to 300 people and destroyed most of the city east of the north and south branches of the Chicago River. The fire left roughly one-third of Chicago's population homeless.

The fire which followed the San Francisco earthquake of April 18, 1906, spread very rapidly due to the fact that gas mains were ruptured and kerosene lanterns were tipped over by the initial shock of the quake. Loss of life was estimated at 500 people, and about $350 million worth of property damage was done. It is uncertain how many deaths were due to the earthquake and how many were due to the fire.

Additionally, about 600 Americans die of gas poisoning each year, with about 400 of these deaths coming in the home. Some of these deaths involve natural gas leaks or an unlit gas stove. But, most of these deaths involve carbon monoxide poisoning. Carbon monoxide is produced by the incomplete combustion of natural gas and gasoline.

Although it is difficult to arrive at an exact total for the number of accidental deaths that occur each year in the U.S. due to the use of natural gas and various oil derivatives, this estimate is probably reasonable:

1. Deaths by suffocation due to natural gas leaks, carbon monoxide poisoning, etc.: 300 yearly.

2. Deaths from burns suffered as a result of the use of natural gas and the oil derivatives: at least 500 yearly.

Total: about 800 deaths per year.

The Real Unprecedented Disaster

For 20 years now, antinuclear activists have prevented the widespread use of nuclear power by claiming that it is too unsafe, and that its use could lead to an "unprecedented disaster" which might kill 100,000 or more people.

Well, there's an unprecedented disaster waiting to occur all right, but it doesn't involve the use of nuclear power. The real unprecedented disaster involves the shipping and storage of oil and liquefied natural gas (LNG). These are two highly flammable, very explosive substances, and it's only a matter of time before their present unwise placement and risky handling lead to the worst conflagration since the Chicago Fire of 1871. Although it isn't a well-known fact, a 200,000-ton oil tanker carries the energy equivalent of a two megaton hydrogen bomb. This exceeds the destructive force of all of the bombs dropped on Iraq during the first 24 hours of the 1991 war.

According to the experts, this unprecedented disaster involving oil or liquefied gas is actually much more likely to occur than a nuclear accident of equal severity. Unlike nuclear power, some lesser disasters involving the use of oil and LNG have already resulted in several hundred fatalities. Plainly, the handwriting is on the wall regarding this disaster. We can't say that we had no warning.

But, let's start at the beginning. In the early 1970s, as air pollution became more of a pressing problem, many cities on both coasts sought to replace coal-burning power plants first with oil, and then with natural gas. The use of oil creates less air pollution than coal, but natural gas produces even less pollution. Natural gas burns cleanly, producing largely carbon dioxide and water vapor, and leaves no ashes which must be disposed of somewhere. It's definitely by far the cleanest, least polluting of the fossil fuels.

As the U.S. demand for natural gas increased, foreign countries, which had been treating natural gas as an unwanted waste product, sought to get their share of this lucrative market. Soon, tankers from the Middle East carrying natural gas were unloading their cargoes at Boston, New York, Los Angeles, and Houston.

In order to ship natural gas in a cost-efficient manner, it is necessary to convert the gas to a liquid, which greatly reduces its volume. This is done by compressing and cooling the gas to approximately -260°F. The super-cooled liquid, which takes up only 1/600 as much space as the gas did and is therefore cheaper to ship, is then pumped into the tanks of lique-fied natural gas (LNG) tankers. These tankers are basically giant floating refrigerators, for the LNG must be kept cold during transit, or it will expand, rupture the tanks, and escape.

Incidentally, these tankers are huge vessels. Many of them exceed two-tenths of a mile in length and carry over 4 million cubic feet of LNG. They can cost over $200 million to build and $100,000 a day to operate.

You might think that at a cost of $200 million, LNG tankers would be the safest ships afloat. But, this is far from the case. In the past, both LNG and oil tankers were single hulled. Only in recent years have double hulls become more common. And, the tanks on LNG carriers are single walled. There is no second layer of containment in the event of a collision.

These hulls have been breached by collisions many times. For example, on June 2, 1973, the oil tanker *Esso Brussels,* which was moving slowly, collided with another slow-moving vessel in the port of New York, spill-ing 1.3 million gallons of Nigerian crude oil. A fire ensued which killed 16 people.

Heavily Populated Fire Hazards

Next, let's look at some of the U.S. ports where oil and LNG tankers will dock. The port of New York is one of the largest and busiest in the world. Between the New York islands and the New Jersey shoreline are 1,500 square miles of bays, rivers, and inlets. Docks, jetties, and wharfs line mile after mile of the shoreline. And, only a short distance from these docks is the densest concentration of highly flammable storage tanks, oil refiner-ies, and petrochemical plants in the U.S.

There are 34 main oil terminals, hundreds of big oil and LNG storage tanks, some of which are 14 stories high, dozens of refineries, and scores of petrochemical plants. Over 40 percent of all of the flammable petro-chemicals in the U.S. are produced or stored in this dangerously explo-sive, highly flammable corridor.

To add to the danger, within a 20-mile radius of the port of New York and this heavy concentration of explosive, flammable LNG, oil, and pet-rochemicals live many of New York City's 7.2 million people. Included in this area are the boroughs of Staten Island, Brooklyn, Queens, the Bronx, and Manhattan Island. And, within the same 20-mile radius are the New Jersey towns and cities of Woodbridge, Union, Rahway, Elizabeth, Bayonne, Irvington, Perth Amboy, Newark, Hoboken, Jersey City,

Bloomfield, Clifton, Patterson, Englewood, Passaic, and Nutley. Many of these cities are reasonably large: Newark has a population of 314,000 and Jersey City, 223,000.

And, this is the most densely populated area in the U.S. New York City, with 23,494 people per square mile, is the nation's most densely populated city. Jersey City comes in second, with 16,934 people per square mile. Newark, with 13,718 is fourth.

In addition to New York harbor, oil and LNG tankers routinely dock at Houston. Not only is Houston our fourth largest city at 1.7 million people, but it is surrounded by nearly as great a concentration of explosive storage tanks, flammable oil refineries, and petrochemnical plants as New York City. Texas City, which serves as a port for Houston, holds the dubious distinction of being the site of the nation's worst industrial disaster. In 1947, two vessels carrying explosive ammonium nitrate blew up while docked at Texas City, killing 468 to 1,000 people and injuring at least 5,000 more. Roughly 70 percent of the cargo entering the port is considered flammable or explosive.

Other large ports at which LNG tankers routinely dock include Everett, Massachusetts, only 1.5 miles from downtown Boston, and Terminal Island just outside Los Angeles. These are both heavily populated areas: Boston has 570,710 residents; and, as the nation's second largest city, L.A. now has a population of over 3 million.

So, both oil tankers and ships carrying liquefied natural gas will dock in ports which are often ringed by the U.S.'s greatest concentration of huge, explosive LNG and oil tanks, oil refineries, and flammable petrochemical plants. Finally, this tremendous fire hazard has been placed in close proximity to three of our four largest cities, where population density is at its greatest. This sounds more like an outline for disaster instead of wise city planning. If the antinuclear activists were really interested in protecting the public from a disaster, they would have spent their time protesting these unsafe conditions instead of trying to prevent the use of nuclear power, which has an almost spotless safety record.

Some Disasters Have Already Happened

Earlier, it was pointed out that there have already been a number of accidents involving oil and natural gas tankers, and that we can't say that we've had no warning. The details of some of these accidents follow.

We'll begin by looking at just a few of the hundreds of accidents involving oil tankers.

1973 - An oil tanker, the *Esso Brussels,* collided with the *Sea Witch* on the

Kill Van Kull, part of the port of New York. Over one million gallons of Nigerian oil caught fire, and 16 people died.

1974 - The *Yuyo Maru,* a tanker carrying naphtha and liquefied petroleum gas, was heading into Tokyo Bay when it collided with a second vessel. The tanker caught fire immediately. Flames covered the sea for several hundred yards in all directions. Dozens of firefighting ships were dispatched to put out the fire, but these efforts were unsuccessful. The *Yuyo Maru* was still burning 19 days later, when the Japanese Navy sank it. At least 33 people died.

1975 - The *Edgar M. Queeney* collided with the Liberian oil tanker, the *Corinthos.* The *Corinthos* was only half loaded. The accident occurred in the Delaware River, and 26 people died.

1976 - *The Saninema,* an *empty* oil tanker, exploded at the San Pedro docks near Los Angeles. Windows were broken 20 miles away, and the blast was heard by people 40 miles away. Nine people died.

1977 - The Panamanian oil tanker *Claude Conway* exploded and sank off the North Carolina coast. Twelve people died.

There have been many other accidents involving oil or LNG tankers, but these five accidents should serve to establish the fact that an accident involving an oil or LNG tanker is a very real possibility. A total of 96 people were killed and several times this number injured in just these five accidents.

Next, we'll take a brief look at the safety record of LNG (liquefied natural gas) storage tanks.

1944 - In Cleveland, a 50-million-cubic-foot LNG tank ruptured, spilling 1.2 million gallons of liquefied natural gas. The liquid poured into sewers and the basements of homes before exploding. Flames shot a mile into the air. The blast and subsequent fires killed 133 people. A total of 14,000 people were left homeless.[11]

1973 - An *empty* two billion cubic foot LNG tank on Staten Island exploded. Of the 43 men working on the tank, only three survived.

A total of 173 people died in these two accidents.

Now, we'll take a quick look at the flawed safety record of oil refineries and the petrochemical industry.

1947 - The freighter *Grandcamp* caught fire and exploded while being loaded at the Texas City docks near Houston. The explosion ignited the Monsanto Chemical plant only 700 feet away, and it, too, exploded. The blast was felt 150 miles away, and it was noted 1,000 miles to the north on a seismograph in Denver. On the following day, another ship loaded with explosive nitrates blew up, and hundreds of people fled the city. The three explosions and the resulting fires killed at least 468 people, and possibly as many as 1,000. Because many migrant workers were involved, the exact number was difficult to establish. This stands as America's worst industrial accident to date.

1970 - No one was killed, but an explosion at an oil refinery in Newark, New Jersey, shook northern New Jersey, Staten Island, Brooklyn, and Manhattan. Over 13 million people felt the shock wave.

1977 - An explosion at the Texaco oil refinery at Port Arthur killed seven people.

1978 - Disaster struck again at Texas City, when a dozen explosions at an oil refinery killed six people.

1989 - A series of explosions rocked the Phillips Petroleum Company's Pasadena, Texas, plastics plant. (Pasadena is adjacent to Houston.) Twenty-three workers died.

From 504 to over 1,000 people died in these five accidents involving oil refineries and the petrochemical industry. This should establish the fact that oil refineries and the petrochemical industry are among our potentially most dangerous industries, largely because of the flammable, explosive nature of the substances involved.

Finally, there's the matter of the smoke produced by oil fires. When one of these fires occurred at Bayonne, New Jersey, on January 6, 1973, the smoke produced was much thicker than that of the infamous killer fogs of London. Fortunately, the wind was strong enough to disperse the smoke produced during the Bayonne fire, and no temperature inversion, which might have trapped the smoke, was present. With conditions more favorable to a catastrophe, this could have become a U.S. version of London's killer fogs.

Three years later, on January 3, 1976, New York's heavily populated boroughs had a second close call. This time, a 90,000-barrel oil storage facility in South Brooklyn caught fire. The fire ignited one tank after another, and it burned for four days before being brought under control.

Again, the people of New York and New Jersey were lucky, and winds dispersed the clouds. Had a temperature inversion, or a stagnant air mass, been present, several thousand people, or more, might have died. Accidents such as these are much more likely to happen than are nuclear accidents. First of all, the law prevents building nuclear power plants in the midst of heavily populated areas, but oil-fired power plants and refineries are often present in the very heart of these areas. Secondly, oil or natural gas storage facilities have no multiple containment layers, or defense-in-depth systems in place which might keep a minor accident from becoming much more serious.

Worse, according to the experts, not only are disasters involving petroleum products more likely to happen, but the consequences are likely to be worse than those of a major nuclear accident. In a *Report to the State of California on the Safety of Steam-Generating Power Stations,* C. Starr estimated the probability and consequences of an oil fire, and these were subsequently compared with those of a nuclear accident.[12] Starr concluded that serious oil fires were much more likely to happen than nuclear power plant accidents. And, he also decided that oil fires were much more likely to kill large numbers of people than nuclear power plant accidents.

So, according to this expert assessment, oil fires in storage facilities are likely to be a much greater threat to the public's safety than are nuclear accidents. This conclusion is partially confirmed by the oil fires which have occurred (1939, Venezuela, 500 dead; and 1957, West Pakistan, 300 dead, etc.) and by the nuclear accidents which have not occurred in Western-built nuclear power plants during their 42 years of use.

Nuclear Power Plants: Targets for Terrorists?

By 1975, antinuclear activists had so frequently voiced the fear that a nuclear power plant might explode that it was becoming stale news. Then, one of the leading activists claimed that the radioactive materials used in nuclear power plants were very vulnerable to theft, and that a police state might have to be created to prevent theft or sabotage by terrorists.

After this, a number of scenarios for terrorism involving nuclear power plants quickly surfaced and were widely circulated, causing the public to further doubt the safety of nuclear power plants. Let's look at some of these scenarios.

In one scenario, terrorists fire a bazooka at the containment dome of a power plant, blowing a hole in it; radioactive materials from the reactor escape, and the wind carries them to a nearby city, contaminating hundreds of thousands of people. In a second, related scenario, terrorists take over a nuclear power plant, set explosive charges on the inside of the containment dome, and blow a hole in it, allowing radioactive materials to escape.

Fortunately, both of these scenarios are highly unlikely, which is probably why they haven't happened during the 40 years in which nuclear power plants have been around. To begin with, the outermost containment dome on a nuclear power plant is three to four feet thick. It is made by forcing concrete in between a tight lattice of layers of large metal bars, some of which are as big as your wrist. This is essentially the same construction which the Germans used to cover their submarine pens in World War II. Despite a furious attack with bombs weighing up to 2,000 lbs., the Allies were unable to put these facilities out of action. So, breaching a containment isn't as easy as it might initially seem. Next, the terrorist would have to steal the weapon or obtain it from a government sponsoring terrorists. While this might be difficult, it's far from impossible.

Then, it's unlikely that a single shot from a bazooka would accomplish very much. It would undoubtedly take a number of shots to breach the containment dome. Also, there are two eight-inch layers of solid steel to breach as well. This would give the plant operators plenty of time to summon SWAT teams and shut the plant down. It would be much easier for a terrorist to fire a surface-to-air missile at a passenger airplane, and his chances of success would be much greater.

Were terrorists successful in taking over a nuclear power plant, trucking several tons of explosives into the plant, unloading them, and setting them in place, they would have a better chance of breaching the containment dome. But, they would also have to blowholes in the eight-inch thick layers of solid steel before any radioactive materials could escape. When the Allies' warships shelled the beaches at Normandy, most of the steel and concrete pillboxes remained intact, and it was necessary for Allied infantry to disable these pillboxes with hand grenades thrown through gun ports, or with flamethrowers, both of which killed the occupants but did little damage to the pillbox itself. None of these steel pillboxes were anywhere near eight inches thick, despite having been designed to withstand naval shellfire and aerial bombing.

Of course, all of these measures would take the terrorists a lot of time, giving the authorities time to react and recapture the facility. Besides, even *if* successful, the attack wouldn't give terrorists what they want, which is to kill a lot of people immediately. Instead, if they did succeed in blowing holes in all of the metal and concrete containments, and blowing up the reactor itself, forcing radioactive materials out of the power plant and into the air, if weather conditions were exactly right, the terrorists might cause a number of cancers over the next 50 years, but no immediate loss of life. And, it is likely that all of the terrorists would be captured.

All of this sounds like a lot of risk and trouble to accomplish very little evil, which is probably why terrorists instead chose to bomb the World Trade Center in New York City and the Murrah Federal Building in Oklahoma City. These were simply better, easier targets.

In another scenario, terrorists would steal plutonium (which misinformed activists call "the most toxic substance on earth") and release it into the ventilating system at a rock concert, or some similarly crowded place.

Is this likely to happen? First, it is extremely difficult to steal plutonium, at least in the U.S. It's very difficult to remove plutonium from a reactor which is in operation. While plutonium is being shipped to or from a reactor might be a better time to steal it, but it is shipped in heavy lead containers and surrounded by layers of shielding to prevent the escape of radiation. And, the truck carrying the plutonium is carefully guarded. Armed guards with radios are constantly in contact with others, and in the attempt of an attack, help would be on the way immediately. Over the years, many tons of plutonium have been shipped to nuclear weapons makers without incident.

Finally, if terrorists were successful in obtaining plutonium and dispersing it into the air at a crowded event, no people would die immediately. There would be a small number of cancers 20 to 50 years down the line, but this isn't what terrorists want: They want an immediate body count.

In yet another scenario, terrorists would steal enough plutonium to build a nuclear bomb which could be used to blackmail governments into acceding to the terrorists' demands. To begin with, it is not easy to steal even a very small quantity of plutonium in the U.S. Any plant handling plutonium has a security fence, electronic surveillance, and armed guards. Detection devices sound an alarm if anyone tries to exit the facilities with plutonium. The stolen plutonium can be detected even if the thief were foolish enough to swallow it, as drug smugglers often do with drugs. FBI clearance is required for anyone handling plutonium. The FBI investigates every aspect of a nuclear power plant applicant's life, and rules out anyone who is the least bit questionable.

Most important, stealing reactor-grade plutonium won't help the terrorist make a bomb. The plutonium used in a bomb has to be weapons-grade plutonium, which is more concentrated. Reactor-grade plutonium has to be reprocessed to separate it from the uranium oxide mixed in with it to make reactor fuel. Reprocessing and enrichment are necessary to convert reactor-grade to weapons-grade plutonium. These processes might be carried out by a rogue government, but it is out of reach for a group of terrorists. What the terrorist needs is weapons-grade plutonium. Of course, weapons-grade plutonium is even more carefully guarded, and it isn't produced or used in nuclear power plants which generate electricity. This grade of plutonium must be stolen from the weapons industry.

Even if terrorists were able to steal sufficient weapons-grade plutonium to build a small nuclear bomb, their work has just begun. To build a bomb which has any chance of working, the terrorists' group must include a number of people who have very specific skills. A nuclear bomb certainly can't be built by even a knowledgeable college student, as the antinuclear activists and the media once claimed.

Any nuclear bomb-building team has to include a theoretical physicist, a mathematician, a chemist, an electronics specialist, and a very good demolitions expert. The last two people will build the triggers, devices which require carefully shaped explosive charges, and 100 or more triggers, all of which must explode simultaneously. These technicians will not only have to be good—they had better be lucky, as well. The endeavor would also call for a place to work, at least $100,000 in cash, and a full-time effort. Then, if the bomb worked, it *might* level a city block.

No wonder the terrorists at Oklahoma City used fertilizer and diesel fuel to accomplish their dirty work.

India's experience illustrates the difficulties involved in building a nuclear bomb. Despite the fact that India had a very well-trained scientific community, full government financial support, and a good source of weapons-grade plutonium, it took them ten years to produce a nuclear bomb, and then it failed to explode when tested. They went back to work, improved the trigger, and were successful on the second try. Apparently, nuclear bomb making isn't as easy as the antinuclear activists would have us believe.

Several conclusions can be drawn from all of the preceding. First, the scenarios of terrorists attacking a power plant and blowing it up are probably not very likely to occur. And, if an attack should occur, it is unlikely to succeed. Much the same can be said for attempts to steal plutonium and disperse it into the air. And, to steal reactor-grade plutonium from a nuclear power plant or a convoy bringing plutonium to a power plant would not serve the terrorists' purpose. Even a well-financed group of terrorists will not be able to use reactor-grade plutonium to make a nuclear bomb.

So, it seems safe to assume that if a terrorist group ever does succeed in making a nuclear bomb, the raw materials will not come from the nuclear power industry. This is simply too difficult a route to take, and too unlikely to succeed. And, anyone smart enough to be able to build a nuclear bomb is going to be smart enough not to try this futile undertaking.

Let's pause a moment and make one thing clear—nuclear power plants and the nuclear weapons industry are two separate, different, unrelated enterprises. We could close down every nuclear power plant in the U.S., and it wouldn't decrease the chances of nuclear terrorism very much.

Terrorists will have to use materials intended for the nuclear weapons industry if they want to make nuclear bombs. And, as we'll see, there is an increasing chance that terrorists might be able to obtain weapons-grade plutonium.

How Nuclear Power Plants Might Diminish the Threat of Terrorism

After the Cold War ended, the superpowers agreed to reduce their fearsome nuclear arsenals. As a result of the Strategic Arms Reduction Talks, the U.S. agreed to dismantle 15,000 nuclear warheads, and the Russians 30,000. This will result in over 1,000 tons of weapons-grade plutonium and enriched uranium being removed from these weapons.

In the U.S., these dangerous materials are likely to be closely guarded. But, with the Russian economy on the ropes, funds for the tight security needed to adequately protect this weapons-grade material simply are not available. As a result, stories have circulated about how easy it is to buy plutonium on the Russian black market—if the buyer has cash.

Let's consider a possible scenario for a moment. Suppose a well-heeled terrorist group or a rogue nation such as Iraq were to buy some of this weapons-grade plutonium. If they were then to hire out-of-work Russian scientists and technicians with experience in nuclear-bomb construction, there's no reason why they couldn't make a workable nuclear bomb.

Further, suppose that this rogue nation decides to attack its neighbor. When the first nuclear bomb goes off, all of the countries which presently do not have nuclear weapons will insist on obtaining them for self-defense. Suddenly, the world has become a much, much more dangerous place to live. Gone is any hope of preventing the proliferation of nuclear weapons. Now, all the world can do is pray that sanity will prevail. But, will it? Or, are there madmen similar to Adolf Hitler in power who might build up a small nuclear arsenal, and then launch a nuclear surprise attack on a long-hated nation?

There were 273 terrorist attacks in 1998, and these attacks killed 741 people and injured almost 6,000. About 40 percent of all terrorist attacks were aimed at U.S. targets, and the bombing of the U.S. Embassy in Kenya, which killed 291 people and wounded 5,000, was the worst single attack. Seven nations—Cuba, Iran, Iraq, Libya, North Korea, Sudan, and Syria are thought to sponsor terrorist groups.

A number of these nations are also working to improve their capabilities for mass destruction. It is no secret that Iran has acquired missile technology from Russia, or that North Korea and Iraq have sought to develop nuclear weapons.

Plainly, the weapons-grade plutonium and uranium from dismantled Russian nuclear weapons is extremely dangerous. It seems to constitute nearly as big a threat to world peace as the original nuclear missiles did. Yet, everyone agrees that nuclear disarmament is the first step toward a safer world.

Dr. Michael Higatsberger formerly of the Institute for Experimental Physics at the University of Vienna in Austria reports a way out of this dilemma: A nuclear physicist, Alvin Radkowsky, has devised a method in which the weapons-grade uranium and plutonium coming from the dismantled nuclear weapons may be used as a fuel in most Western-built nuclear reactors now in operation. Little or no modification is required for most reactors.

Radkowsky's method uses the weapons-grade uranium (diluted to 20 percent) or the plutonium from nuclear warheads to initiate the fissioning of thorium. As thorium fissions, it releases energy in the form of heat, just as U235 does in conventional nuclear reactors. Named the Radkowsky Nonproliferative Light Water Thorium Nuclear Reactor, this method has the additional advantage of not producing new plutonium, as most reactors currently do.

Although Radkowsky's reactor is still being tested in the U.S. and in Russia, it shows great promise. If successful, it could help prevent the dangerous nuclear proliferation previously described by reducing the amount of weapons-grade uranium and plutonium presently on hand throughout the world.

So, not only do civilian nuclear power reactors offer little possibility for terrorism, but they may also have the potential for actually reducing the threat of nuclear terrorism and nuclear proliferation.

Fossil Fuel Facilities: Targets for Terrorists?

Throughout this book, we've stressed the fact that civilization cannot survive without the consumption of massive amounts of energy, and that there are only two ways to produce this energy: Nuclear power plants, or fossil fuel-burning power plants and furnaces. So, the question we seek to answer here is: Which source of energy is more vulnerable to terrorism? We've already looked at the very limited possibility of terrorism in nuclear power plants. How vulnerable are fossil fuel facilities to terrorism?

Some of the most vulnerable fossil fuel facilities are the 14-story-high tanks containing liquefied natural gas on Staten Island. These tanks, each of which hold 37.8 million gallons of LNG, are single-walled. Their security measures include an earthen dike to contain small to moderate spills, and a chain link fence like the one you might have to keep the neighbor's dog away from your evergreens. A terrorist attack on these facilities would probably be far more productive than one on a nuclear power plant.

This is a far more real danger than anything the antinuclear activists can invent; yet, they're apparently unconcerned about the possibility of such terrorists' acts. In fact, antinuclear activists from New York City and northern New Jersey are often arrested miles from home, at Seabrook, New Hampshire, where it has long been fashionable to try to delay the construction of a nuclear power plant whose use poses none of the dangers described for oil and natural gas. Of course, the increased use of nuclear power could lessen the need to import such large quantities of oil and LNG, which would in turn make New York, Houston, Los Angeles, and Boston much safer places to live. Somehow, this thought eludes the antinuclear activists.

Terrorists Have Already Attacked Oil Pipelines

In other countries, terrorists often attack oil pipelines in an attempt to steal oil or force various governments to yield to their demands. Two such incidents were reported simultaneously in U.S. newspapers on October 19, 1998. The first of these incidents occurred in oil-rich Nigeria, near Jesse. Apparently, a spark from a vandal's pipeline-cutting tool ignited escaping oil, and an explosion ensued. Fire spread to three nearby villages, and from 700 to 1,000 people died from the explosion and the fire. It was not certain whether or not this was the work of thieves or terrorists, who in recent weeks had attacked oil installations as part of their demands for better roads, schools, and greater political representation. But, it illustrates how vulnerable pipelines are to attack, and the potential death toll when this happens.

The second attack on an oil pipeline occurred thousands of miles away, near Bogota, Colombia, and was definitely the work of terrorists. Forty-five people died when a pipeline explosion resulted in a huge fireball which ignited wooden, straw-roofed homes. The authorities blamed the National Liberation Army, who had attacked the pipeline several times previously. In the past, rebel groups have claimed that they blew up the pipelines because "the government had sold out to foreign oil interests."

When was the last time 1,000 people died during a single weekend because of a terrorist attack on a nuclear power plant? To date, terrorists have not attacked any nuclear power plants, probably because they are far more difficult targets than oil pipelines. Oil pipelines often thread their way through hundreds of miles of jungle or desolate country, and a terrorist can take his time and rig his explosives carefully with little fear of being discovered or caught. But, a nuclear power plant is a compact facility usually located close to police.

Much the same can be said for terrorist attacks on trains moving oil or coal. Railroad tracks are as vulnerable as pipelines.

Clearly, fossil fuel facilities are far easier to attack than nuclear power plants. And, the chance to kill large numbers of people immediately is much better.

Air Pollution Episodes: The Killer Fogs

As you know, one of the worst problems associated with burning fossil fuels is the release of large quantities of dangerous pollutants into the air. These pollutants damage the human respiratory tract and lead to additional numbers of deaths from bronchitis, emphysema, heart disease, pneumonia, influenza, and lung cancer. In the past, the best estimates by the experts place the number of these deaths at an average of 50,000 per year in the U.S. alone.

A number of air pollution episodes have occurred in which large numbers of excess deaths have been related to high levels of air pollution. In order of the fatalities produced, these episodes follow.

The Five Greatest Air Pollution Disasters

1. December, 1952. The first of London's killer fogs. A four-day long inversion over the city trapped the air pollutants produced from coal-burning furnaces and automobiles. 8,000 died.

2. January, 1956. Another in the series of London's killer fogs, this one resulted in 1,000 excess deaths.

3. December, 1962, London. 850 excess deaths.

4. December, 1957, London. 800 excess deaths.

5. March, 1944, Salerno, Italy. Carbon monoxide, sulfur dioxide, and other toxic gases produced by a coal-burning train standing inside a tunnel killed from 426 to 521 passengers. From the standpoint of the number of people killed, this was also the worst railroad accident of all time.

These are just five of the more serious disasters. There are any number of other disasters in which fewer people were killed. And, as the Greenburg study on air pollution indicated, there must have been many such disasters which went completely unnoticed. In fact, one of the most dangerous aspects of air pollution is that it constantly kills many people without even being noticed. So, since the end of World War II, when the use of fossil fuels dramatically increased, there must have been hundreds—perhaps even thousands—of minor air pollution episodes in which a number of people died an early death.

Because we mentioned Chernobyl's estimated long-term death toll of 20,000 people, we should also mention the fossil fuels' continual, long-term death toll. Worldwide, during the twentieth century, fossil fuels have probably killed 20 million people. Therefore, for each future Chernobyl-related death which has yet to occur, there have already been 1,000 air pollution deaths due to the use of the fossil fuels. Worldwide, there have also probably been several million accidental deaths which can be attributed to the use of fossil fuels.

A Summary of the Record

Now, let's take a moment and summarize what the record shows concerning coal, oil, natural gas, Western-built nuclear power plant accidents, and Russian-built nuclear power plant accidents. Table 7.2 does this nicely for us.

Table 7.2 *Energy-related Immediate Accidental Death, Worldwide*

The Five Worst Accidents in Each Area				
Coal Mining	Oil and Natural Gas	Air Pollution Episodes	All Nuclear Power Reactors, Worldwide	Commercial U.S. Nuclear Power Reactors
Manchuria (1942) 1,549 Dead	Nigeria (1998) 700-1,000 Dead	London (1952) 4,000-8,000 Dead	Chernobyl (1986) 31 Dead	0 Dead
France (1906) 1,060	Brazil (1984) 508	London (1956) 1000		
Japan (1963) 447	Venezuela (1939) 500	London (1962) 850	(No other fatalities involving radiation)	
West Germany (1946) 439	Texas (1937) 413	London (1957) 800		
Wales (1913) 439	Russia (1989) 400	Salerno (1944) 426-521		

Plainly, the record shows that nuclear power plants are much safer than using fossil fuels. And, as mentioned earlier, these are just the five worst accidents in each area. Worldwide there have probably been several million fatal accidents involving the fossil fuels, but not one fatal accident due to the nuclear aspect of Western-built nuclear power plants.

When you compare the actual accident record of fossil fuels and nuclear power plants as we've just done, it's hard to understand how the anti-nuclear activists have been able to convince 15 percent of the American public that all nuclear power plants should be closed, and another 48 percent that no more nuclear power plants should be built.[13] But, that's exactly what has happened.

Any reasonable person has to admit that nuclear power's established safety record over the last 42 years is far superior to that of the fossil fuels.

CHAPTER 8

What Are the Alternatives?

Oil, which is one of our two present major sources of energy, is in limited supply, and our very civilization could be in terrible jeopardy if these supplies run out before we are able to develop and put into operation an acceptable alternate source of energy.

Recent estimates indicate that our supply of crude oil could be exhausted within 45 years. When our oil is gone, this will place a much greater strain on our coal supply, and it could be exhausted within less than 50 years.

To further complicate the situation, estimates of how much oil remains are so uncertain that it could run out without giving us a lot of warning. And, the development and implementation of a new, large scale source of energy could easily take 20 years or more. Finally, modern civilization can't exist without the consumption of large quantities of energy. If our energy sources run out and no new ones are in place, it will be "back to the cave" for civilization. But now there are so many of us, that about half of the people presently living would die of disease or famine as civilization made the painful transition to bare subsistence farming.

In this chapter, we'll look briefly at some of the more promising alternatives to coal and oil, including the possibility that conservation could solve this critical problem.

Solar Energy

There has been a lot written about solar energy. Some of the more interesting bits follow:

> In 15 minutes, the sun radiates as much energy on our globe as mankind consumes in every other form during an entire year.

and:

> Sunlight provides the U.S. every two days with energy equal to all our remaining fossil fuel reserves. (Mitchell Wilson, *Energy*, 1967.)

In only 3 days we receive as much energy from the sun as could be obtained by burning all potential reserves of coal, petroleum, natural gas, and tar, together with all of the earth's forests. (Ayres and Scarlott, *Energy Sources,* 1952, as quoted by H. Brown in *The Challenge of Man's Future,* 1954.)

If we total the incident energy over the whole surface, we find 1.78×10^{17} W [watts], which is 10,000 times what we need to supply world energy needs in the year 2000. (Richard Wilson and William Jones, *Energy, Ecology, and the Environment,* 1974.)

When you read passages such as those quoted, it's only natural to think that solar energy, that is, energy from the sun's rays, is the answer to all of civilization's energy problems. After all, solar energy *appears* to be free. It doesn't pollute our air, and it won't run out until the sun dies, millions and millions of years from now. No wonder solar energy is the choice of the media, most movie stars, most antinuclear activists, and anyone else who gives the situation a quick, effortless, superficial glance.

Unfortunately, the great promise of solar energy hasn't come true yet. Scientists are working to make this promise become reality, but it hasn't happened yet. Going into the late 1990s, solar energy accounted for less than of 1 percent of all of the energy generated yearly in the U.S. And, there were several very good reasons why solar energy was not more widely used: There are some serious scientific and technological problems which must be solved in order for solar energy to become a practical source of energy. Mobil Oil discontinued its 19-year old solar energy research program in 1993. Apparently, Mobil believed that these problems would not be solved in the near future.

The first of these problems involves finding a way to collect solar energy. Basically, there are two ways to do this. They are known as "active" and "passive" solar energy collection. In passive collectors, the sun passes through properly oriented windows or glass surfaces, and strikes a second surface which can absorb heat. When the sun goes down, these surfaces release the heat which they absorbed earlier, and help to keep the building warm during the night. To date, passive solar energy has found only limited use, appearing largely in new homes in the $150,000 plus price range.

Several factors have prevented passive solar collection systems from becoming more widespread. Large glass surfaces are expensive to install. On cloudy days, more interior heat escapes through the glass than heat enters. And, it is not always possible to orient the building properly. Finally, backup heating systems are almost always required for use on cold, dark days.

As the technical bugs are worked out, passive solar energy systems will probably gain increased popularity. And, as fuel prices increase in the future, these systems will begin to look like a better investment. However, residential heating accounts for only about 20 percent of our energy demands, and passive solar techniques are not applicable to much more than at the most, a quarter of this 20 percent, so this still leaves the energy problem 95 percent unsolved, even without considering the energy required for backup systems.

Active solar collection is an entirely different story because it can be used to generate electricity. In active solar collection, sunlight falls on a photovoltaic cell. The energy of the sunlight ejects an electron, which in turn, produces an electron "shower" of a hundred electrons or more. These electrons move out of the photovoltaic cell and become part of an electrical current which can light electric light bulbs, heat homes and water, operate motors, and power other devices. You may have seen solar powered calculators or even small radios. These devices use photovoltaic cells.

On the surface, this looks good. But, the first problem is that sunlight is a very diffuse form of energy. At high noon, when the sun is directly overhead, on a cloudless day near the equator, about 129 watts of thermal energy land on each square foot of earth. *If* all of this solar energy could be captured and converted to electricity, it would light a 125-watt bulb. However, even in the sunny deserts, which are in near-tropical latitudes, the sun doesn't shine 100 percent of the time. The minimum monthly average, even in these usually sunny locations, is only about 22 watts per square foot.

In the photovoltaic cell, solar energy is converted to electrical energy. When one form of energy is converted to a second form, some of it is always lost. Most photovoltaic cells have an efficiency of only about 10 percent, so the average electrical power produced drops from the 22 watts received per square foot to only 2.2 watts generated per square foot.

This means that if we want to build an electrical generating station which uses solar energy, it will have to collect ten times more solar energy than the electrical energy it will dispense to its customers. To build a solar powered generating station with a capacity of one billion watts, which has the same capacity as the newer fossil fuel and present nuclear power plants, will require about 16 square miles of photovoltaic collectors. Space must be left between the rows of collectors so they can be kept free of dust and snow, which would decrease the efficiency of the photovoltaic cells. If we allow only a 30 percent increase in plant size for these maintenance roads, 21 square miles will be required for each plant. This figure is for the equator. At more northern latitudes, the figure increases to 50 square miles per plant. By contrast, fossil fuel or nuclear power plants which have the same capacity usually occupy less than a square mile.

We'll Have to Evacuate Five States

If 500 solar generating plants each 50 square miles in size were to be built, over 25,000 square miles of ground would be covered with solar energy collectors and maintenance roads. This is almost exactly the total area covered by the states of Connecticut, Delaware, Rhode Island, New Hampshire, and New Jersey.

This large area requirement wouldn't be so bad if electricity could travel over great distances without loss, but this can't be done. As electricity moves through transmission lines, a "voltage drop" occurs, and this makes the transmission of electricity over long distances unfeasible. Electricity must be generated reasonably close to where it will be used. Because the Northeastern states are the most densely populated, this is where many solar generating stations would have to be located. Unfortunately, it isn't easy to find large plots of unoccupied ground near, say, Boston or New York City.

Ideal sites for solar generating plants are easy to find in any number of Western states, but the population of these states is low, so not many plants are needed where they would be easiest to place.

Solar Energy Isn't Free

Although many antinuclear activists think solar energy is free, it's not. Although it may *appear* to be free, in actual practice, electricity generated by a solar generating station is so expensive that it is far from being competitive even with oil, our most expensive fuel. When you consider that 16 square miles of expensive photovoltaic cells are required to generate one billion watts at the equator, it isn't hard to see why solar energy is so expensive. A really enormous capital investment would be required if we were to shift to solar energy. Tremendous quantities of glass, copper, and other raw materials would be needed. The cost of electrical energy would skyrocket for years to come.

And, this short analysis doesn't say anything about the fact that most experts think that solar energy could be more dangerous than nuclear energy. Nor does it address solar energy's unsolved problem of waste disposal. (Solar energy collectors often use cadmium compounds, some of which are extremely poisonous and must be disposed of periodically.)

In the future, as fossil fuel reserves are depleted, their prices will probably rise steeply. When this happens, solar energy could become more competitive. Meanwhile, research may provide answers to some of the problems which have thus far prevented solar energy from becoming more widely used. However, until this happens, solar energy remains one of our most expensive, least practical ways to generate energy, which is exactly why we see so little of it in use today.

Alcohol as a Fuel

Most people have used "gasohol" in their automobiles from time to time. This fuel is usually a blend of 10 percent ethyl alcohol and 90 percent gasoline, although other blends and other alcohols can be used. Automobile carburetors can be built which will burn 100 percent alcohol, although these automobiles are hard to start.

Alcohol for use in automobiles is produced by the fermentation of plant materials rich in simple sugars. This is essentially the same process used to produce beer, wine, and whiskey. To make alcohol for use in automobiles, sugar cane is often used. In the future, crop wastes such as corncobs, leaves, and stalks may be used. These materials are rich in complex sugars, which can be broken down chemically.

The prospect of using such worthless plant material to produce valuable liquid fuels sounds *inviting*. *But,* there is a drawback: At present, it requires more energy to produce a gallon of alcohol than burning the alcohol will produce. For example, it takes 110,000 BTUs of heat to produce a gallon of alcohol which, when burned, yields only 76,000 BTUs of heat, so there is a 34,000 BTU deficit per gallon.

Still, when our oil runs out, there will be an enormous demand for liquid fuels, so in the future we may see large quantities of coal being burned in order to produce alcohol which will then be used to power trucks and automobiles. Of course, this would more rapidly deplete our supply of coal.

In 1989, President George Bush proposed that a fleet of alternative fuel vehicles be on the highway by 1997. By mandate, these two million cars would burn methanol or some fuel other than gasoline. However, it was quickly pointed out that the combustion of methanol can result in the production of from three to five times as much formaldehyde as gasoline produces. Unfortunately, formaldehyde reacts in the air to produce ozone, the very pollutant which the use of methanol was supposed to prevent. New York was the last state to abandon this program in August of 1998.

It's easy to set timetables for scientific and technological progress, but Mother Nature reveals her secrets grudgingly; and, as time has shown, she pays no attention to government mandates. Far more certain progress would be made toward ending the problem of air pollution if the government would turn its attention to the political problem of controlling the antinuclear activists, which it has now ignored for almost 30 years. After all, political problems, not scientific problems, are what politicians are best prepared to solve.

Hydrogen as a Fuel

The use of hydrogen as a fuel is so appealing that at one time, people spoke of the "coming hydrogen economy." Hydrogen's high energy content and the fact that it forms water vapor when it burns were two of the big advantages most often mentioned.

However, even though hydrogen itself burns cleanly, its use is not pollution-free. As you may know, 78 percent of the air is nitrogen. When combustion of any fuel produces a high enough temperature, the nitrogen of the air, which is ordinarily inactive chemically, reacts with the oxygen of the air to form nitrogen monoxide. In turn, nitrogen monoxide can further react to form nitrogen dioxide, which is an air pollutant. So, even if hydrogen, which burns cleanly, is used, there would still be some air pollution. However, its use would not result in the emission of sulfur dioxide, carbon monoxide, or any of the other usual pollutants. The use of hydrogen would go a long way towards alleviating our air pollution problems.

Hydrogen does not occur in the air in appreciable quantities, so it must be produced chemically. At present, most hydrogen obtained is produced from natural gas, which is itself a valuable fuel.

It is also possible to produce hydrogen by passing an electrical current through water. Of course, the electricity used in this process must be produced by burning coal or oil. So, thus far, neither one of the two processes for making hydrogen seems to be an improvement over what now is being done.

As a matter of fact, these two processes will use more energy than the hydrogen they produce will generate. In any conversion from one form of energy to another, some energy is always lost. That is, the efficiency of the process is always less than 100 percent. For example, when heat energy is used to turn a turbine to produce mechanical energy and then electrical energy, 65 percent of the heat energy is wasted. The process is only 35 percent efficient.

The storage of electrical energy in large quantities has long remained an unsolved problem. It has been suggested that the cheap electricity produced during low demand hours could be used to generate hydrogen, and later, hydrogen could be burned to generate electricity during high demand hours. Again, energy losses during conversion complicate this otherwise interesting idea.

Unless some of the many technical problems which exist at present are solved, it may be a long time before the day of the hydrogen economy arrives.

Hydroelectric Power

When water behind a dam is at a higher level than the river into which it will flow, it has potential energy because of its height. This potential energy can be converted into mechanical energy as the water falls. And, this mechanical energy can then be converted into electrical energy. In 1998, about 5 percent of our electrical energy was generated by hydroelectric power. Unfortunately, not too many practical sites for dams remain undeveloped. Further, because rivers carrying suspended solids such as mud empty into dam reservoirs, the reservoirs usually silt up in from 100 to 300 years. So, the energy from hydroelectric sources cannot be depended on forever, nor can its present capacity be increased very much.

Because of these considerations, it is unlikely that hydroelectric power will ever be able to play a much larger role in meeting our energy demands than it now does.

Incidentally, if you asked 100 people which was safer, hydroelectric power or nuclear power, at least 99 out of the 100 would probably pick hydroelectric power as safer. However, the facts show otherwise. For example, 110 workers lost their lives during the construction of Boulder Dam, and dams do collapse, often drowning large numbers of people. When the Vaiont Dam in Italy burst in 1963, from 2,000 to 4,000 people died. Closer to home, when the Saint Francis Dam in California collapsed in 1928, at least 600 people, and possibly 1000, were killed. According to estimates, the failure of the Folsom Dam, on the American River above Sacramento, could result in the death of 260,000 people. And, earthquakes do occur in California. Keep in mind that in the U.S., not one member of the public has ever died as a result of the use of nuclear power. Death due to the use of nuclear power has been limited to a few hundred uranium miners.

Oil Shales and Tar Sands

So far, every alternative source of energy we've discussed has some very difficult-to-solve problems associated with it which prevent its widespread use. Here's one that looks somewhat more promising except for the fact that it will pollute the air.

Three large deposits of oil shale are present in Utah, Wyoming, and

Colorado. Together, these three deposits have been estimated to contain 1,800 billion barrels of oil. This means that there is almost 68 times as much oil waiting to be recovered from oil shale than there is crude oil remaining to be pumped from U.S. oil wells. And, this makes oil shales our second largest potential source of the fossil fuels, right in back of coal.

Actually, the term "oil" shales is not correct, although widely used. The "oil" removed from oil shales is a waxy organic mixture called kerogen. The oil shales are mined, crushed, and heated. When this is done, the liquids collected can be chemically processed to yield liquid fuels, which are known as "synthetic crude oil," or more commonly, "syncrude."

Syncrude may also be obtained from tar sands. Although the U.S. does not have any tar sands, Canada has significant deposits. Like the oil shales, the tar sands are heated strongly, and a thick syrupy mixture known as bitumen is obtained. This is chemically processed to produce synthetic crude oil. You should note that the extraction of syncrude from both oil shales and tar sands requires heat. Therefore, energy must be expended to produce fuel from both sources.

The net gain in energy, if any, is uncertain at this time.

At present, both of these sources of fuel are too expensive to compete with crude oil. This will undoubtedly change, because as crude oil supplies diminish, its price will certainly increase. Meanwhile, there are a multitude of technical problems to be solved before large-scale production of synfuel from oil shales can begin.

The combination of oil shales and nuclear energy could solve our energy problems for centuries to come. Nuclear energy could be used to generate electricity and for many large stationary uses. Electric cars and heat pumps would further eliminate the need for other energy sources. Synfuel from the oil shales could then be used to power the larger trucks and locomotives which might too quickly deplete electric batteries. The use of this combination would also go a long way towards solving the air pollution problem, too.

However, as promising as the oil shales look as a source of energy, a note of caution is called for. Recent technological reviews of the methods of extraction being considered are discouraging. In fact, according to scientists David Bodansky and Fred Schmidt, these methods are so uncertain that we shouldn't count on the oil shales, at least at present.[1]

Windmills and Wishful Thinking

Utilizing the energy of the tides, geothermal energy, the energy of the wind, and nuclear fusion to make power are all being studied even as this is written. However, unless some spectacular breakthroughs in these areas occur, these methods will either be limited to a relatively small role in solving our future energy problems, or they will not be usable at all. All of these methods have technical problems which must be solved, or a limited number of locations where their use is economically feasible.

Take windmills for example. Farmers in windy areas have used windmills to pump water for years, and the idea of using them to generate electricity is appealing. However, as a large-scale method of generating electricity, they've been a dismal, multimillion dollar failure so far. One big problem is that the wind doesn't blow 24 hours a day, and unlike water, electricity can't be stored for later use. But, their unreliability is only one of the drawbacks to windmills.

Windy Altamont Pass, in Alameda County, California, looked like a promising site for windmills, so Kenetech Windpower and others built 7,000 windmills on 80 square miles of hills east of San Francisco. Although there are few windy sites as promising as this, Altamont's windmills haven't worked out very well. Maintenance problems have been much greater than expected, and on any given day, many of the windmills are down, awaiting repairs. And, when they do operate, the noise is so loud that many homeowners have sued the operators, who now routinely buy out angry homeowners rather than go to court. Worse, thousands of birds are killed each year by the huge, whirling blades, including several hundred birds of prey such as federally protected golden eagles.

No wonder that many windmill projects have gone the way of Southern California Edison's $30 million windmill, which was sold for scrap in 1983 for less than two-tenths of a cent on the dollar.

Even if a technological breakthrough were to occur today which might make one of the alternative sources of energy look more promising, it might be decades before it was perfected and ready to be pressed into service. Often, several significant discoveries in seemingly unrelated fields are needed before a dream becomes a reality.

For example, landmark discoveries by Greeks, Germans, Italians, Danes, British, French, Belgians, and Americans were needed to bring electricity into American homes. Starting with the discovery of static electricity by the ancient Greeks, it took almost 2,500 years before electricity became useful.

Although we can hope that the discoveries which will convert solar energy or one of the other alternative sources of energy from a dream to reality will come at a faster pace than this, we can't be sure that this will happen. Nature reveals her secrets slowly, and pays no attention to human needs or suffering.

What the Experts Think about Alternative Sources of Energy

In 1980, social scientists Stanley Rothman and S. Robert Lichter polled 279 scientists who could be considered "energy experts" regarding the contributions that various sources of energy could be expected to make toward meeting our energy needs in the next 20 years.[2]

Only 1 percent or 2 percent of the 279 experts thought that biomass (alcohol, etc.) and passive solar energy would be able to make a large contribution to our future energy needs. None—not one—of the 279 experts thought that solar electricity would be able to make a large contribution to our energy needs by the year 2000. Sixty-one percent, and 80 percent, respectively, predicted that oil and coal would be large contributors. Even though the poll was taken after Three Mile Island, 45 percent of the experts thought that nuclear power would make a large contribution to meeting our energy needs.

It is interesting to note that time has proven that these energy experts knew what they were talking about.

Conservation: The Most Dangerous Alternative

Whenever you get an antinuclear activist to admit that coal and oil have serious problems associated with their use, and solar energy is still but a dream, they fall back on their old standby: Conservation. And, this method of meeting our energy needs sounds so simple and appealing that a lot of people are taken in by it.

As you know, the antinuclear activists are preventing us from using nuclear energy because they claim that it's too dangerous to use. But, I'm sure that it will surprise you to learn that conservation could be the most dangerous approach to solving the problem of meeting our energy needs.

Physics professor Bernard Cohen has calculated some of the risks associated with various activities.[3] There's nothing particularly mysterious about Dr. Cohen's calculations; they are similar to the ones made by insurance companies all the time, and life insurance rates are based on the tables constructed from these calculations. These tables have to be right, or the company could lose some big money.

Dr. Cohen points out that smaller cars use less gasoline and, therefore, are an important part of any conservation program. But, reliable statistics show that driving a smaller car is significantly more dangerous than driving a standard sized car. According to Dr. Cohen, driving a smaller car poses a greater danger to the average person than do falls, fire, or firearms.

If more people rode bicycles to work, this would save even more gasoline than smaller cars do. But, as it turns out, bicycles are even more dangerous than small cars.

Another conservation measure is adding weatherstripping around doors and windows to prevent the loss of warm indoor air, thus decreasing the amount of fuel needed to heat your home. But, this, too, can be hazardous to your health. Radon, an invisible, odorless gas, is released by the uranium found in many soils. Unfortunately, radon is radioactive and is known to cause lung cancer in uranium miners. Radon is constantly escaping from the soil, and some of it finds its way into homes via foundation cracks and unsealed crawl spaces. Weatherstripping slows down the interchange between inside and outside air and causes the radon level to increase in well-weatherstripped homes. Because radon is currently thought to cause 14,000 lung cancer deaths a year, sealing your house very tightly—as conservationists advise you to do—is not a good idea.

As Dr. Cohen points out, tightening up homes to reduce air leakage in accordance with government regulations makes conservation by far the most dangerous energy strategy from the standpoint of exposure to radiation. According to Dr. Cohen's figures, this one act of conservation exposes us to 800 times more radiation than we would receive if all of our electricity were to be produced by nuclear power plants. (It should be noted that Dr. Cohen is widely recognized as one of the foremost authorities on radon. He recently supervised research in which the radon level was measured in 350,000 homes.)

But, these aren't the worst risks that conservation poses. The really big danger is that overzealous conservationists or misguided environmentalists might adopt measures such as the Kyoto Treaty, which will cut into our industrial production and make us poor. According to Dr. Cohen's figures, from the standpoint of average longevity, being poor is more dangerous than being in an army unit sent to the Vietnam War. And, being poor constitutes a greater danger than stroke, motor vehicle accidents, homicide, or hurricanes and tornadoes.

Now, there isn't anything wrong with trying to cut down on waste. Waste is always foolish; but, it is especially foolish when something as valuable as energy is concerned. However, Americans are already among the most efficient in terms of energy used per dollar of gross national product turned out. So, while some conservation measures might eliminate some waste, too much conservation would cut into production, and that's when the big slide into Third World poverty, squalor, and disease starts.

Earlier, we pointed out that our standard of living depends on our ability to produce goods. And, in turn, our ability to produce goods depends on our having access to a reliable source of usable energy. This is an important idea, and everyone who claims to be well-educated should be aware of this relationship.

We can think of energy as a tool which enables us to produce more goods, thus increasing our income. Perhaps you remember earlier mention of the Turkish production worker who labored without the help of very much electricity, and was able to earn only 41 cents an hour. At the same time, the average Norwegian production worker used over 32 times more electricity, so he was able to produce more goods and earn 46 times more, or $18.92 an hour. Of course, this big difference in income makes a lot of difference in how the two workers live. The Norwegian can afford to go to a doctor when he needs to, and the Turk can't. When the Norwegian needs to take medicine for high blood pressure, he can afford to buy it. But, the poor Turk may be unaware that he even has high blood pressure. Over the years, poor food, poor medical care, and other income-related things begin to take their toll, and the average Turk dies almost 12 years before the average Norwegian dies. (Since this was written, Turkey has closed the gap somewhat, increasing both electrical usage and longevity.)

If, under the guise of conservation, we cut back on our use of energy beyond the point of eliminating waste, we also cut back on our industrial production. If carried far enough, these cuts can hurt all of the services supported by high industrial production. Soon, we may be unable to support our medical researchers and our teachers (both of whom we don't support in any too grand a style even now), our doctors, our water purification technicians, and so on. Cuts in these services will lead to a decrease in our life expectancy. If you have any doubt about the relationship between industrial productivity and longevity, spend a minute or two looking over Table 8.1.

The second column from the left shows the electrical energy generated per person in the various countries. This can be thought of as a rough measure of industrialization and production. The next column to the right shows the gross domestic product per person generated by this production. And, the last column shows the average life expectancy which people in each of the various countries can enjoy.

You should note that generally speaking, countries that use very little energy have lower incomes and a shorter life expectancy. Conversely, the more energy a country uses, the richer it is, and the longer the life expectancy of its people. When you see the short life span that people in the poorer countries have, you can understand why Dr. Cohen says that being poor is more dangerous than being sent to Vietnam. Earlier, we said that conservation could be the most dangerous approach to solving the

Table 8.1: Electrical Energy, Per Capita Domestic Product, and Life Expectancy in Various Countries

Country	Electrical energy generated per person in kilowatt hours	Gross domestic product per person	Average life expectancy in years
United States	12,579	$28,600	76.3
Germany	6,274	$20,400	77.0
Spain	4,165,	$15,300	77.7
Hungary	3,233	$7,500	70.5
Mexico	1,562	$8,100	71.7
India	410	$1,600	62.9
Haiti	61	$1,000	51.5
Ethiopia	22	$430	40.9

(Source: 1999World Almanac. Most figures are for 1997.)

problem of meeting our energy needs. This statement was based on the possibility that we might let an overzealous conservationist who doesn't understand the relationship between energy usage, industrial production, and our prosperity sell us on the idea of cutting our energy usage beyond the point of eliminating waste. If our energy usage is cut far enough, we could become poor.

According to Dr. Cohen's figures, in terms of the average loss of life expectancy which accompanies both risks, if, as a nation, we became poor, we would run a greater risk than we now do, on the average, from air pollution. In fact, coal burning could double, or triple, and being poor would still be a greater risk.

So, conservation, if carried past the point of waste reduction (which is what would have to be done when we run out of oil) is the most dangerous alternative solution of all. It's even more dangerous than burning more coal, and it's much, much more dangerous than turning to nuclear power.

For some time now, the use of the fossil fuels has been on a collision course with the quality of the environment.

Burning coal and oil pollutes the air, causing millions of cases of respiratory disease, tens of thousands of air pollution-related deaths, acid rain, and forces us to run the risk posed by the greenhouse effect. On the other hand, without access to energy, our civilization will perish.

As the increased use of fossil fuels led to further deterioration of the environment, the cry of "Conservation!" was heard more and more frequently. By the summer of 1989, there was evidence that the predicted collision between rising energy demands and environmental concerns was about to occur. On August 30, 1988, the Environmental Protection Agency (EPA) announced that it was banning construction of large factories in the metropolitan Los Angeles area because this area had failed to meet EPA air pollution standards.

In effect, this ban sent a signal that the industrial growth of certain areas would have to cease until better ways of controlling air pollution were developed. If this ban on new industry was limited to only one area struggling to to solve its environmental problems, it might not be particularly serious. But, if it is a sign of things to come throughout much of America, it does indeed cast a dark shadow over the land.

To curtail industrial growth is to strangle progress in all the other areas which depend on industry. Our health, our standard of living, our abundant leisure time, and our progress in science, medicine and innumerable other fields depends on our ability to produce goods.

At present, the best way to decrease air pollution is to build nuclear power plants which do not pollute the air. Stopping industrial growth is a last-ditch measure to be avoided if at all possible. To stop industrial growth would be a great step backward we would all eventually regret.

More non-air-polluting nuclear power plants would be in use in California today if not for the antinuclear activists. On one occasion, in 1976, a moratorium which would have prevented the use of nuclear power in California appeared on the ballot, and the people of California promptly rejected it, despite a barrage of misinformation by the antinuclear activists which was widely reported in the media.

Thirteen years later, in 1989, persistent antinuclear groups did succeed in closing the Rancho Seco nuclear power plant in California. Fifteen prior attempts to prevent the use of nuclear power in California had failed, but at last, the antinuclear activists finally succeeded. It is worth noting that a *U.S. News and World Report* poll of December 7, 1992, reported that only 15 percent of all Americans wanted to close all nuclear power plants. Clearly, the antinuclear activists are a stubborn, persistent minority.

The Only Alternative to Fossil Fuels

Most new technologies are not particularly safe when first introduced, but become safer as measures are taken to eliminate the dangers that appear as the new technologies are used. For example, when passenger trains first started running at high speeds in the U.S., 30,000 casualties a year was the result. Not until safety improvements such as air brakes were instituted did this toll diminish.

But, the classic story of the improvement of safety over time is that of coal mining. In the early years of the twentieth century, it was not unusual for coal mine accidents to cause almost 2,000 deaths a year in the U.S. Between 1900 and 1930 there were 33 coal mine accidents which claimed 75 or more miners. But, the last coal mine accident to claim 75 or more lives occurred way back in 1968. A lot of changes have been made, and today's coal mines are much safer. In recent years it's not unusual for fewer than 50 miners to be killed in mining accidents during a given year. This is only 2.5 percent of the death toll at the beginning of the twentieth century.

Plainly, time is needed to learn where danger lurks in a new technology, and correct it.

That wasn't the case with nuclear power, however. Nuclear power made its appearance in the U.S. late in 1957, and in the 42 years since, its use has not caused a single death in the public sector. Several hundred or so uranium miners have died from accidents and from breathing the radon gas produced by uranium, but like coal mines, uranium mines are much safer places to work today.

Today, a new generation of nuclear power reactors is waiting to be built. Initial studies indicate that these reactors will be from 10 to 1,000 times safer than their predecessors. This new generation of nuclear reactors is going to be smaller, safer, simpler, and more economical to build and operate.

One problem with today's big reactors is that they produce a lot of heat, which is what they were designed to do. But, the only two nuclear accidents in Western-built nuclear power plants both involved a loss of coolant and the subsequent overheating of fuel rod assemblies.

Although neither of these accidents—at Fermi and Three Mile Island—harmed or endangered anyone in any way, the media's handling of the Three Mile Island accident so frightened the public that a loss of coolant accident is now a utility company's worst nightmare.

Today's big reactors require an "active" cooling system composed of valves, pumps, and backup pumps. The backup pumps are diesel-powered pumps which start up should the electrically powered pumps fail. This is necessary because unless cool water is pumped into the reactor, the core will overheat, even if fission has stopped.

With a reactor about the size of today's new reactors, the cooling system can be "passive." That is, the coolant circulates by convection, and no pumps are needed. In these new, improved, smaller reactors, a meltdown is virtually impossible.

Because there are only about half as many valves, pumps, feet of pipe, and similar parts, these new reactors are simpler. And, simpler is good. It means less equipment to malfunction, periodically test, and maintain.

All of today's reactors were custom-built on the site, and no two are alike. The second generation of reactors from a given manufacturer will all be identical, and they'll all be built in "modules" to be shipped to the building site and set in place. Installation will be quick and easy, and workmen will be less likely to make mistakes because they will be installing modules that are factory-built.

Let's look briefly at several of these new, improved reactors. The AP600 is a smaller reactor much like our present pressurized water reactors which have been the standby since 1957. But, this new reactor has passive cooling. If there's a coolant loss, huge water tanks situated above the reactor release water into the reactor by gravity. The high pressure inside the reactor is overcome by pressurizing the emergency water tanks with nitrogen gas. Studies suggest that this, and other safety features, will make this reactor approximately 1,000 times safer than its predecessors. The design for this reactor will be standardized, and it will be simpler, which will make it less expensive to build and operate than today's reactors.

Breeder Reactors

Everyone in the nuclear power field agrees that in the future, most nuclear reactors will be "breeders." Although breeders were first developed in the U.S., France's "Super Phoenix" is now the world's best known breeder.

Breeders convert our most abundant form of uranium, U238, into plutonium, Pu239, which is a nuclear fuel similar to U235. An efficient breeder always produces more fuel than it consumes, often doubling the fuel it has used within several years. And, it generates electricity as it does this.

The process of breeding begins when a U235 nucleus fissions, producing two or three fast neutrons. These neutrons may then collide with the more abundant U238 nuclei present. The U238 nuclei each readily capture a fast neutron, and the U238 atom undergoes a short series of transmutations as it briefly changes into other elements before forming plutonium. Since each U235 nuclei releases two or three neutrons, more fuel in the form of Pu239 is formed than was consumed. Plutonium 239, as with U235, can be used as a nuclear fuel, but it must be recovered from the reactor's fuel and separated from the other fission products, so provisions for reprocessing are necessary.

The advantages of breeder reactors are very important: They allow us to use the most abundant isotope of uranium, U238, which is otherwise wasted. This allows us to obtain energy from all uranium atoms, not just from U235, which makes up less than one percent of naturally occurring uranium. This means that with breeders, each gram of uranium potentially can generate 385 million times more energy than a gram of coal, not the 2.7 million times more energy described in chapter 2.

Without breeders, our supply of fissionable atoms could be consumed in 50 years or less. But, with breeders, we have enough uranium to last for thousands of years. And, if we can effectively extract uranium from the ocean—and there's no reason why we can't do this—we will have enough uranium to last infinitely. Estimates place the supply of uranium in the oceans at five billion tons, and more is washed into the ocean each year. The cost of the extraction process is not a big factor, because fuel costs per kilowatt-hour are so low in a breeder that a 20-fold increase in extraction costs would result in only a 1 percent increase in electrical costs.

When our supply of the fossil fuels is exhausted, we will have to get our energy from breeder reactors unless some unforeseen breakthrough occurs in some other technology.

The PRISM reactor, which was developed at Argonne National Laboratories, is a small, second-generation breeder. The fuel used is an alloy of uranium, plutonium, and zirconium. Because fast neutrons are more efficient for breeding than slow neutrons, a moderator is not needed. This means that water cannot be used as a coolant, because it also acts as a moderator. The coolant used in PRISM is liquid sodium. Ordinarily, sodium is a light, soft, metallic solid which melts at 210 degrees Fahrenheit and boils at 1,640 degrees. These melting and boiling points, plus the fact that liquid sodium can readily transfer heat, makes it an excellent coolant. Unfortunately, liquid sodium has several drawbacks; it's so active chemically that it will react with water, and it will burn readily. These problems can be solved by confining the liquid sodium to a closed system where there is no water or air.

If PRISM comes into use in the U.S., any antinuclear activists still around will probably claim that sodium is the most dangerous of all metals, or some such nonsense. But, the fact is, it used to be on the shelf in almost every high school chemistry lab in the U.S., and chemical engineers have had plenty of experience in handling liquid sodium safely.

PRISM's fuel cell assemblies sit in a large tank of liquid sodium. There are no pumps to fail, and the reactor shuts itself down in the event that overheating occurs.

Like many of the second generation of reactors, PRISM will be factory-built in the form of three 155,000kw modules, which are shipped to the building site for final assembly. Both construction costs and time to build will be greatly decreased. It should be possible to build a nuclear power plant in three to five years, instead of the 10 to 12 years it formerly took. Of course, this assumes that antinuclear power activists will be prevented from interfering with construction as they have done in the past.

The plutonium produced by breeding will be separated from the other unwanted fission products in the spent fuel by electrochemical refining right on the site. By design, the end product will be very radioactive and must be handled by remote controls with the operator situated behind heavy shielding. This insures that the theft of plutonium, a fear often expressed by the antinuclear crowd, is an impossibility.

At present, there is no reprocessing of spent nuclear fuel in the U.S. As a result, today's reactors use only a small fraction of the fissionable substances present, and the rest becomes waste. The U.S. government made the decision not to build reprocessing facilities in the 1970s, and it was a bad, wasteful decision. This decision was made under a lot of pressure from antinuclear activists, and might not have been made had this political pressure not been present. Unless things change, we will end up burying valuable nuclear fuel which would have served our children well.

The experts estimate that not only will PRISM bring an end to this waste, but it'll be a lot safer than today's reactors. And, PRISM will be able to generate electricity that's 20 percent cheaper than coal-produced electricity. Apparently, Japanese nuclear engineers have faith in these estimates, because Japan has invested 20 million dollars in the development of PRISM. This kind of support, from a country that was on the receiving end of two atomic bombs, speaks highly of the rationality of the Japanese, and their ability to deal with antinuclear activists.

Other countries are also working on the second generation of reactors. In Sweden, which also has its share of antinuclear activists, the PIUS reactor (an acronym for "process inherent ultimate safety") has been developed. As the name implies, PIUS is supposed to be extraordinarily safe and depends almost entirely on passive systems which rule out the chance of operator error.

Switzerland plans to build "Geyser," which is a small reactor that requires almost no supervision. Geyser will be used to heat water which will then be used in hot water heating systems in homes and businesses.

The Bad News about the Second Generation of Reactors

Unfortunately, none of these super-safe, highly efficient reactors will ever be built in the U.S. unless we change our licensing procedures. Antinuclear activists have used the courts, the government, and the media to stop construction on every nuclear power plant ordered since 1974. Sometimes construction was stopped on many nearly completed nuclear power plants at a cost of tens of billions of dollars to the utility companies or the public.

To illustrate how this could happen, let's look briefly at the history of the Seabrook, New Hampshire, nuclear power plants.

Seabrook

When Seabrook was in the planning stage, in 1971, almost everyone was enthusiastic about it because air pollution from coal was beginning to become a more serious problem. Several nuclear power plants had already been built in the area, and not only had they been finished on time, but the construction costs had been less than expected. Although the two big reactors planned at Seabrook would have generated 70 percent of New Hampshire's electricity, they would have only consumed a few pounds of uranium daily. By contrast, if the plant used coal or oil, 20,000 tons of coal and the ashes it produces, or 3.6 million gallons of oil would need to be handled each and every day. These are enormous quantities, and not having to deal with them each day was a huge advantage.

The first sign of the multitude of problems to come surfaced on January 6, 1977. The Environmental Protection Agency (EPA) had already approved the project, but the regional administrator suddenly changed his mind. Construction was already well underway, but the contractors were forced to put a hold on it pending the EPA administrator's new decision. This reversal of approval was largely due to antinuclear protests that the plant's cooling system would discharge warm water into the Atlantic Ocean. "Thermal pollution" had become the antinuclear activists' battle cry.

Although common sense should have indicated that the discharge of 80°F water into the Atlantic Ocean wouldn't affect its temperature significantly, the ploy was successful in halting construction.

Earlier, in 1970, on a prime-time TV special on the environment carried by NBC, commentator Edwin Newman had repeated the antinuclear activists' prediction of rivers which would boil and then evaporate, when he said,

> [By] the end of the decade, our rivers may have reached the boiling point; three decades more, and they may evaporate. One of the causes of thermal pollution is the spread of nuclear power across the land.[4]

Thirty years have now passed, and no rivers have boiled or even warmed up more than a degree or two. But, at the time, many people must have believed this ridiculous exaggeration. On January 7, 1977, one day after the regional administrator's decision to stop construction of Seabrook, CBS reported:

> Some people are worried about the attention that the plant is receiving. They fear that it will become a national staging ground for opponents of nuclear power. Opponents say that's exactly what will happen unless work on the project is stopped.[5]

On May 1, 1977, an estimated 2,000 protesters converged on Seabrook, forced their way past security guards and police, and occupied the construction site. The police arrested 1,414 people.

The next day, May 2, ABC reported:

> In New Hampshire, today, a team of four judges working around the clock completed the arraignment of 1,400 protestors who were arrested yesterday. They were jailed for refusing to end a peaceful sit-in on the site of a nuclear power plant in Seabrook. The demonstrators, mostly in their twenties, were charged with criminal trespassing. Most of them were unable, or unwilling, to post bail, which ranged from 100 to 500 dollars. The jails in the area are full and National Guard armories are being used to hold the protestors.[6]

With expenses for feeding and holding the prisoners approaching $50,000 a day, the state soon released the protesters. Some refused to leave jail, but eventually got bored and left anyway.

After a delay of over six months, on June 17, 1977, the Environmental Protection Agency once again gave the go-ahead to Seabrook by approving the disputed cooling system which would release warm water into the Atlantic Ocean. It had taken six months for the EPA to decide that the 80°F water which Seabrook released would not significantly affect the temperature of the Atlantic Ocean. Although no warm water from Seabrook had been released yet, at the EPA meeting in Washington, one arrogant protester even waved dead fish in the face of the EPA officials. Now, the final go-ahead for the plant was in the hands of the Nuclear Regulatory Commission (NRC). A little over one month later, on July 26, 1977, the NRC gave Seabrook's contractors approval to resume construction. In all, there had been a costly seven and one-half months delay.

In the spring of 1978, protesters again tried to stop construction. Although they initially failed, the NRC later stopped construction on July 2, 1978. On August 4, the EPA again approved the controversial cooling system, and six days later the NRC gave permission to resume construction at Seabrook.

At this point, the combination of frivolous lawsuits by protesters and design changes mandated by the EPA and NRC had put Seabrook three years behind schedule and 50 percent over budget.

In order to understand why construction delays are so expensive, it's necessary to look at the procedures used to finance this construction. Whenever a construction project is undertaken, be it a nuclear power plant or a home, money has to be borrowed to pay the builders. This is called a "construction loan." As work is completed by each sub contractor they are paid from this construction loan, and the utility company must then begin paying interest on the money paid out.

Because public utility companies have a monopoly, the rates a public utility can charge its customers are generally set by state utility commissions. These rates are based on the actual cost of operation plus what would amount to a reasonable return on the capital investors have put into the utility over the years to build the plants in operation. The value of these operating plants is known as the "rate base."

By law, in many states a power plant must be completed and in operation before the utility company can include the cost of its construction in the company's rate base. This way, present users of electricity will not be charged for construction work which is for the benefit of future customers. And, this means that the interest on construction loans must be paid out of cash reserves the utility company has accumulated over the years, or financed by other means. However, once the plant is completed and is actually in operation, its cost can be added to the rate base, so at that time the utility can begin earning money to pay for the cost of construction.

Now, suppose that a utility company has borrowed one billion dollars to construct a nuclear power plant. The plant is nearing completion, and it will soon go into operation, at which time its construction costs can be added to the rate base, and the plant can begin earning money to repay the funds which were borrowed to construct it.

If, at this time, protesters can hold up completion by filing a lawsuit of some sort, the utility company must go on paying the interest on the construction loan out of its reserves until the suit is settled by the courts. It was not unusual for such delays to cost a utility company as much as $274 thousand dollars a day in the 1980s. Of course, at this rate, not many utility companies have enough of a reserve to withstand the financial strain imposed by long, continual delays. Even a six-month delay will cost the utility company $50 million. It's little wonder that so many utility companies which tried to build nuclear power plants have ended up being forced into bankruptcy by the protesters.

Originally, Seabrook's first unit had been scheduled to begin generating electricity by 1983, and the second unit was to begin operation in 1985. But, by February 1984, unit one was two years behind schedule, and there was speculation as to whether unit number two would ever be finished. The estimated cost of building just unit number one was almost $6 billion, or six times the original estimate for building both units. Most of this unexpected increase in cost was due to lawsuits and illegal "sit-ins" staged by groups such as the Clamshell Alliance and the Boston-based Coalition for Direct Action at Seabrook. In 1979, the latter vowed to occupy the construction site and turn it into an "anti-nuclear village with victory gardens and alternate energy exhibits."

Part of the blame for these costly delays must be placed on the ease with which the protesters were able to force the EPA and NRC to reverse their previous approval of construction. It would seem that the time for protests would be before construction is approved, and that once approved there would be no changes and no delays. However, this is not the case at present. As Cincinnati Gas and Electric's William Dickhoner said, "You can't build something when you have 285 regulatory changes while it's being built."[7]

Although the government may get the blame for these costly delays, the protesters' role here has to be recognized. A government responsive to its citizens is usually one which is likely to be reelected. And, this is as it should be. But, thus far, largely because of media attention, the protesters have been far more effective than the pro-nuclear forces or common sense in terms of influencing governmental agencies.

Each lawsuit to stop construction, no matter how ridiculous, has had its day in court, has been argued, considered, and won, or more often, lost. But, the democratic process has been slow, and for the utility companies and the users of electricity the delays have been disastrously expensive. A simple change in laws, which places approval in the hands of only one agency and which limits protests to preconstruction time periods, could prevent the protesters from frivolously using the courts and governmental agencies as they now do.

Under the present procedure, it's little wonder that comments such as the following have become commonplace in the nuclear industry:[8]

> No utility executive in the country would consider ordering one [a nuclear power plant] today—unless he wanted to be certified or committed.
> —Robert Scherer, chairman of Georgia Power

The first lesson we've learned is, "Don't build nuclear plants in America." You subject yourself to financial risk and public abuse.
—Don Beeth, director of nuclear information at
Houston Lighting and Power.

It's almost a punitive deal to open a nuclear plant these days.
—William Dickhoner, president of Cincinnati Gas and Electric.

If you think these comments might be somewhat exaggerated, consider the following list of a few of the protesters more detrimental civic "accomplishments." In each case, protests and legal suits by the protesters substantially increased the actual cost of the nuclear power plants as shown:

• Diablo Canyon, California: original estimated cost $450 million; actual cost $4.4 billion (a tenfold increase).

• Shoreham, New York: original estimated cost $242 million; actual cost $4 billion (a sixteenfold increase).

• Trojan, Oregon: original estimated cost $235 million; actual cost $460 million (almost double).

• Midland, Michigan: original estimated cost $267 million; actual cost $4.4 billion (a sixteenfold increase).

• Marble Hill, Indiana: original estimated cost $1.4 billion; actual cost $7 billion, before being abandoned.

The difference between the original projected cost and actual cost of just these five power plants and Seabrook is over $21.6 billion. An estimated 120 nuclear plants in various stages of planning or construction met a similar fate. No nuclear power plant ordered since 1974 in the U.S. has ever been completed.

Seabrook 2 was abandoned late in 1984, even though it was 22 percent complete. At that time, the fate of Seabrook 1, which was 80 percent complete, was in doubt. This unit now had cost the utility in excess of $6 billion, over six times that of the $973 million cost originally estimated for both reactors.

Without Energy, a Prosperous Area Will Become a Slum

While the fate of Seabrook 1 was in doubt, the people in the five northeastern states continued to pay the highest heating and electric bills in the nation. In June of 1984, the New England Power Pool, which includes 86 utility companies in the region, entered into a tentative agreement with Quebec's provincial utility, Hydro Quebec, to purchase 2,000 megawatts of power yearly for ten years at a total cost of $4.5 billion. And, Canada's New Brunswick Electric Power Commission said that it was prepared to build a nuclear power plant whose entire electrical output would be sold to New England.

Although reliance on Canadian utility companies for electrical power was seen as a risky move because Canadians were uncertain of their own long-term energy needs, New England had little choice. Faced by the possibility of increasing some of the worst air pollution problems in the nation, cities such as Boston and New York could hardly turn to coal. And, although oil is a cleaner fuel than coal, it is the most expensive fuel of all, and much of it comes from the dangerous, uncertain Middle East. As the prospect of increasing energy costs or increasing air pollution plagued utility companies and public health authorities, the protesters sat back, unconcerned. Although they had created these problems, they didn't have to solve them. Nor did they have to pay the $5.5 billion cost overruns they had caused at Seabrook.

During 1983, 1984, and 1985, the demand for electricity in New England increased by four percent a year. This demand increased to five percent in 1986, and there were 19 times that year when the New England Power Pool had all of their electrical generators running at maximum capacity, and yet were unable to meet demand. When this happens, the utility has no choice but to buy emergency power from other utilities, if they can spare it. In the summer of 1999, New Yorkers paid 30 times higher prices than usual for the purchase of Canadian power.

If no emergency power can be purchased anywhere, the utility company is forced to take the next step to prevent a shortage of electricity. It gradually reduces the voltage supplied to consumers until it reaches a maximum reduction of about 8 percent. At this point, some computers may automatically switch off, television pictures may shrink so that they do not fill the screen, and all electric motors will heat up. And, because all light bulbs will dim, this is known as a "brownout."

However, at this point, the utility company cannot further reduce the voltage, because if it does, electric motors will overheat and may burn out, causing fires. If the demand for electricity still continues to exceed what the utility company can generate, it has no choice but to cut off the electricity to entire areas. This is the intentional "blackout" which utility companies dread. Although few people realize the consequences of a blackout, it's definitely not something to take lightly.

When this happens, all industrial production is stopped. Lights go off in businesses. No water is pumped into water tanks, and water companies must hope that the electricity goes on before the water in their tanks is used up, or there will be no water to drink. Life support systems in private homes go off. Iron lungs, dialysis machines, and oxygen generating devices become inoperable. Hospitals with their own emergency generators can continue to operate, but they do so under a severe handicap. Traffic lights and elevators cease to function. Schools must close. All activity in the electrically deprived area comes to a halt.

A short-term blackout is a tremendous aggravation for everyone involved. But, it's very much a minor-league affair compared with what will happen if electrical demand continues to exceed supply over a long period of time. Then, the utility company has no choice but to black out large areas on a set schedule: No electricity in Staten Island from 6 A.M. to 10 A.M.; no electricity in Queens from 2 P.M. to 6 P.M.; no electricity in Manhattan from 6 P.M. to 10 P.M., and so on. This is the "rolling blackout" which utility companies hate.

If this repeatedly happens, the results will be catastrophic. Business and industry will flee from the electrically-deprived area en masse. As their jobs vanish, people will be forced to move out of the area. Unemployment will soar. State and local governments, medical services and schools will suffer from lack of financial support. Soon, a once prosperous area will become a poverty-stricken slum.

In January of 1994, the nightmare just described began for much of the eastern half of the U.S. Unusually cold weather caused the demand for electrical energy to soar to the point were utilities serving 21 million people from Washington D.C. to New Jersey were forced to institute rolling blackouts.

On January 19, the federal government shut down for two days because Washington D.C. was scheduled for such a blackout. City and state governments all over the area also closed.

In Louisville, Kentucky, Ford Motor Co. closed both of its plants and cut working hours at 11 plants in five other states and Canada. Honda, Chrysler, Nissan, and Toyota in Ohio, Missouri, and Illinois also closed their plants. In Pennsylvania, the entire state was put under a disaster emergency and state offices closed. Thermostats were set at 60°, and the governor recommended that everyone turn off unnecessary electric lights and equipment such as televisions, dishwashers, and clothes washers and dryers.

In New Jersey, Maryland, Delaware, Virginia, Ohio, Pennsylvania, and the District of Columbia, power companies were forced to temporarily halt service to thousands of customers. Workers all over the area were sent home. Without electricity, work was impossible.

During a heat wave in the summer of 1999, a shortage of power produced similar problems. When riots and looting took place during blackouts, an angry mayor of New York promised to investigate everyone involved in the fiasco. But, he neglected to mention the antinuclear protesters who had stopped the construction of a number of nuclear power plants in the area over the past years.

Because lack of power can be the economic death knell of a region, these events caused serious concern throughout much of the industrial Northeast.

Once frequent brownouts indicate that an area is on its way to a disaster such as this, immediate steps must be taken, because it takes at least five years to build a coal or oil burning power plant, and three to five years for the second generation of nuclear power plants. This warning is not something to be ignored.

But, brownouts had long been experienced in sections of the Northeast, and they had been ignored.

From 1986 to 1990, only Seabrook, Hydro Quebec of Canada, and a few other small sources of electrical power were scheduled to come on line in the New England area. Fearful of more delays by the protesters, utility officials hastened to point out that a continued 4 to 5 percent a year growth rate in demand, plus failure of any one of these sources to become operational, could mean very real power problems for New England. These problems surfaced in 1994 and 1999.

What Needs to Be Done

Plainly, some changes in licensing procedures are needed. The nuclear industry has done its part to simplify things by going to several standardized reactor designs. This way, once a design has been approved, getting approval for subsequent plants of the same design should be almost automatic.

In past years it was necessary to get a construction permit, build the plant, and then obtain a license to operate the plant. Often the many bureaucratic agencies involved succumbed to pressure from antinuclear protesters and mandated expensive design changes while the project was underway. For example, to placate those who protested Seabrook's cooling system, two tunnels, each 19 feet in diameter, were bored through three miles of solid bedrock leading away from the plant and out under the ocean floor. But, this concession to the protesters was followed by more lawsuits and protests over other frivolous matters.

The present federal regulations require that regional, state, and local officials work together in order to develop the best possible emergency response plan. This is as it should be, because all parties will be involved in the situation. However, when several groups must cooperate in order to get anything done, even regulations originally created with the best of intentions can become a bureaucratic quicksand. For example, when it came time to license Seabrook, the Department of Public Safety of the state of Massachusetts gave one ear to the protesters and the other ear to its anti-nuclear power boss, Governor Michael Dukakis, and declined to participate in the emergency response planning for Seabrook, thus throwing a monkey wrench into the licensing machinery.

The Massachusetts Department of Public Safety devised an unreasonable concept as an excuse to avoid its responsibility in this matter: They insisted on "zero risk." What this meant was that unless it could be shown that Seabrook posed absolutely no risk to the people of Massachusetts, the Department of Public Safety would not approve it. This led to three more years of delay, at a cost of almost one billion dollars. In the end, the NRC finally ruled that Seabrook could start up without Massachusetts entering into the emergency response planning usually required.

Of course, there a very few things which are entirely risk-free. Under zero risk, no airplanes would fly and no cars would move. The use of stairways would be forbidden because of the danger of falls; and to avoid the possibility that someone might get electrocuted, no electricity would ever be generated. Plainly, zero risk doesn't exist in the real world. But, this is the yardstick that the Massachusetts Department of Public Safety insisted on applying to Seabrook.

People are routinely evacuated all over the U.S. whenever a chlorine or ammonia tank car is derailed, so the arrangements for an evacuation aren't particularly complicated. Because of Seabrook's exceptionally safe construction, evacuation procedures were actually easier to plan for it than for most potential disasters.

In March of 1990, after 17 years of legal battles, Seabrook was finally granted a license to operate. But, the victory had been so expensive that no utility company planned to build another nuclear power plant.

A touch of bitter irony is added to the whole situation when the anti-nuclear activists proclaim "Nuclear power plants are more expensive to build than other power plants." Of course, this would not be true if we could build a nuclear power plant in six years, as other countries do, rather than the twelve years needed in the U.S. because of delays caused by the activists.

Until some way is found to prevent delays such as we've described, none of the modern, second generation of nuclear power plants will be built in the U.S. They'll be built overseas, and the countries which build them will have the most modern, safest, cleanest, cheapest energy of all at their disposal. Meanwhile, we'll limp along using fossil fuels, an eight-hundred-year-old, dangerously outmoded technology which has killed approximately five million Americans during the past century.

This isn't what the country's foremost physical scientists want to happen, of course. In June of 1975, 34 of them, including 11 Nobel Prize winners, said, "We can see no reasonable alternative to an increased use of nuclear power to satisfy our energy needs."[9]

The Heidelberg Appeal

Internationally, there is great concern over the dangers posed by ignorant, irresponsible political activists such as the anti-nuclear power group. In recent years, these irresponsible groups have done so much to stop progress in so many areas that 2,700 intellectual leaders, including dozens of Nobel prizewinners from 102 countries, recently endorsed the Heidelberg Appeal. These extremely intelligent, accomplished people condemned "the emergence of an irrational ideology which is opposed to scientific and industrial progress and impedes economic and social development."[10]

The Heidelberg appeal did not receive very much attention from the media, which has done much to publicize the irrational ideology mentioned.

Why Progress Should Not Be Rejected

There's an old saying: "Every dog shall have its day." Centuries ago, Greece was the dominant nation on earth. We still learn Euclidian geometry in high school and read Plato and Aristotle in college. The Greeks left their mark on the world, and twenty centuries later it still persists.

But, intelligent, creative, and strong as the Greeks were, they fell to a bunch of well-trained, highly disciplined Roman farm boys. Rome spread its empire northward to England, westward to France, eastward to Persia, and southward to Egypt. It built roads all over Europe which can still be seen even to this day. And, the Romans accomplished what Adolf Hitler's fearsome war machine could not: They successfully invaded England.

Then, the mistakes piled up, and Rome fell. Other countries ascended to the throne, sat there briefly, made some errors, and then watched other countries surge past them. The Spanish Armada is no more; and the sounds of Napoleon's marching armies no longer echo over Europe.

In more recent times, the machinery of the Industrial Revolution allowed England to become the world's mightiest industrial power. English rule spread to Canada, the Colonies, Australia, South Africa, India, Singapore, Hong Kong, Africa, and Afghanistan, where the English were able to stay much longer than the Russians. Then came Hitler, who thought he knew more about waging war than his generals did. Hitler's mistakes quickly piled up and led to the quick downfall of what he had called the "Thousand Year Reich."

Today, Greece is a second-rate country with a per capita income of $3,260 per year. Italy has fared a bit better, but it is far from being a world force, which is equally true of Spain. France and England are still powerful nations, but they are hardly the dominant forces they once were. Hitler is gone, and Germany is involved in the painful process of becoming reunited into a single country.

Each of these once-dominant nations made mistakes which allowed other nations to overtake and surpass them.

After World War II, America and Russia began their reign as the dominant world powers. And, for a while, they looked invincible. Today, Russia's economy is a well-known disaster, and the antinuclear activists have forced the U.S. to turn its back on the age of nuclear energy. Although other nations realize the advantages and benefits of nuclear energy, we seem destined to forsake them.

Our Achilles' heel could be the antinuclear activists, whose misinformation and deceitful tactics have caused us to reject what time has shown to be the safest, cheapest, most powerful source of energy known. Because few things are as important to modern civilization as energy, this is an extremely important mistake.

As it now stands, the rest of the world is moving into the nuclear age, but we are not. Other nations will prosper from the use of uranium, which contains up to 385 million times more energy than coal. Other nations will see their health problems and death rate due to air pollution diminish. Other nations will cease to contribute to global warming and will see the environmental damage done to their lands by acid rain decrease greatly. Not only will we be unable to enjoy the progress described, but we will continue to be one of the few industrial nations threatened by oil embargoes and the specter of running out of oil.

Superstition is defined as an unreasonable belief based on fear and ignorance. For almost thirty years, the unreasonable fear that a catastrophic accident might occur in a nuclear power plant has shaped our national energy policy.

No first-class nation can remain so it if lets superstition determine its course on critical matters. When this happens, it is only a matter of time before it's goodbye progress, prosperity, good health, and the good life. Then, it's hello to longer working hours or unemployment, less income, more disease, and more poverty.

It doesn't have to be this way, of course. Although superstition dies hard, when enough people become aware of the facts, superstition ultimately gets rejected. You are now more knowledgeable about the advantages of nuclear power than most people, and you should put this knowledge to use. All you have to do is become as vocal as the antinuclear activists. When a newscast is blatantly biased against nuclear power, pick up the phone or write the station a letter pointing out this bias and then demand an unbiased report.

When an unfair anti-nuclear power article appears in the newspaper, write the editor. For example, the next time some uneducated reporter writes that getting rid of nuclear waste is an unsolvable problem, write and educate the writer about the real unsolved problem—that of getting rid of the wastes produced by burning coal.

When a politician jumps on the antinuclear bandwagon to pick up a few cheap votes, write him and tell him that he will lose your respect and your vote.

And, don't forget to write to your congressmen. When *Time* magazine of October 23, 1989, called Washington "the Can't-Do Government," and said that it was "paralyzed by special interests and shortsightedness" and was "no longer capable of responding to its growing challenges," *Time* was at least partially right. In any event, Washington has let political activists dictate our nation's energy policy for over 20 years now, and no change in this increasingly critical area seems forthcoming. Only thousands of letters and numerous protests by special interest groups seem to be capable of moving the government. Only when pro-nuclear voices are louder than those of the antinuclear activists will the politicians begin to break the nuclear logjam.

Finally, pass this book on to a general science teacher in your local high school. He or she should already be aware of the truth about nuclear power, but you can't be sure of this because the antinuclear activists' propaganda mill has been extremely efficient. Most teachers reach 125to180 students a day. One thing is certain: We can't afford to have any antinuclear activists teaching our children if we are to enter the nuclear age.

All of this sounds like a nuisance, but better a little inconvenience now than a badly diminished standard of living later, or a massive worldwide catastrophe such as the one discussed earlier. If every informed person screams loudly enough and long enough, their voices will be heard, sweet reason will prevail, and this war against ignorance and fear can be won.

It's not a war we can afford to lose; the stakes are too high.

Wasn't it H. G. Wells who said that "civilization was more and more a race between education and catastrophe"?

Notes

Chapter 1

1. This topic is more completely covered in chapter 4. See notes 1, 2, 3, 4, 5, 6, 7, 8, and 9, chap. 4.

2. EPA National Air Pollutant Emission Trends, 1900-1996. EPA-454/R-97-011 U. S. Environmental Protection Agency, Research Triangle Park, NC Dec. 1997, p. ES4.

3. Elsa C. Arnett, "Poverty Ranks Among Most Consistent Health Risk Factors," Knight Ridder Newspapers, *The Indianapolis Star*, Aug. 16, 1998, sec. D, pp. 1 and 5.

Chapter 2

1. Samuel Glasstone, *Sourcebook on Atomic Energy* (New York: D. Van Nostrand Company, Inc., 1958), p. 417. See also, Allen L. Hammond, William D. Metz, and Thomas H. Maugh II, *Energy and the Future* (Washington, D.C.: American Association for the Advancement of Science, 1973), p. 37.

2. Spencer R. Weart, *Nuclear Fear* (Cambridge, MA.: Harvard University Press, 1988), p. 171.

3. Edith Efron, *Barrows* vol. 56, no. 23, June 7, 1976, p. 3.

4. Bernard L. Cohen, *The Nuclear Energy Option* (New York: Plenum Press, 1992), p. 171.

5. Bernard L. Cohen, *The Nuclear Energy Option* (See ch. 2, note 4), p. 171.

6. "Report of the President's Commission on the Accident at Three Mile Island." J. B. Kemeny, chairman, Washington, D.C., Oct. 1979.

7. Petr Beckman, *The Health Hazards of Not Going Nuclear* (Boulder, CO: Golem Press, 1976) p. 19.

8. "Health Evaluation of Energy Generating Sources," American Medical Association, *Proceedings of the House of Delegates*, 127 convention, June 18-22, Report C of the Council on Scientific Affairs, American Medical Association, pp. 286-89.

9. Bernard Cohen, *Before It's Too Late* (New York: Plenum Press, 1983), p. 2.

10. Stanley Rothman and S. Robert Lichter, "The Nuclear Energy Debate: Scientists, the Media and the Public," *Public Opinion*, Aug./Sept. 1982, pp. 47-52.

11. Stanley Rothman and S. Robert Lichter (See ch. 2, note 10), p. 49.

Chapter 3

1. The Media Institute, *Television Evening News Covers Nuclear Energy: A Ten-Year Perspective* (Washington, D.C.: The Media Institute, 1979), Appendix IV.

2. BernardCohen, *Before It's Too Late* (See ch. 2, note 9), p. 121.

3. "Environmental Aspects of Commercial Radioactive Waste Management," U.S. Dept. of Energy Document DOE/ET-0029, May 1979.

4. Bernard Cohen, *The Nuclear Energy Option* (See ch. 2, note 4), p. 182.

5. Ibid, *pp. 204-205 and pp. 211-12.*

6. The Environmental Protection Agency, *National Air Pollutant Emission Trends, 1900-1996* (Research Triangle Park, NC, 1997), p. ES-4.

7. Beckman, *The Health Hazards of Not Going Nuclear* (See ch. 2, note 7), p. 114.

8. Richard Wilson and William J. Jones, *Energy, Ecology, and the Environment* (New York: Academic Press, Inc., 1974), p. 253.

9. Spencer R. Weart, *Nuclear Fear* (Cambridge, MA: Harvard University Press, 1988), p. 333. (See ch. 2, note 2).

10. The Environmental Protection Agency (See ch. 3, note 6), pp. 1-1.

11. The Environmental Protection Agency (See ch. 3, note 6), pp. 3-15.

12. Cohen, *Before It's Too Late*, p. 2. (See ch. 2, note 9).

13. The Environmental Protection Agency (See ch. 3, note 6), pp. 3-13.

14. James Cornell, *The Great International Disaster Book* (New York: Pocket Books, 1979), p. 180.

15. Ibid., p. 279.

16. Beckman, *The Health Hazards of Not Going Nuclear* (See ch. 2, note 7), p. 107.

17. Dixy Lee Ray, *Trashing the Planet* (New York: Harper Collins, 1992) p. 147.

18. Beckman, *The Health Hazards of Not Going Nuclear* (See ch. 2, note 7), pp. 110-111.

19. Bernard Cohen, *The Nuclear Energy Option* (See ch. 2, note 4), pp.211-12.

Chapter 4

1. L. Lave and E. Seskin, "Air Pollution and Human Health," *Science* 169, (1970), p. 723.

2. L. Lave and E. Seskin, "Does Air Pollution Cause Ill Health?" University of Pittsburgh Report, Pittsburgh, PA (1971).

3. L. Lave and E. Seskin, "An Analysis of the Association Between U.S. Mortality and Air Pollution," University of Pittsburgh Report, Pittsburgh, PA, (1971).

4. R. Wilson, S. Colome, J. Spengler, and D. Wilson, *Health Effects of Fossil Fuel Burning: Assessment and Mitigation* (Cambridge, MA: Ballinger Publishing Co., 1980), p. 219

5. Cohen, *Before It's Too Late*, p. 99. (See ch. 2, note 9).

6. L. Lave and M. Chappie, "The Health Effects of Air Pollution: A Reanalysis," *Journal of Urban Economics* 12 (Nov. 1982): p. 346.

7. Office of Technology Assessment, *The Direct Use of Coal* (Washington, D.C.: Government Printing Office, 1979), p. 217.

8. Office of Technology Assessment, *Acid Rain and Transported Pollutants* (Washington, D.C.: Government Printing Office, 1985), p. 258.

9. "Air Pollution Found to Be More Deadly than Thought," *Herald Times,* Bloomington, IN, March 10, 1995, p. A3.

10. Derek M. Elsom, *Atmospheric Pollution* (Oxford, U.K.: Blackwell, 1993), p. 27.

11. Office of Air Quality and Standards, *National Air Quality and Emissions Trends Reports, 1997* (Triangle Park, NC., 1998) p. 117.

Chapter 5

1. Dixy Lee Ray, *Environmental Overkill* (New York: Harper Collins Publishers, Inc., 1993), p. 23.

2. Ibid., p. 23.

3. Dixy Lee Ray, *Trashing the Planet* (ch. 3, note 17), p. 34.

4. Paul and Anne Ehrlich, *Healing the Planet: Strategies for Resolving the Environmental Crisis* (New York: Addison Wesley, 1991), p. 72.

5. John Gribbin, *Hothouse Earth* (New York: Grove Weidenfeld, 1990), p. 17.

6. Robert Engleman, "Hotter Times: Greenhouse Effect Gains Credence," *Herald Times,* Bloomington, IN, June 16, 1988, p. A6.

7. "U.N. Scientists Warn of Global Warming," *Electric Consumer* 39, no. 1, (July 1989): p. 2.

8. Gribbin, *Hothouse Earth* (See ch. 5, note 5), p. 201.

9. Ibid., p. 1.

10. Ibid., *Hothouse Earth*, p. 133.

11. Ibid., *Hothouse Earth*, p. 195.

12. John Gribbin, *Carbon Dioxide, Climate, and Man* (Nottingham, England: Russell Press, 1981), p. 44.

13. Ibid., p. 45.

14. "U.N. Predicts Disaster from Global Warming," *Herald Times,* Bloomington, IN, June 30, 1989, p. 1.

15. Ray, *Environmental Overkill* (See ch. 5, note 1), pp. 6-7.

16. Ronald Bailey, *Eco-Scam* (New York: St. Martin's Press, 1993), p. 159.

17. Ibid., p. 159.

18. Ibid., p. 159.

19. Al Gore, *Earth in the Balance* (New York: Houghton Mifflin Co., 1992), p. 14.

20. Chris C. Park, *Acid Rain: Rhetoric and Reality* (New York: Methuen and Co., 1987), p. 103.

21. W. H. Vogelman, "Catastrophe on Camel's Hump," *Natural History* (Nov. 1982): pp. 8-14.

22. Acid *Rain and Transported Air Pollutants.* John H. Gibbons, Director, office of Technology Assessment, U.S. Congress, Washington, D.C., UNIPUB, (New York, 1985), pp. 42-3.

23. Park, *Acid Rain: Rhetoric and Reality* (See ch. 5, note 20), p. 11.

24. Ray, *Trashing the Planet* (See ch. 3, note 17), p. 64.

25. *Acid Rain and Transported Air Pollutants.* See note 22, chap. 4, pp. 218-19.

26. National Acid Precipitation Assessment Program: 1990 Integrated Assessment Report, NAPAP Office of the Director (Nov. 1991), p. 45.

27. Lee M. Thomas, "The Next Step: Acid Rain," *EPA Journal,* June/July 1986, pp. 2-3.

28. Fred L. Guiles, *Jane Fonda: An Actress in Her Time* (New York: Doubleday and Co., 1982), p. 267.

29. Bill Jordan, *Daily Camera,* Boulder, Colo., April 26, 1974, p. 40.

30. Cohen, *Before It's Too Late* (See ch. 2, note 9), p. 16.

Chapter 6

1. William M. Brown, *Petroleum Prices: Past, Present, and Prospective* (Indianapolis, IN: Hudson Institute, 1987), p. 29.

2. Kenneth C. Crowe, *America for Sale* (Garden City, New York: Anchor Press/Doubleday, 1980), p. 19.

3. "Trade Deficit Has Cost 5.1 Million Jobs, Study Says," *Herald* Times, Bloomington, IN, Oct. 16, 1988, p. A4.

4. "Fuel Tax Proposal Aggravates Industry," *Indianapolis Star,* Indianapolis, Ind., Feb. 21, 1993, Business section, pp. 1-2.

5. Stanley Rothman and S. Robert Lichter (See ch. 2, note 10), p. 52.

6. Ray, *Environmental Overkill* (See ch. 5, note 1), p. 68.

7. Harrison Brown, *The Challenge of Man's Future* (New York: Viking Press, 1954), pp. 167-68.

8. Ibid., p. 236.

9. Ibid., rear cover.

10. Fred Hoyle, *Energy or Extinction?* (London: Heinemann, 1977), p. 28.

11. Ibid., p. v.

12. Edward Teller, *Chicago Tribune*, Oct. 17, 1979, pp. 10-11.

Chapter 7

1. Sheldon Novick, *The Electric War: The Fight Over Nuclear Power* (San Francisco: Sierra Club Books, 1976), p. 315.

2. Greg Adamson, *We All Live on Three Mile Island* (Sidney, Australia: Pathfinder Press, 1981), p. 43.

3. "Chernobyl Babies Appear Normal; Have Higher Risks," Associated Press release, in the *Indianapolis Star*, April 23, 1987.

4. Carol J. Williams, Associated Press release, in the *Indianapolis Star*, April 19, 1987.

5. "Chernobyl Babies Appear Normal; Have Higher Risks." (see ch. 7, note 3)

6. Richard Wilson, "Back to Chernobyl," *NOVA*, (Feb. 14, 1989).

7. Bernard Cohen, *The Nuclear Energy Option* (See ch. 2, note 4), p. 113.

8. Cornell, *The Great International Disaster Book* (See ch. 3, note 14), p. 282.

9. *The World Almanac and Book of Facts 1988* (New York: World Almanac, 1988), pp. 529-30.

10. Cornell, *The Great International Disaster Book* (See ch. 3, note 14), pp. 255-69.

11. Ibid., pp. 262, 265.

12. C. Starr, M. A. Greenfield, and D. F. Hausknecht, *A Report to the State of California on the Safety of Steam Generating Power Stations* (1972). Available from the Engineering Dept., University of California at Los Angeles, Los Angeles, CA.

13. *U. S. News and World Report* (Dec. 7, 1992): p. 12.

Chapter 8

1. Fred Schmidt and David Bodansky, *The Energy Controversy: The Fight Over Nuclear* Power (San Francisco: Albion Publishing Co., 1976), p. 17.

2. Stanley Rothman and S. Robert Lichter, (See ch. 2, note 10), pp. 47-52.

3. Cohen, *Before It's Too Late* (See ch. 2, note 9), pp. 85-117.

4. Edwin Newman, "In Which We Live," NBC-TV, June 1970. Quoted by

Petr Bechman in *The Health Hazards of Not Going Nuclear,* (Boulder, CO: The Golem Press, 1976), p. 123.

5. The Media Institute, *Television Evening News Covers Nuclear Energy: A Ten Year Perspective* (Washington, D.C.: The Media Institute, 1979), Appendix IV.

6. The Media Institute. See note 5, chap. 8.

7. Peter Stoler, "Pulling the Nuclear Plug." *Time* (Feb. 13, 1984): p. 42.

8. Ibid., pp. 35-41.

9. Petr Beckman, *The Health Hazards of Not Going Nuclear* (See ch. 2, note 7), p. 21.

10. Alston Chase, "The Anti-Social Traits of Literacy and Genius," *Indianapolis Star,* Nov. 28, 1993, sec. F, p. 3.

Recommended Reading on This Topic

Petr Beckman, *The Health Hazards of Not Going Nuclear,* The Golem Press, Box 1342, Boulder, CO. 80302, 1976.

Bernard L. Cohen, *Before It's Too Late,* Plenum Press, 233 Spring Street, New York, NY 10013, 1983.

Bernard L. Cohen, *The Nuclear Energy Option,* Plenum Press, 233 Spring St., New York, NY 10013, 1990.

Dixie Lee Ray, *Trashing the Planet,* Harper Collins Publishers, Inc., 10 East 53rd St., New York, NY 10022, 1990.

Index